THE PASSION OF
POLAND

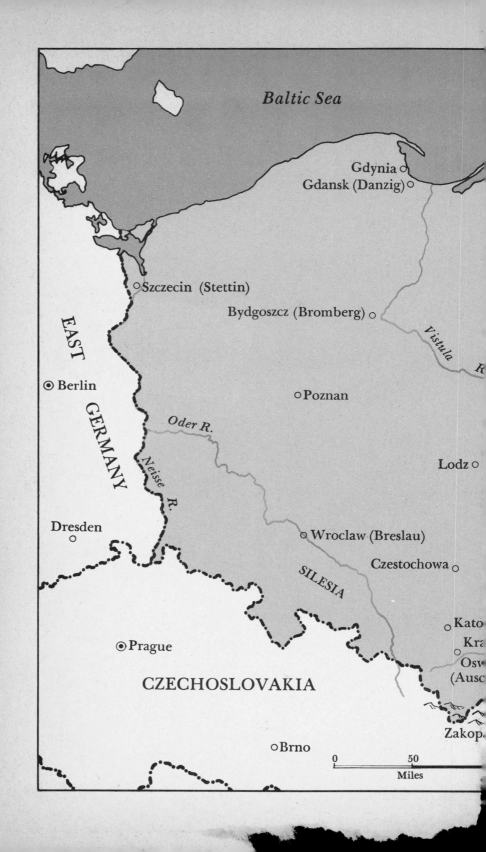

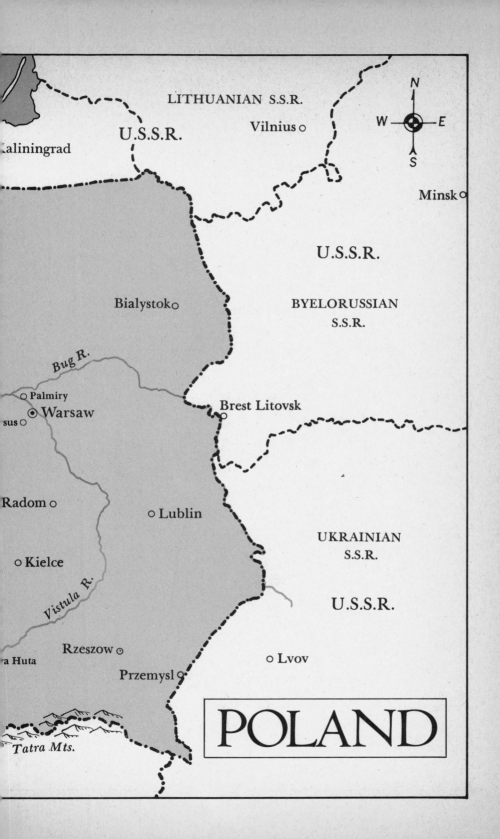

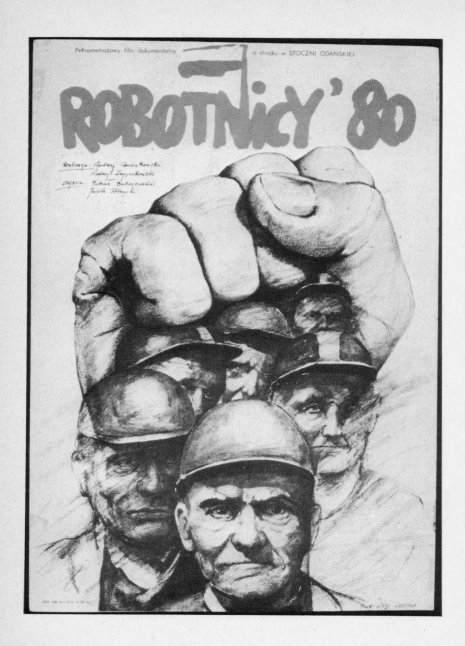

LAWRENCE WESCHLER

THE PASSION OF POLAND

From
SOLIDARITY
Through the
State of War

 PANTHEON BOOKS, NEW YORK

Parts of this book previously appeared in *The New Yorker* magazine in November 1981 and April 1983.

Grateful acknowledgment is made to Stanisław Baranczak to quote from his poems, "Those Men, So Powerful" (translated by Magnus Jan Krynski and Robert Macguire) and "Restoration of Order" (translated by Richard Lourie).

Library of Congress Cataloging in Publication Data

Weschler, Lawrence.
   The passion of Poland, from Solidarity through the state of war.
   Includes bibliographical references and index.
   1. Poland—History—1980–   . 2. NSZZ "Solidarność" (Labor organization) 3. Weschler, Lawrence. I. Title.
DK4442.W47 1984   943.8′056   83–24942
ISBN 0–394–72286–8 (pbk.)

Map by Dyno Lowenstein

Manufactured in the United States of America

First Pantheon Paperback Edition

Frontispiece art: The poster for *Workers '80*, a documentary film of the August 1980 strike in Gdansk. Both film and poster were widely displayed throughout Poland during 1981. (*Artist: A. Pagowski*)

*For My Mother
with Love and Appreciation*

Start with the logo, designed during the August 1980 strike by J. and K. Janiszewski, two unemployed graphic artists in Gdansk. The word taps into a reservoir of communal memories of over a century of worker activism on behalf of a socialist ideal which had been betrayed by thirty-five years of inept, corrupt state bureaucratic practice. The word reclaimed that ideal, and the flag pegged it as specifically Polish. The image acted almost like a Rorschach pattern during the sixteen months of Solidarity: everyone agreed the letters formed a crowd, but part of the time people saw the crowd as surging forward, led by the S and the C; while much of the time, people saw the letters standing around, milling, the A and the R leaning into each other, waiting to see what was going to happen...

Contents

Contents

A STATE OF WAR— OCTOBER–DECEMBER 1982 | 97

EPILOGUE—SEPTEMBER 1983 | 181

APPENDICES | 207

Acknowledgments

To begin with, I must acknowledge several nameless Poles—my translator (an absolutely invaluable guide), various taxi-drivers, a psychologist, a mathematician, an ex-architect, several editors, filmmakers and journal-ists, several workers. "Oh, don't worry," they'd tell me during my first two visits. "Use our names. Everything's out in the open. What can they possibly do to us?" Sometimes, indeed, almost giddy with their new-won freedom, they'd insist upon it: "Make sure you use them and spell them correctly. We want to be on record. We want our children to be able to look back and read about this." In most cases—except where individuals were already well known by the authorities or well exposed through their own work—I demurred. In November 1981, when much of the first half of this chronicle appeared in *The New Yorker*, my caution may still have seemed excessive. Following the desolate events of December, how-ever, that hesitation perhaps appeared more wise. And yet, upon my return to Poland in September 1982, in the midst of martial law, many of my defiant Polish friends still insisted that they would rather have been on record with their names, and I apologize for having less nerve than they.

As for those Poles whom I do mention by name in the pages that follow, I will not make anyone's job easier by listing them here. Suffice it to say that this book came into being through the extraordinary graciousness, generosity, and warm fellow-feeling of many wonderful Poles, and I worry for them.

Carl Ginsburg traveled with me during my first trip, my uncle Henry Feiwel during the second, and my brother, Raymond Weschler, during the third. Many of the impressions and insights recorded here derive from hours and hours of mullings shared with all three of them. Conversations with John and Nina Darnton, the Warsaw correspondents for the *New York Times* and National Public Radio, respectively, also proved extremely useful, as did my few meetings with the London *Observer*'s Neal Ascherson. Anna Maksymiuk, who has in the meantime moved to the United States, was gracious both in guiding me through the shipyard in Gdansk and in helping to sort through some of the intricacies of Polish history once she had resurfaced here. Roman Laba, an American Fulbright scholar in Warsaw who compiled perhaps the most complete documentary archive on Solidarity and its underground afterlife (and even managed to spirit most of it out of the country), was a splendidly generous guide during my third visit. Daniel Singer, one of the most insightful observers of the Polish scene, and his wife, Jeanne, were lovely hosts to me as I returned each time by way of their Paris home.

Roman Harte, a onetime Polish producer now based at the American Film Institute in Los Angeles, provided me with a series of invaluable initial contacts in Poland. On the other side of the work, Debbie Young and, again, Carl Ginsburg provided excellent assistance in preparing the chronology.

My own thinking on the general problems of authority and legitimacy —issues which pervade these reports—was shaped in large part several years ago during my studies with Sheldon Wolin (then at the University of California at Santa Cruz, now at Princeton, from where he edits the seminal journal *Democracy*). My thinking on the specific problems of political organizing and practice owes a great deal to years of conversations with Cheryl Parisi, Wretha Wiley Hanson, and Michele Prichard.

During the months since my October 1982 visit, many of my impressions as to the significance of events back in Poland have derived from conversations with newly arrived Polish émigrés and visitors here in New York. Of particular value were the insights of Joanna Stasinska, which were both passionate and exceptionally lucid.

Several journals and newsletters, especially in the months since the coup, allowed interested observers outside Poland to keep current with events and attitudes inside. Of particular value to me were *L'Alternative*, the Paris-based bimonthly specializing in coverage of "human rights and democratic freedoms in Eastern Europe" (4, rue Trousseau, 75011, Paris); the French Solidarity Support Committee's biweekly *Bulletin d'Information* (10, passage des Deux Soeurs, 75009, Paris); the New York-based *Committee in Support of Solidarity Reports* (275 Seventh Avenue, 25th floor, New York City, 10001); and the London-based biweekly *Uncensored Poland News Bulletin*, perhaps the most exhaustive of these documentary sources, put together by the Information Centre for Polish Affairs (115 Redston Road, London N87HG). Anyone wishing to pursue further explorations on Polish themes would be well advised to start with these chronicles.

Rob Tiller and Peter Canby did exceptional jobs fact-checking the "Solidarity" and "State of War" segments, respectively, as they were being prepared, at often breakneck pace, for publication in *The New Yorker*. John Bennet provided calm, smooth, and thoughtful direction with both segments in what could have been, but never became, a hectic editing process. Tom Engelhardt at Pantheon Books supplied wise perspectives and an overarching unity as the separate reports were being hooped together to form this single volume. For the past several years, Jonathan Schell has consistently been offering his resonances, and they have been consistently evocative. And finally there has been William Shawn, whose book this is: without his steady support and continuous encouragement, it would never have crossed beyond the musing stage.

—L.W.

Anna Walentynowicz, the popular crane operator whose firing sparked the August 1980 strike in Gdansk, addresses her co-workers during a break in the negotiations. She is flanked by Lech Walesa. (*Jean-Louis Atlan/SYGMA*)

Preface

I'D BARELY INTENDED to go and I certainly wasn't planning to write.
Poland of course had been in the news a lot during the months before
spring 1981, when I was in Europe anyway on a writing assignment. I
decided to venture a visit, more out of curiosity than anything else. But
being there was an altogether transforming experience.

There are stories, when you're a journalist, which tend to turn entirely
opaque: you spend months and months digging and all you come up with
is slurry. In Warsaw and Gdansk, however, during the spring of 1981,
every place I turned was ore. People who hadn't been allowed to speak
their minds for thirty-five years had suddenly come unstopped. They'd
talk to you—*as if talking mattered*—and their talk would seem to rise
from some deep, clear core of truth and value. You walked down the
street and there were jewels everywhere: all you had to do was open your
pockets and stuff them in. The sad, grey, lumpish geode of the place had
split open, and the internal patterns were magnificiently crystalline.

So that leaving, I couldn't help but write; and writing, I couldn't help but return. That, then, is the genesis of this book: Poland made me do it. Everything I saw and reported was framed in quintessentially Polish terms, steeped in the often quirky particulars of the Polish situation. And yet the lessons were more general. In a way, I began to realize I was reporting on what it is that comes alive when a place—any place—comes alive, and then what it is that gets repressed when a place, any place, gets repressed.

These last few months, back here in New York, as I've been compiling my various *New Yorker* pieces into this book, I've spent many hours talking with Polish émigrés and exiles, people who happened to be out of the country at the time of the coup and knew that going back would only mean incarceration; people who chose exile rather than whatever fate (prison, lifetime unemployment, military service) the martial-law regime was prepared to threaten in its stead; people who couldn't take the sorrow any longer and finally contrived some means of escape.

Escape to freedom and happiness.

And yet I seldom found joy or ease in the eyes of these people. Outside Poland, Poland seems always on their mind. They suffer homesickness for the land and the language and for particular people. They suffer for lack of precise knowledge about what is happening to family and friends— mail is sometimes censored, always takes weeks to get through, and when it finally does it sometimes takes days to decipher the cryptic allusions laced amidst the pleasantries. They feel useless and riddled with guilt. Over and over again, these are themes to which the émigré poets for example, return. Stanislaw Baranczak in Cambridge, Massachusetts:

> With so much barbed wire, so many seas in between,
> This canister of gas which had not been shot
> at me at all, has, despite everything,
> landed at my feet;
>
> there's no chance of this doing any good,
> it's pointless, their masks are air-tight,
> and it will make my eyes sting even longer
>
> but still I pick it up and throw it back at them.

Beyond the particular sources of their particular melancholies, however, I sense a homesickness for a sense of meaning—the sort of meaning that once coursed and even today still trickles through daily life in Poland. Lech Walesa, speaking recently with journalists, reportedly hinted at some of the content of his June 1983 conversation with the Pope in the Tatra Mountains: "During this meeting I expressed my thought that the Polish nation is more happy than any other, even though it has less bread and less shoes than any other." His is no naive celebration of the charms of poverty; rather it is a defiant assertion of value. Philip Roth recently commented that his years of serving as the general editor of a series of books by Eastern European authors have taught him to appreciate the difference between places where everything goes and nothing matters and those where nothing goes and everything matters. That's the point: even today in the midst of miasmic repression, Poland remains a place where fundamental values are at stake, where meaning is in contest.

One can get homesick for things mattering.

New York City
December 1983

August 31, 1980: the triumphant conclusion of the seventeen-day strike. From the walls of the Lenin shipyards, Lech Walesa thanks the townspeople of Gdansk for their support. Poles often refer to this popular photograph as "Lech the Angel," the Polish flag rippling behind him like wings. (*Alain Keler/SYGMA*)

SOLIDARITY TIME

———————— + + ————————

May 1981

JUST TRYING TO GET IN, you can quickly see what drove the Poles crazy. For most Americans, the visa-application process is the first exposure to the maddening pace of the Polish state bureaucracy. By the time you're finished, you can easily end up dealing with three separate offices—one in Washington, one in New York, and one in Chicago—each of which shuttles you back to the two others for further paperwork. And at some point you just end up having to wait. During that time, you may have the opportunity to meditate on the *character* of an entrenched bureaucracy's power: *the tyranny of information.* The clerk knows something you need to know, and not only won't he tell you now, he won't tell you when he will tell you. As the days pass and your anxiety increases, you may also begin to sense the *function* of a bureaucracy: in a society on the verge of shaking itself to pieces, where the socioeconomic pressures of modernity are wreaking havoc on the structures of traditional life, bureaucracy serves *to slow everything down.* To a bureaucrat, what and why don't matter in the least as long as he can slow things down.

1

Somebody ought to write a novel about this purgatory of waiting, you may find yourself grumbling. And then, of course, you realize that somebody already has—Franz Kafka, the insurance clerk from Prague. In realizing this, you also realize that this bureaucracy is not an exclusively Polish phenomenon and indeed, that it predates the imposition of Communism. For decades—centuries—the Middle Europeans have been refining the theory and practice of purgatorial bureaucratics. Poland is merely one of the world champions. Or anyway, it used to be.

Eventually, you may give up on the visa process in America and head straight for Europe, where the tyrannical bureaucracy seems less deeply entrenched. Indeed, the closer you get to Poland today the less invincible the bureaucracy's authority seems. In Poland itself, that authority is in substantial disarray. My visa, when it finally materializes early in May, in West Berlin, comes so fast that I don't even have time to buy a ticket before boarding the Berlin–Warsaw night train. I figure I'll buy one on board. At the station, I befriend a Pole I'll call Krzysztof—the top DJ in Lublin, according to his own account. His backpack is bulging with singles, the treasure hoard he amassed during a week in Hamburg, Cologne, and Düsseldorf. He is 25, and his English is derived principally from song lyrics. Nevertheless, as the train pulls out of the station he is able to regale me with stories and pantomimes of his life and good times as an itinerant disc jockey in the country towns around Lublin. He passed some sort of state exam, but it sounds as if he basically free-lances. Organizations or schools call him and he takes his records: he is very up to date and can discourse at length on Aretha Franklin, the Rolling Stones, John Lennon, disco, and even punk. He tells me about a Polish punk group he once heard named Deadlock; later they merged with another group and formed Crisis. He believes they made a record in Paris. Their leader, a punker named Mirek, identifies a lot with reggae music—the way it combines rebellion and religion. Language fails us somewhere in here, but apparently Mirek's music grows out of some sort of mystical identification with Our Lady of Czestochowa, the Black Madonna, whose miraculous protection turned back an invading Swedish army in the seventeenth century.

I ask Krzysztof about Solidarity, and his eyes brighten. He doesn't care much about the politics and the economics; what he keeps returning to is how Solidarity has opened up the borders. This has been his first trip to West Germany. He had no trouble getting a travel visa in Poland, whereas a year ago he wouldn't have even bothered to try.

We cross the border—the grim East German customs officials giving way to open-faced and easy Poles. About half an hour later, we hear the conductor scuttling toward us down the corridor. I reach for my wallet and suddenly feel Krzysztof's brusque slap. *"Nie, nie,"* he insists, forcing the wallet back into my pocket. The door slides open, and the conductor asks for our tickets. The other people in the compartment proffer theirs, and Krzysztof proffers his, but when it comes time for me, Krzysztof uncorks a torrent of commiseration, explanation, and elaboration. I have no idea what he is saying. The conductor, a kindly, thick-spectacled old hand, seems by turns bewildered, annoyed, and amused. The two of them go at it as if I weren't even there. At one point, Krzysztof telegraphs to me that he is telling the conductor I was attacked in Berlin and my ticket was stolen; then he returns to the fray. Finally, the conductor gives up, retreats to the corridor, closes the door, and moves on. Krzysztof is beaming. "Poland, my country!" he exclaims. "These, my trains! You, my guest!" It's a simple question of hospitality. "Poland," he concludes, "free country!"

I arrive in Warsaw at 6:30 A.M. on May 5th (Krzysztof continues to Lublin) and trundle sleepily over to the Hotel Forum. (From all indications, this first week in May constitutes a relatively calm period in the ongoing Polish crisis. Tempers have cooled considerably since the last frenzy—the police action in Bydgoszcz, in March.) As I wait to check in, I strike up a conversation with an American who is checking out. He is the project manager for a 68-million-dollar RCA contract to build a color-picture-tube factory here that the Poles will subsequently staff and manage. The project, he tells me, was launched in 1975 and is now almost completed. He'll be back one or two more times. RCA has already been paid off except for the final million or so dollars. He leaves for the airport.

Before I can register, it turns out, I have to exchange my travel vouchers. Poland requires the American visitor to buy in advance 15 dollars' worth of travel vouchers for each day of his stay—thus, 150 dollars' worth for my ten-day visa. As soon as you arrive, you can exchange the vouchers for zlotys at the official rate of 32 zlotys to the dollar. You must show a record of that transaction before you check into a hotel. I process my vouchers and register for my room. All of this becomes significant when, a few seconds later in the elevator, the bellboy offers to exchange money at the rate of 140 zlotys to the dollar. Later in the day, taxi-drivers and various gentlemen milling around the hotel entrance offer 150, 160, and even 170 zlotys to the dollar.

There are several ways of trying to describe the economic chaos in Poland today. Perhaps I should begin by noting that thanks to, among other things, the country's dismal balance-of-trade deficit and its resultant huge debt to Western banks, Poland's currency, the zloty, is considered virtually worthless not only abroad but even in its own country. There are many items (lumber, for instance) that for all intents and purposes are unobtainable with zlotys but can be readily procured with foreign dollars. This dismal situation has been officially sanctioned through the institution of PEWEX shops—government-run stores that accept *only* foreign currency. Indeed, the government is so eager for foreign money that some items at PEWEX shops sell for substantially less than their Western retail price. (A large bottle of Drambuie is available for $8.40, a large bottle of J&B whiskey for $6.20, and a pack of Dunhill cigarettes for $.70.) There are even PEWEX apartment houses—government-built condominiums which can only be had for dollars. I pass one of these one day. "The only people who live there," my Polish guide informs me, "are prostitutes and priests."

One result of this morbid situation is the vigorously thriving black market in currency. The people who are willing to offer you five times the official rate for your dollar either accumulate large quantities of dollars and then exchange them at a still higher rate or—more often—use the dollars directly to buy otherwise unavailable goods, either for themselves or for steep resale. These exchange practices render all money transactions in Warsaw a bit dreamlike for Americans. On the one hand, wherever you have to provide proof that your zlotys were obtained at the official rate—when you pay for a hotel room, for example—life can be expensive. A passable double room at the Hotel Forum runs 80 dollars (2,560 zlotys). But nearly everything else can be obtained with unofficial zlotys—"Monopoly money," as it's called by American tourists—and once you've crossed over into the black market you reap a double benefit: you can get five times the official rate for your dollar, and everything you'd want to buy can be had for half its Western price. You start living like royalty. Lavish dinners—pheasant, duck, veal—go for between 170 and 220 zlotys. You can entertain a couple of friends for a night of dinner and film and be hard pressed to crack five dollars. Meanwhile, outside most hotels there are private citizens, usually old ladies, eager to rent you a private room in their small, two-room apartments for between 600 and 1,000 zlotys a night (under $6.50). They'll even be happy to change the money themselves, right along with the sheets.

The Polish government needs the foreign currency so badly that it generally turns a blind eye to this rampant practice. One day, I ask a Polish friend about all the money changers massed outside the Hotel Forum. Isn't it dangerous? Aren't some of them police agents?

"*Of course* some of them are police," he readily concurs. "But they give good rates, too."

It's not so much the police you have to worry about as the con artists. One morning, I get snookered. In exchange for my dollars, this guy is supposed to hand me a wad of 1,000-zloty notes. He counts them out, drops the wad, picks it up, and hands it over. When he's long gone, I realize he's switched wads, and I'm left with a bunch of fifties wrapped in a single thousand note. But still I come out better than if I'd exchanged at the official rate! Which is to say that when you trade at the state bank they're literally robbing you blind.

The Muzak at the Hotel Forum is up-to-the-minute Western rock (music which, for that matter, saturates the entire country). The bar is agog with fancy prostitutes—all of them available for ridiculously small amounts of hard currency—and hordes of Western businessmen dazzled by their sudden good fortune. It can get a little disconcerting, sitting there amidst the prostitutes and the money changers in Warsaw, Poland, to suddenly hear Bob Dylan come wailing over the P.A. system, "When you gonna wake up, strengthen the things that remain?" And it can get downright eerie, sitting there at the fanciest restaurant in town, wolfing down your succulent duck, to look out over the plaza at the lines queuing outside a grocery store where a few patchy lettuce heads adorn the window. It can stop your fork dead in its tracks halfway to your mouth: What in the hell is going on in this country?

Which brings us back to my acquaintance from RCA. "What on earth does Poland want with a color-picture-tube factory?" a Western economist visiting Warsaw asks me in exasperation a few days later. "Hardly anyone in Poland can afford a color TV set, and no one anywhere else in the world is going to want a color set made in Poland. The Poles have managed to pour 68 million dollars into a plant that will probably have to be written off as a total loss. RCA is home free with its 68 million, and Poland is left owing that, plus interest, to a consortium of Western banks. Add a few dozen boondoggles like that together, and you end up with a total foreign debt of more than 25 billion dollars. And it's not even as though RCA came to them with some hard sell—*they* went to RCA! Back in the early seventies, Edward Gierek"—Gierek was the head of the Polish Communist Party between 1970 and 1980—"and his boys decided Poland could have a grand economy with color TVs and cars and all sorts of luxury goods. Only, they forgot to build the infrastructure. And they were so scared of outside criticism that they refused to listen to anyone but their closest advisers, who were all a bunch of cowering yes-men. During the past 15 years, Poland may well have suffered the worst central planning of any economy in Eastern Europe. I mean, take Hungary by comparison. The Hungarians, too, enlisted the aid of Western companies when they decided to build a big manufacturing complex—only theirs manufactures electric-light bulbs. Now, everybody in Hungary needs electric-light bulbs, and if there's a small surplus the Hungarians don't have to worry—they're never going to prove threatening enough on the world market to provoke any multinational corporations into seeking the kind of trade sanctions that Poland quickly ran up against on another occasion, a few years back, when it tried to corner the American golf-cart market. That was another fiasco."

The Polish Communist Party, perhaps more than any other Communist Party in Eastern Europe, was imposed on its people. (In Czechoslovakia, for example, there was a Socialist tradition, and even, in the early days of the regime, a Communist electoral victory.) It was imposed as one of many factors in Soviet national-security considerations following the Second World War—considerations that may have made sense from the Soviet point of view but left the Polish Communists with a tremendously difficult task in achieving legitimacy. They failed dismally. Lacking a solid, organic connection with the country's working class—the kind of connection that had been claimed, for example, by the London-based government-in-exile, which coordinated most of Poland's indigenous resistance during the Nazi occupation—the Party leadership in Poland tended to drift into an increasing insularity. When workers became restless, the Polish Communist Party, instead of addressing the fundamental issue of the roots of authority and accountability, repeatedly tried to buy off its discontented workers with higher paper salaries or with subsidies designed to defer increases in food costs—strategies that the national economy could not support and that in the long run led to a serious undermining of the workers' real standard of living.

Meanwhile, as public-spiritedness declined among Party officials and managers, a pattern of cynical privilege-hoarding degenerated into a system of rampant petty and not-so-petty corruption. It's easy to see, for example, how anyone whose job involved contact with the West could quickly conjure an extraordinary fortune in zlotys. Poles refer over and over to the case of Maciej Szczepanski, the head of the state television network, who, it is said, managed to obtain a yacht, a private jet, and a villa in Kenya before his recent ouster. Gierek is said to have spotted himself ten villas around the country; the one in which he is currently living, according to a recent exposé, cost 27 million zlotys to build—funds skimmed off the budgets of a variety of highway and mass-housing projects. Such corruption, in all fairness, is relatively small-time compared with some of the scandalous examples one finds in the West; but in a country as poor as Poland, and one that at least claims to aspire to an egalitarian ideal, this pattern of inequality has been a cause of increasing public frustration. It isn't even the grossest national examples that so gall most Poles; rather, it's the petty corruption pervading the country at the local level: the Party boss who can always count on fresh, lean ham; the plant manager with two extra rooms and a color TV in his house.

Whatever the progress of the current political renewal, the economic situation of Poland has been getting steadily—and now precipitately—worse. This deterioration stems in part from the economic effects of all the recent political turbulence—loss in productivity because of strikes, the shorter work week conceded to many workers by the government, and so on; but it is more generally a result of the cumulative damage to the economy of the 35 years of mismanagement that spawned the political turbulence in the first place, especially the mismanagement of the last ten years. Giving Gierek the benefit of the doubt, for a moment, one can perhaps argue that his economic master plan made a certain amount of sense in 1970. Gierek hoped to turn Poland into a major manufacturing power. Western banks were only too happy to lend Poland the money to build the new factories, highways, and other support systems, and Western contractors were likewise delighted to oblige. Poland began to starve its agricultural sector in favor of these new initiatives. Gierek and his men felt that eventually the hard-currency profits from the manufacturing would more than make up for the predicted shortfall in agricultural production. Poland would be able to import food and still make a net profit. At first, things seemed to go well, as was to be expected: billions of crisp, hard dollars were giving the Polish economy a good, stiff rush. But several problems began to develop early on, not the least of which was the worldwide recession of the mid- and late seventies. After the petroleum crisis of 1973, the West could no longer be counted on to provide Poland with a market for its newly manufactured goods; the country was left with a horrendous national debt, and no way of paying it off. Indeed, by 1981 something like two-thirds of whatever hard currency Poland could manage to muster was going merely to service the *interest* on the debt.[1] The remainder of the hard currency was desperately needed to import food, consumer goods, spare parts, and raw materials—and there simply wasn't enough. The shelves in stores began to empty; factories fell idle for lack of raw materials or spare parts; buses broke down and couldn't be repaired; electrical blackouts and coal shortages became rampant; and productivity in general plummeted. This was the backdrop for the strikes of 1980: Solidarity didn't cause this situation—if anything, Solidarity was caused by it.

Retracting the benefit of the doubt, one should note that there were many economists back in 1970 who predicted that Gierek's initiatives would come to precisely this end. That Gierek and his advisers didn't listen was partly a function of the insular situation of the Party. But it was also the result of a pattern of vested interests: There was a class of high- and middle-level bureaucrats and professionals—Poland's Red bourgeoisie—who stood to reap substantial improvements in their standard of living under the Gierek policy, and they did. While the rest of the country's economy was becoming riddled, many people were making a killing during much of the seventies. (This social milieu has perhaps been best captured in the films of Krzysztof Zanussi—most recently in *Contract*.)

There are other, somewhat related reasons for Poland's current economic predicament. One is the matter of prices. A Warsaw friend of mine puts the matter succinctly: "Prices bear no relationship whatsoever to actual values in this country." Because the ruling authorities—not the market—set prices for most goods in Poland, and because those authorities lack any legitimacy whatever in the eyes of most Poles, when economic factors have dictated the need for an increase in prices the government has seldom been able to make the increase stick. Workers go on strike and extract either compensatory wage increases or price rollbacks, or, often, both—and the government gives in because not to do so would be to raise the question of its own legitimacy. Meanwhile, to cover its flank (so that at least on paper the columns jibe), the government prints up new zlotys. The result is that, since production is based on real factors (supply of raw materials, spare parts, the length of the work week, etc.), the output of products declines while the number of zlotys in circulation increases. More zlotys chase fewer goods. Is it any wonder that the zloty has become virtually worthless in its own country? The problem in this case is particularly vexing because the workers themselves share a certain complicity.

Another source of trouble is the overcentralized character of planning in Poland. "For example, Poland has long had a serious housing problem," a Solidarity staff member in Warsaw explained to me one afternoon. "So the government decided that the way to attack this problem was with huge standardized-housing complexes. They nationalized all the small local construction concerns and consolidated them into these huge operations that could produce only massive gray housing complexes. The trouble was that once everything became so centralized the slightest crimp in supply or deployment tended to bring everything to a stop. If, say, because of our trade deficit we were momentarily unable to afford to import some ingredient for cement, virtually all housing construction had to come to a halt. Meanwhile, the kind of small-scale local operations that in the past could have worked around such momentary shortages had ceased to exist. Here's a case where we once had an infrastructure and it's been destroyed."

People who grew up in Europe before the Second World War recall a time when France and Poland were considered the twin breadbaskets of Europe. This year, however, Poland is expected to spend two and a half billion dollars of its scarce hard-currency reserves on food imports. When you ask Poles what happened, the reply you most often get is, "That's a good question. We can't believe it ourselves." There are long-term causes and more immediate causes. One fundamental problem is that, unlike any other Eastern European country, Poland never succeeded in collectivizing the bulk of its agriculture; even at the outset of Communist rule, the Party's hold on the allegiance of the people, especially in the heavily Catholic countryside, was simply too tenuous. The result is that today approximately 75 percent of the country's arable land is farmed by more than three million independent small farmers, who in turn account for 75 percent of the country's agricultural output. This would be fine except that, for ideological reasons, the government lavishes tractors, fertilizers, and other supplies and equipment on its collectivized farms, making it terribly difficult for private farmers to gain access to similar supplies and thereby reducing most Polish agricultural activity to an astonishing primitiveness.

The peasants one sees in the countryside are usually either trailing scrawny horses or pushing plows themselves. One man tells me he must wait for up to three weeks to rent a grass cutter or a harvester from the government. "By then, the harvest is over," he says. The government charges him 300 zlotys an hour for the cutter, 2,000 for the harvester; in turn, it pays him 400 zlotys for 100 kilos of potatoes and 8,000 zlotys for a large fattened pig. But, the peasant tells me, most of the tractors have now broken down; there are almost no spare parts; and the collectivized farms are hoarding what few vehicles remain. According to a recent article in the *New York Times*, Polish independent farmers in 1980 received only half of the fertilizer and 40 percent of the fodder they needed to run their farms. In Poland, as in America, young people are tending to leave the country for city life. "Farmers have less money than workers," I was told by a young man working in a field about 40 miles outside Warsaw. "The workers spend theirs—whatever little they have left—on pleasure. Peasants never have time or money for pleasure." In America, the departing youths are being replaced either by machines or by a tenant-farmer class. No such alternative possibilities exist for Poland.

The government's pricing policy—or, rather, its inability to enforce a realistic one—accounts for further problems. Because workers reject price increases, the government cannot offer farmers prices that would make it worth their while to produce more. ("This is hard work," I heard an exhausted peasant tell an anxious city dweller outside Lodz. "If you're so eager for more food, come out here and grow it yourself.") The situation can result in outlandish aberrations. Sometimes the government actually has to sell certain goods for less than it paid for them, and I heard of a farmer who sold the government a given quantity of potatoes, went to the city, bought them back, and then sold them to the government once again, netting himself a tidy profit. More generally, such aberrations take the form of the rapidly growing black market. Indeed, many farmers living close to the cities could hardly be described as suffering: in Gdansk, for example, I often saw peasants drive up to the open-air market in Mercedes-Benz automobiles, whose trunks were filled with fresh eggs being sold at many times the official price.

In 1970, Poland was still a net agricultural exporter. But here again Gierek's administration was responsible for a series of almost insane miscalculations. Notably, Gierek's people took it into their heads that meat consumption somehow betokened modernity, so, to the extent that they aided their agricultural sector at all, they focussed on building up livestock herds—at a cost of millions of dollars in Western feed and of billions of zlotys' worth of indigenous supplies—all for a program that never really coalesced anyway.

The practice of small farming in Poland is terribly inefficient even in ways unrelated to the complications created by government policy. At least five percent of Poland's arable land lies perpetually fallow, in the form of unfarmed boundary strips between the countless small private plots. At some point, a compromise must be achieved; in the meantime, the Polish breadbasket will continue to provide mere crumbs compared to its potential.

The rest of Poland's economy is likewise surprisingly mixed. There is a large sector that is officially state-owned, a small sector that is officially private, and a remarkably large sector occupying an undefined region between the two. Thus, some people own their own homes, some rent theirs from the government, some buy into government-built complexes, some rent out space in the homes that they own or rent. Some can pass their property on to heirs, and some can't. All this activity is subject to the incredibly complicated bureaucracy. The waiting list to get one's own apartment in a government-built complex is currently over ten years long. (A phone, I am told, can take 20 years: one day you simply receive a note saying that your phone is ready; from that point you have seven days to amass the 10,000-zloty down payment, or else you fall back to the end of the line.) In the meantime, Poles have contrived some ingenious ways of burrowing between the cracks of the pervasive bureaucracy—in some cases, almost literally. I met one man who had given up on his waiting list. He and a group of his friends found a Stalinist-style apartment building on the edge of Warsaw, vintage 1950s. The building had a large, pompously imposing entrance hall, which they commandeered, and into which they slotted four apartments and a store. They procured all the supplies and did all the construction themselves. This man currently lives in one of the nicest apartments I've seen in the Warsaw area, and he pays not one zloty for it: after years of trying to fit his particular situation into one of its categories—to figure out how much to charge him—the bureaucracy has either given up or lost track of him altogether.

In recent months, all sectors of the Polish economy have been experiencing extreme constrictions, and the possibilities for ingenuity are wearing thin. The results, everywhere, are shortages and lines. "It used to be," my friend in the free apartment tells me, "that when I saw a line, I passed it by—who needed the bother? You could always find your product later in the day somewhere else, without a line. Now whenever I see a line I immediately join it—I'm excited to find a store with anything to sell."

One evening, I attend a Polish film that was shot about four years ago. At one point in the film, the action moves to a grocery store where there are no lines and the shelves are amply stocked with all kinds of goods—the way things apparently were about four years ago. The scene has the audience rolling in the aisles.

"Products appear and disappear, reappear and then disappear again," a woman tells me. "And then sometimes they just disappear for good. It used to be that our stores were stocked with many different kinds of cheese. I haven't seen cheese in six months." The shortages seem to roll from one product to another. During the time I am there, there are sequential shortages of milk, sausage, matches, beer, toilet paper, chocolate, and cigarettes. These shortages translate into long lines wherever the items happen to surface. Conversation within the lines often involves intricate analyses of the causes of the particular shortage of the day. With cigarettes, for example, the theory is that enough tobacco and paper exist but because of the national debt the government hasn't been able to import the specific type of adhesive needed to seal the rolled papers. With matches, some people feel that it's a question of sulfur, others, of wood. People pass the time of day patiently waiting, parsing all the possibilities, joking over their misfortune. Meanwhile, the country's productivity is drip-dribbling away: everyone comes in late for work.

One of the most fascinating features of the lines is the institution of self-policing. For example, a rumor spreads that a particular store will be receiving a shipment of sewing machines. A line spontaneously forms. The person at the head of the line takes out a sheet of paper and people sign up in order of appearance. After a while, when it becomes clear that the sewing machines aren't coming that day, they disperse. Each morning, they queue up once again to reassert their position in the line —each name on the sheet is followed by a series of checks—and when the sewing machines eventually materialize they are apportioned according to the list. You find the lines everywhere—even in front of police offices, where the people queuing for travel visas or other bureaucratic appointments first register with the woman at the head of the line, with her tattered list.

"These lines," a woman says to me with a sigh. "This is what kills our time. This is what wears us down—the time we waste in strategizing our daily lives. How you have to remember to buy bread on Thursday, because the line's too long on Friday, and that it has to be brown bread, because white won't last till Monday—all these tiny, petty details, cluttering up your mind until you don't have room for anything else." Another acquaintance tells me she feels that the shortages are a calculated strategy on the part of the government to wear the people down, to slowly rob them of hope and enthusiasm. But a third person—a sociologist—feels that while the lines started out as an inconvenience, they are fast becoming an institution. "It's not that bad," he assures me. "This is where people meet, slow down, talk, exchange ideas on what's happening in the country. And then, the miserable situation of our economy changes the dimensions of living—now we take tremendous satisfaction in the smallest things. Just finding two bottles of milk becomes an adventure. A pack of cigarettes can make my day—it feels like a triumph."

Along a low plateau above the west bank of the Vistula in the north-central part of Warsaw stretches Stare Miasto, the Old Town: a quaint cobblestone quarter virtually unchanged since the seventeenth century— except that not a wall there is more than 35 years old. Toward the end of the Second World War, after the Nazis had extinguished successive uprisings in the ghetto and the rest of the town, and before the advancing Soviet Army got around to liberating the few ravaged Warsavites who had survived, the Germans systematically levelled the entire city of Warsaw. In the Historical Museum, off the Old Market Square, one can see old films of the devastation: German soldiers spraying emptied buildings with flame and then dynamiting the burned-out shells. But after 1945 the returning residents of Warsaw refused to accept history's verdict. In an extraordinary community effort, they set about rebuilding the Old Town exactly as it had been. Long-lost crafts of metalworking and glassmaking had to be reinvented, masonry and woodwork meticulously grafted. The result, after decades of painstaking work, is a virtually exact replica of the original Old Town.

Nothing happening in Poland today makes sense without reference to its tortured history, and particularly the grim legacy of the war. This is true in two respects. First, however much mismanagement and corruption may have aggravated Poland's current economic situation, Poland is a poor country. Only 35 years ago, it lay in total ruin, its housing and its industry completely devastated. Unlike Western Europe, which could rebuild with the aid of enormous infusions of capital from the United States—the one world power whose industrial base had received no damage whatsoever—the Poles had to pull themselves up by their own bootstraps. The Soviet Union did extend some assistance, but it was in the process of repairing its own overwhelming devastation. It's easy for Westerners and Americans to ridicule the state of the Polish economy, but we must remember that the existence of any Polish economy at all is evidence of a certain dogged triumph. Second, the tragedy of what the Second World War did to Poland highlights the larger tragedy of Poland's entire history. "This low, flat country is the cesspool of Eurasia," a Warsaw intellectual tells me. "Whenever history backs up to either side of us, the chaos and the carnage spill over into Poland." The Polish people may win the prize for history's least enviable geographical placement. During the past 500 years, their very existence as a nation has been a sporadic achievement: their statehood disappears, reappears with new boundaries, disappears again. Poland exists within the German sphere of influence during one generation and within the Russian the next. ("The thing you must never forget about Poland," a friend in

Warsaw tells me, "is that we lost the Second World War.") Amid it all, the Polish people breed martyrs in endless profusion—a profusion reflected, in turn, in the abundance of flowers with which they then adorn the martyrs' monuments. Every few blocks on almost any Warsaw street, one will come upon a plaque commemorating some gruesome carnage, and the plaque will invariably be draped in bright fresh blossoms. Out of this sorry history the Poles have distilled a fierce, romantic nationalism, and nothing in Poland today makes sense unless one understands that temper.

No one has understood it better than the Catholic Church. Diagonally across the street from the University of Warsaw, you will find the Church of the Holy Cross. It's a modest baroque structure. Inside, plaques along the side walls commemorate a cavalcade of Polish national heroes: musicians, artists, scientists, political leaders. In one alcove, there's a bust of Chopin. Beneath the bust lies an urn; inside the urn lies the composer's actual heart. The alcove is strewn with flowers, and tiny student badges from Poznan, Lodz, Lublin, Bydgoszcz, Krakow. . . . Similarly, in the crypt beneath the venerable Wawel Cathedral, in Krakow, one comes upon the sarcophagi of Adam Mickiewicz and Juliusz Slowacki, the two greatest poets of nineteenth-century Polish Romanticism. In Czestochowa, about 70 miles northwest of Krakow, a miraculous painting of the Black Madonna, Queen and Protector of the Poles—the holiest shrine of Polish Catholicism—draws thousands of pilgrims to the 600-year-old Jasna Gora monastery *every day*, and hundreds of thousands each August, during the Feast of the Assumption. Dozens of priests hear confessions at all hours, while hundreds of visitors—of all ages, in all sorts of garb—jam forward for a view of the shrine's icon, their faces streaming with tears. (For a moment, one fancies oneself not in Central Europe but rather—where? Iran?) Atop the chapel tower, a huge sign announces, simply, "600," anticipating the six-hundredth anniversary, in 1982, of the founding of the monastery, and Pope John Paul II's promised return visit. "Look at that," my Polish guide tells me. "Six hundred years. Compared to that, what can *they* offer us, with their pathetic thirty-six?"

In the battle between Catholicism and Communism for the hearts of the Polish people, only the former has been able to tap into and express Polish nationalism, while the latter's inability to do so accounts in part for its inability to rule. For Poles, the Catholic Church is an organic national institution, the Communist Party an imposed colonial one. In a courtyard at the University of Warsaw, a 21-year-old literature student tells me that she and 80 percent of the young people of Poland regularly attend church on Sundays—"some as believers, some as some sort of believers." When you try to get a take on the precise character of Polish Catholic belief, however, things become a bit hazy (just as they do when you try to pin a Solidarity leader down on what, precisely, he sees as

13

the future of economic organization in his country). The student tells me that she and most of her classmates tend to ignore the Church's teachings on birth control and abortion. (Polish families are generally modest in size; finding families with more than three children is unusual, at least in the cities.) She also thinks that the Church's posterboard campaign on behalf of Creationism, as opposed to evolutionary theory, is only marginally effective. "For us," she concludes, "the Church signifies patriotism, tradition, continuity, and stability."

One frequently comes upon young men in priests' robes—one sees priests of all ages, for that matter, but the young priests stand out. "They become priests," a friend tells me, "partly out of a religious vocation, perhaps more out of a patriotic one, but also because the priesthood is the path to the finest education—in every field of endeavor—available in this country. The Church preserves and transmits the knowledge of Poland much more than any secular institution."

A highly educated sociologist tells me that although he himself seldom attends church anymore, he sends his six-year-old son to Sunday school. "The Church has preserved Polish history and culture," he explains. "If my son did not receive exposure to the Church, there isn't a single Polish poem he'd ever understand."

But the Church in Poland offers its congregations something even more profound than cultural heritage; fundamentally, the Church extends to the Poles a limitless *solace*, and Polish history being what it is, such solace just about has to be limitless. This became clear to me on the evening, during the second week of May, when we received word that the Pope had been shot. I had intended to visit a regional meeting of the Warsaw Solidarity branch, but the meeting was summarily cancelled. Instead, I wandered into a neighboring church. In the crepuscular stillness, hundreds of Poles were kneeling in the pews; a priest was saying Mass; the organ occasionally underscored the moment's solemnity. Behind the priest, a huge, ornate gold-leaf altar framed a dark baroque painting of the Crucifixion. Here were these people facing yet further calamities: the life of their Pope (doubly theirs) in peril; their own Cardinal Wyszynski old and badly ailing; their economy in shambles; the Russian tanks at the border—in short, a nation, as ever, on the rack. And here before them, as ever, was the dark, strangely calm image of a man splayed in crucifixion, both a figure for their situation and the promise of a kind of redemption, or at least a solace. "Poland," wrote Juliusz Slowacki, the great Romantic poet, "is the Jesus Christ of nations."

Perhaps the most poignant war memorial in Poland lies about ten miles to the north of Warsaw, at Palmiry, in a flat clearing surrounded by birch forest. This is one of the places where, in the early days of the Occupation, the Nazis brought prominent Polish citizens in the middle of the night and herded them together for summary execution. In the clearing today, you find row upon row of uniform cross-shaped head-stones—5,000 of them. At the entry gate, an engraved inscription pre-serves a bit of anonymous graffiti found in a Gestapo prison cell after the war:

> *It is easy to talk about Poland,*
> *Harder to work for Poland,*
> *Harder still to die for Poland,*
> *Hardest of all to suffer for Poland.*

On the far side of the clearing, rising serenely out of the birch forest, tall and lean and gleaming white, are three simple crosses, the middle one slightly taller than the others. They suggest nothing so much as a benign eternal vigilance.

"If it hadn't been for the election of John Paul II in October 1978," a young student tells me in the courtyard at Warsaw University, "August 1980 would never have been possible. I do not consider myself a be-liever, but even I was choked with emotion at the news. It gave us a tremendous surge of pride, a sense that we were perhaps something after all, that maybe we didn't have to be resigned to all this."

Another friend, a Catholic intellectual now active in Solidarity, tells me, "It wasn't so much his election as Pope as his visit here that June [in 1979] that really inspired the country. Here we were, facing a tre-mendously complicated series of logistical tasks—setting the itinerary for his trip, making arrangements for several huge rallies, providing for crowd control, and so forth—and the government was pointedly declin-ing to help us. Generally speaking, the authorities were trying to ignore the Pope's visit as much as possible; television coverage, for instance, was limited. The police pulled back, made themselves scarce, partly out of tact, I suppose. And so, completely independent of anything that John Paul had to say, we discovered an extraordinary and quite unsus-pected competence *within ourselves*: we could do all kinds of things by ourselves, we didn't need the authorities. We developed communications networks, planning procedures—all kinds of skills that would become tremendously useful a year later."

The Pope's Masses during the visit drew millions of rapt Poles, and one phrase of his in particular has fixed itself in the people's imagina-tion. It was uttered at the conclusion of a prayer, and has since been inscribed as a commemorative frieze on the wall outside the shipyard in Gdansk: "Let the Holy Spirit come into this country and this ground. Amen." The woman who translated the frieze for me in Gdansk sighed emotionally and whispered, "Imagine! He said that in 1979 and then we had August in 1980. It was as if he said, 'Let there be light,' *and there was.*"

The relationship between the Catholic Church and the Solidarity movement is particularly curious. For while the Church seems to be inspiring all sorts of democratizing tendencies within society—by way of its rhetoric concerning "individual human dignity"—it is at the same time one of the most rigidly hierarchical institutions around; indeed, it's the only thing in Poland remotely as hierarchical as the Communist Party. While the Church has long provided a context for resistance, the Church during the recent crises has in practice been a force for moderation—some Poles go so far as to say, for capitulation. There can be no question, however, that John Paul II himself presides over the entire Polish renewal like a guardian angel. Poles will tell you over and over again that John Paul has informed the Soviet leaders in no uncertain terms: if they and their allies should decide to invade Poland he will immediately fly to Warsaw. (The Poles think that this threat is a major reason for Russia's reluctance to invade.)

"The Pope!" scoffed Josef Stalin in 1935, dismissing a request that he sanction Catholicism in Russia. "How many divisions has he got?" The fact of the matter, as Stalin's Kremlin successors have come to realize, is that in Poland today the Pope's divisions are legion.

There is a dark side to Poland's overwhelmingly Catholic consensus. Perfectly thoughtful and sensitive Polish intellectuals will tell you, without a moment's circumspection, that Poland today is probably the most ethnically homogeneous nation in Europe. "Ninety-eight percent pure" is a phrase I often heard uttered without a trace of irony.

In September 1939, more than 30 percent of the population of Warsaw was Jewish, and the proportion was similar in other Polish towns. (More than three million Jews lived in the entire country.) Long before the arrival of the Nazis, the Jews of Poland had been subject to considerable indigenous persecution, and there is substantial historical evidence to indicate that some elements of Polish society welcomed Hitler's invasion, at least to the extent that it promised to solve the perennial problem of Jewish "contamination." After the war, hundreds of cadaverous Jews returning from the concentration camps were bludgeoned as they arrived in their hometowns. Thousands of others were chased out. In 1968, an official anti-Semitic purge further thinned the Jewish remnant. This month, as I was touring Poland, the figures I heard for the total remaining Jewish population ranged from 5,000 to 7,000. One person in Warsaw estimated that 200 Jews remain in the city.

"Actually," a writer assured me, "many Jews are prominent in several sectors of Polish society."

"What sectors?" I asked.

"Film."

"What other sectors?"

"No other sectors."

"I was brought up on three dead languages," confides the narrative voice at the outset of Isaac Bashevis Singer's 1978 novel, *Shosha*, "Hebrew, Aramaic, and Yiddish (some consider the last not a language at all). . . . Although my ancestors had settled in Poland some six or seven hundred years before, I knew only a few words of the Polish language. We lived in Warsaw on Krochmalna Street."

During the early part of my stay in Warsaw, I, too, lived on Krochmalna Street, in the heart of what had been 40 years ago a walled-in Jewish ghetto. I read Singer and walked along his streets—Mila, Nowolipie, Chlodna, Leszno. . . . The Jews were all gone, the language was gone—not even the buildings remained. Although the Warsavites meticulously resurrected the Old Town, that project of exact reconstruction stopped at the edge of the ghetto. Its streets are now lined by flank after flank of tall, gray mass-produced mass housing. Polish children play friskily at intersections where Jewish resistance fighters perished in the final days of the Ghetto Uprising in the spring of 1943. I saw no memorial plaques on the buildings. In a park, I sat reading Singer and wondered in what sense one could even construe this to be the place he had been writing about. Virtually nothing of the Jews remains; all that persists—strangely unaltered by their disappearance—is the surrounding anti-Semitism.

One afternoon, I wander into a park among the housing units where I do discover a large granite-and-bronze memorial to the ghetto fighters. It is the only memorial I will see during my entire stay in Poland that isn't wreathed with commemorative flowers.

Another afternoon, I wander to the western rim of what was once the ghetto, through a walled enclosure and into another time. There, in the dense underbrush of a lush forest, I happen upon the Jewish cemetery. Four hundred years of memorial slabs pitch into one another—wedged and tilted gravestones, cracked columns, decaying figurines, cratered inscriptions. The cemetery seems to recede for acres and acres, everything dappled in suffused green light. Deep in the forest, a few men are engaged in a Sisyphean labor of reclamation. From a shack over at one side emerges an old man—stooped, it seems, by the weight of a huge metal Star of David hanging from his neck. An elaborately embroidered yarmulke covers his sparse hair. He introduces himself as the caretaker of the cemetery.

I am with an American friend, Carl, who as a child picked up a little Yiddish from his Polish grandfather. With the help of Carl's thin strands of Yiddish, the caretaker leads us on a tour. He shows us *"quartiers"* of bankers, shoemakers, and scholars. He walks us past the tombstones of *"groyse rebes"*—great rabbis—and then past the tombs of S. Ansky and I. L. Peretz, two of the greatest Yiddish writers, and then into the *quartier* of the Socialists and the Bundists. "We leave them here to continue their debates," he says, smiling.

At one point, we emerge from the thick forest into an empty clearing, a narrow scar of a wedge. "Here is what we did," he explains. "Early on, the Nazis ordered us Jews to provide sand for the cement wall they were building to close up the ghetto—and they ordered us to dig it out of the cemetery. So as to desecrate as little of the cemetery as possible, the Jews moved the graves from this area to another section of the forest and then dug here. Here they dug deeper and deeper and deeper, so they wouldn't have to do more damage elsewhere. In the end, there was a huge pit. Later, the Nazis used it for mass burials."

We walk on, past tailors and merchants and resistance heroes. Some of the graves are surprisingly recent. "Her daughter is in America," the caretaker explains at a tombstone dated 1967.

"What is your family name?" he suddenly asks Carl.

"Ginsburg."

"Ginsburg, Ginsburg," he repeats, in perfectly measured cadences. "Let's see, what have I got in Ginsburg?" He then leads us to Ginsburg bankers, rabbis, doctors, merchants. . . .

From the Jewish cemetery, we walk about a mile to Aleje Swierczew- skiego 79, where, according to an old guidebook, we can expect to find the Jewish Historical Institute and a museum commemorating the Ghetto Uprising. What we do find is boarded up. We pound on the door. No answer. It's a Wednesday afternoon, four o'clock. We start to walk away, and the door creaks open. A chubby, toothless old man in a cheap gray coat appears in the doorway and gestures that the museum is closed. He doesn't speak English or Yiddish (I'm pretty sure he's a Catholic Pole), but he speaks zloty, and for a small bribe he lets us in. You can do just about anything in Warsaw for a hundred zlotys.

The interior of the museum is a shambles. Downstairs, sacred Torah scrolls are displayed in a cracked vitrine, drenched in dust; a large menorah has toppled over. Upstairs, it's clear, there was once a substantial exhibition on the history of the ghetto during the Nazi Occupation. Today, tattered, curled photos slide from their moorings, maps lie torn on the floor. Blowups of faces hang upside down—sad, reproachful, resigned faces. In one rickety glass case, a rusty milk can and a few disintegrating metal boxes are displayed. These are the containers for the archives—archives meticulously collected inside the ghetto, perilously maintained, carefully buried for later recovery, then recovered, unpacked, mounted, and now utterly abandoned to this new holocaust of memory. On the top floor, clots of correspondence spill from bursting boxes— letters inquiring after missing relatives, dated 1945 and '46. Ancient photographs lie strewn over the floor, fading in the glare of the skylight—

families lost to life and time. As we leave, I thumb through the guest-book. There have been only two other visitors this year. One of them has scrawled "Shame!"

Everything I am seeing confirms the things I've heard about Poland from Polish Jews now living in Israel, France, and the United States. Over and over, prior to my trip, I encountered sheer hatred of Poland and its people, cold fury in reminiscences of an anti-Semitism that, it was claimed, pervaded Polish society in the years before and during the war. "You think it's a coincidence that the Nazis placed Auschwitz, Birkenau, Majdanek, Treblinka, and so many other concentration camps in Poland?" an acquaintance in New York asked me. "The Poles were only too pleased to accept things that even the Germans wouldn't stand for." A woman in Israel compared the behavior of the Hungarian authorities, who occasionally attempted to protect their Jews and, in fact, saved tens of thousands of them in the last stages of the war, with that of the Poles, who, she insisted, showed little such compassion. "Today, Poland's synagogues are used as garages!" she said. "I hear stories about the lines and the shortages and the hard times in Warsaw," a Jewish emigré from Poland now living in Los Angeles told me, "and I wish I could say I feel compassion, but you know what? It couldn't be happening to a more deserving people." "The history of the Jews in Poland would make a dark book," concluded another Polish Jew, currently residing in New York, "but I'm afraid it's now a closed book. To all intents and purposes, there is no Jewish question in Poland today."

His words were now being echoed in Warsaw by an old, tired man, probably in his seventies, who is a survivor of the Lodz ghetto. "Look," the man was saying. "Human life consists of the passage between two doors. For the Jews of Poland today, only one of them is open."

I was therefore prepared to close the book—to close the door on my impressions of the Polish-Jewish question. Only, for some reason, it wouldn't quite close.

For one thing, I encounter a few, admittedly feeble, signs of Polish concern. Late in my trip, I learn that a Catholic intellectual club is volunteering some labor at the Warsaw cemetery, and that a committee of prominent Polish cultural and intellectual figures is forming to lobby for the preservation of Jewish cemeteries and synagogues throughout the country. Furthermore, on some subsequent visits to the Jewish Historical Institute in Warsaw I do encounter a few people working in the archives. It turns out that the Institute's highly esteemed staff did flee Warsaw during the anti-Semitic purges of 1968, but a few people have come along since, and they are trying to bear a minimal witness—as much as can be borne, given the fact that hardly any of them speak or read either Hebrew or Yiddish. There is talk of someday—someday—opening the display gallery once again.

But the biggest reason for my reevaluation of the Polish-Jewish question comes in the form of a group of young Jews whom I happen upon during my last few days in Warsaw. They aren't even supposed to exist, as far as everyone else is concerned, but there they are, coming together for the holy days, for the Sabbath meal each week, and for mutual support and enlightenment. In most cases, these people—mainly young professionals in their thirties (editors, mathematicians, psychologists, and the like)—themselves learned of their Jewish origins only during the past several years. Since that discovery, they've been spending a great deal of time trying to integrate this sudden, unexpected knowledge.

"Most of us have the same story," one of them, a psychologist, tells me on a walk through the former ghetto. "We are children of middle- or high-level officials in the Communist Party. Our parents were Socialists and Communists in the years before the war and had virtually no sense of their own Jewishness even then. They were Marxist atheists, and when the war came—or, in some cases, even before—they fled to Moscow. The fate of Polish Communists in the Soviet Union during the thirties and forties was often tragic—many were sent into the Gulag. But they were true believers, and the thing you have to realize about these Stalinists is that even in the face of such obvious evidence of tyrannical excess as the imprisonment, exile, and execution of their friends and relatives, and even when they faced execution themselves, they remained true believers. They could offer explanations for the occurrence of such aberrations: Stalin didn't know; such was the nature of revolution; the long-term success of the Soviet experiment required sacrifice. Anyway, after the war the survivors returned to Poland with the Soviet Army and took part in the early stages of Communist rule in Poland. Only, they were Jewish atheists, and we, their children, were never raised as Jews, and often weren't even told we were Jewish. That was something we learned only much later—most of us in 1968, when we were suddenly being attacked in the street as Jews, when the Party turned on its own Jews, our parents, using them as scapegoats and expelling them in large-scale purges. Most of us continued to try to hide our Jewishness—that guilty knowledge—from others, and even from ourselves, but in the last several years some of us have been returning, as you would say, to our Jewish 'roots,' and we've been discovering one another."

I ask him how many Jews exist in Poland today.

"Oh, that figure you generally get—between five and seven thousand—is ridiculous. There are tens of thousands of people like us, and thousands of others who still don't know they're Jewish. For one thing, among those who survived the war here in Poland there was a natural process of selection: in most cases, they don't *look* Jewish."

I ask him if he expects any sort of Jewish renaissance in Poland.

"It's much too early to speculate. Certainly nothing dramatic, at any rate. Most of us have been supportive of and active in the current political renewal, and the fate of any Jewish revival will inevitably be tied to the fate of the entire Polish nation. If things open up for Poland, perhaps they will open up for us, too."

This surprises me. Doesn't he believe, like most of his exiled contemporaries, that the Poles are by nature profoundly anti-Semitic?

"No, it's not as simple as that," he replies. "The history of the Jews in Poland is an incredibly complicated story, but it certainly can't be reduced to the statement that Poles are anti-Semites."

Repeatedly I hear the same assertion from this man and his young Jewish friends, and they all give me substantially the same reasons for making it. What follows is, in all fairness, a simplification, but the basic premise is consistent: that the Poles were never anti-Semitic at heart. They have always been highly nationalistic, a proud, suffering people deprived of and longing for their state. In the past, they were faced with a large Jewish population—a population whose very size proves the prior openness of the Polish people, and particularly the Polish nobility, to Jewish immigration. The Jews tended to keep to themselves, in ghettos of their own choosing. It is easy to understand how during the eighteenth and nineteenth centuries the highly nationalistic Poles might have conceived of these self-possessed Jews as aliens in their midst. The foreign occupying authorities—especially the Russians—exploited that anxiety, playing the Jews off against the Poles, as part of their strategy for dominating both. These young Jews insist that such pogroms as occurred in Poland were spillovers from Russia—that there were no indigenous Polish pogroms. ("Now, the Russians—the Russians were always rabidly anti-Semitic!") During the late nineteenth century, according to this view, capitalism, a foreign import, came to Poland by way of the Germans and the native Jews. Many of the most visible and most brutal large-scale enterprises—especially textile plants—were owned by Jews. "Polish resentment was understandable," I am told. Poles who couldn't get back at either the Germans or the Jewish upper class often directed their anger at poorer Jews. "It's not pretty, but it is understandable."

During the twenties, as this explanation goes, the Poles finally achieved their state, but ten percent of the population was Jewish, and the Jews were still largely concentrated in self-contained communities in urban centers. Many people—both Poles and Jews—felt this presence to be troubling, at once alien and too large. Zionism had its Polish supporters. Other Jews, meanwhile, were active in the Communist Party and were devoted to the Soviet example—this in a country and among a people who had only recently thrown off the Russian imperialist yoke. But although individual Poles were often anti-Semitic, according to this account, there was at no point in Poland's sorry history any state or institutionalized anti-Semitism, as there had been in France, in Russia, and in Germany. The most convincing proof of the relative mildness

of Polish anti-Semitism came precisely during the Nazi Occupation:
Given that many Poles hated the Jews and most Poles wanted them out,
still, these young people insist, during the months between the beginning
of the Occupation and the mandatory segregation of all Jews into walled-
off ghettos, there were no pogroms in Poland. The Nazis would undoubtedly have allowed them, but the Poles did not indulge such a gruesome license.

"It's admittedly a thin spindle upon which to base a claim to human-
ism," my psychologist friend tells me. "But there was simply the belief
that Poles do not behave in such a fashion. They hated the Jews, they
wanted them out, but they wouldn't kill them, because Poles didn't kill
innocent, defenseless people. It just wasn't done. And there were many
recorded instances of 'anti-Semitic' Poles lodging and hiding Jews through
the whole war."

After the war, while most Poles looked to their indigenous nationalist
resistance, based in London, geopolitical factors dictated the imposition
of the Moscow-based Communist "government in exile," a regime that
was disproportionately Jewish. "During the late forties, upward of 40
percent of the Polish Communist Party was Jewish," my psychologist
friend insists. Once again, the Poles felt themselves subjected to alien
forces.

I ask one of the young Jews if he is offended by the virtual lack of
Jewish commemoration at Auschwitz. (Although the situation has improved slightly, until recently the camp was preserved as a monument to
"the martyrdom of the Polish nation and of other nations," with the Jews
listed, when they were listed, alongside the Hungarians, the French, the
Yugoslavs, and other European nationalities.)

"Well, that's a typical objection," he replies. "But one thing that
foreign Jews fail to understand is that millions of Poles—of non-Jewish
Poles—also perished at Auschwitz. Sometimes when you make that objection to a Pole he'll tell you, 'But the Jews have their own Holocaust
memorials in Jerusalem.' And there's a certain validity to that. Furthermore, the reason there were so many concentration camps in Poland was
not, as I've heard foreign Jews claim, because the Poles wanted them
here, but rather, because as far as the Nazis were concerned, after they
finished with the Jews the Poles were slated to be next."

Weren't the 1968 purges an example of Polish state anti-Semitism?

"First of all, you will find few of us who will defend the behavior of
the authorities here since 1945 on any question. Second, that campaign
was largely internal—not so much a Polish phenomenon as a Communist Party phenomenon. It was actually quite clever. Certain elements in
the Party saw a chance to eliminate both the Stalinist fathers and the
dissident sons—both the right and the left wings of the Party—and in
the process open up several bureaucratic slots for themselves—slots that

they retain, by and large, to this day. And, third, it was a pathetic attempt on the part of a manifestly colonial regime to pander to native nationalism, to try to appear more Polish in the eyes of its citizens by identifying and attacking an alien element."

I decide not to pursue the obvious next question: What does it say about a people that their nationalism can be pandered to by way of anti-Semitism?

The young man continues, "But, most important, the true Polish character has shown itself in the more recent period, when various quasi-official groups tried to discredit the current political revival by focussing on its Jewish elements—without any success." He then recounts a joke that is making the rounds: "Question: Why is there such a shortage of soap? Answer: Because the authorities are busy turning the soap back into Jews."

"Don't you find that joke offensive?" I ask, somewhat horrified.

"On the contrary, it's a good joke. Anyone who lives here recognizes its subtext—that in the past the authorities tried to blame problems on the Jews, but now there aren't enough left to make the charge credible, so it must have been invalid even then."

What of the fact that Czeslaw Milosz, the Lithuanian-born essayist and poet who writes in Polish, was celebrated as a national hero when he won the Nobel Prize in Literature in 1980, but Isaac Bashevis Singer, who was born in Poland, and whose tales deal principally with life in Poland before the war, was largely ignored in his homeland when he won the same prize two years before? ("A virtually unknown American writer who writes in Yiddish" is how the official Polish news releases characterized Singer. "They've gone and awarded the Nobel Prize to a sewing machine!" was a common joke, I've been told. None of Singer's books is available in Poland, although a few stories have recently been translated and appeared in magazines.)

"Again, it's not as easy as you're implying," my friend insists. "Singer didn't concern himself with the Poles. Read those stories, as I have— I read them in English. Poles hardly ever appear in them, and when they do they are portrayed as shadowy, alien figures. In a fundamental sense, Singer is *not* a Polish writer—certainly not the way Milosz is."

And so forth. It is strange to hear this kind of account from Jews, but increasingly I have come to see these young people not as Polish Jews but, rather, as Jewish Poles—a new breed altogether. These are people who grew up imagining themselves Polish—imbued with the stubborn, fierce, romantic nationalism of their friends and classmates—and have only recently come to their Jewishness and to the difficult task of trying to integrate that Jewishness into their lives.

I don't quite know what I think of their version of Polish-Jewish history. I do know this: Through my meetings with these young Jewish

Poles, I have come to a deeper appreciation of the tragic nature of the historical interpenetration of these two peoples in this hopeless land where ironies fold in and in and in on themselves. For, apart from anything else, Polish history and Jewish history seem to illuminate each other. If Poland, as Slowacki claimed, is the Jesus Christ of nations, then we are speaking of Jesus the Jew, the martyr to the Roman occupation of Palestine. The situation of the Poles during much of the last two centuries—a people, a language, a religion, a literature, a culture, all without a state—is uncannily congruent with the simultaneous situation of the Jews. Much has been written of the messianic longing with which Polish-Jewish Chassidism was rife during the early nineteenth century—but Polish Catholic Romanticism during that period likewise conceived of a national messianic mission. It is one of the cruellest ironies of history that these two stateless, visionary peoples came to share the same meagre plot of land at the same moment.

One day, I ask a Polish Catholic if she has ever read the Book of Job—it seems so much the book of Poland.

"Well, it's funny you should mention that," she answers. "As Catholics, we seldom read the Old Testament. But Milosz, in exile in America, taught himself Hebrew so he could translate sections of the Bible, and he's just released an extraordinary Polish version of Job. Many people are talking about it."[2]

Adam Michnik, one of the leading theorists of the current political renewal, and himself a Jew (though not a particularly observant one), recently wrote an article in which he cast 1956, 1968, 1970, and 1976 as "dates which stake out the successive stations on the Polish *via dolorosa*." There is a poster that summons the same theme through different imagery. A bright-red pulse line moves horizontally across a white background—a seismograph, or perhaps the record of a heartbeat—erupting periodically in steep, jagged verticals, above which are the dates '44, '56, '68, '70, '76, '80. Approaching the present, the tremors increase in strength and frequency, and on the other side of 1980 the red line opens out onto a single powerful word: "SOLIDARNOSC."

'44   '56   '68 '70 '76 '80

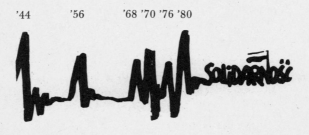

Of all the lines in Warsaw this May, one of the longest always seemed to be queuing outside a small building on the edge of Old Town. People stood patiently waiting for up to two hours at a time, not for food or supplies or bureaucratic approvals, but to see a spare exhibit, compiled by a local photo club, of photographs and documents from "The Events of the Years 1956, 1968, 1970, 1976, and 1980." The unofficial exhibition (it was never advertised in the regular newspapers) consisted of amateur documentation of events that officially had hardly happened at all.

Once inside the building the line snaked slowly along the perimeters of three small adjoining rooms; at eye level, a cavalcade of photos had been modestly pasted to the walls. The photos were generally crude in quality, hasty in execution, haphazard in preservation. The originals of the photos had been surfacing over the past several months, sometimes anonymously at Solidarity offices around the country. They had been taken, often on the run, usually with primitive equipment, by individuals who subsequently risked imprisonment just by keeping them in their homes. In ironic and frequently outrageous juxtaposition to the photographic record, the organizers of the show sometimes displayed copies of contemporary official accounts of the same incidents. Thus, for example, beside photos of the mass protest rallies in Poznan in 1956 were newspaper articles describing "the machinations of a small band of provocateurs."

In 1956: Stalin had been dead for three years when Nikita Khrushchev launched the process of de-Stalinization with his famous secret speech to the Twentieth Congress of the Soviet Communist Party, in February. That process, unsettling as it was within the Soviet Union itself, was wrenching along the periphery of the Soviet empire. In June, in the most dramatic of the Polish confrontations during this period, workers from the Zispo engine plant, in Poznan, set down their tools and marched on the town center, angrily protesting food prices and scarcity. Shots were fired; there were many deaths and many more injuries. In the fall, Wladyslaw Gomulka, a popular nationalist who was by no means the first choice of the Soviet authorities (indeed, he had spent time in Stalinist prisons) was rehabilitated and installed as Party Secretary, inaugurating the famous "Spring in October," a period of renewal as hopeful as it was short-lived. (The attention of the Soviet authorities had in the meantime been distracted by events in Hungary, whose rebellion began as a series of demonstrations in sympathy with the Poles.)

In 1968: Gomulka's regime had stiffened into a traditional autocratic bureaucracy. (Four years earlier, Jacek Kuron and Karol Modzelewski had been expelled from the Communist Party for suggesting, in an "Open Letter to Communist Party Members," that "state ownership of the means of production" did not necessarily produce "social ownership" of those means—and, indeed, that Communism as it was currently being practiced in Poland had veered profoundly from Marxist first principles.) Discontent was rising, particularly among students and intellectuals. (This would become the season of youth movements in Prague, Paris, Berkeley, and Chicago.) By March, the authorities had maneuvered the students into a situation in which they were forced to stage a protest without adequate preparation. The regime responded to this—its own provocation—with a double attack. First, "angry workers" were brought in from the outskirts of various towns, especially Warsaw, to beat up the demonstrating students. (It should be noted that although relatively few workers actually participated in the thuggery, still fewer came to the defense of the students; the "generation gap" of those years was, after all, a global phenomenon, and in Poland the separation between intellectuals and laborers was still quite severe.) Second, certain elements in the Party, including Gomulka himself, launched a rabid anti-Semitic campaign.

In 1970: By December, the economic consequences of Gomulka's tenure had become so serious that the government was forced to post a series of shocking price increases. In a clumsy ruse, the government tried to disguise the increases as a "rearrangement" of prices—the prices for luxury items like television sets, car radios, and tape recorders were lowered, while the prices for necessities like food and clothing went up. The announcement created unrest throughout the country, culminating, in the middle of the month, in a complete shutdown of the shipyards in the Baltic Coast cities of Gdansk, Gdynia, and Szczecin. The workers poured out of the yards, marching on the town centers. (The intellectuals, nursing their wounds from two years earlier, on the whole declined to join or support the demonstrations.) On December 16th, the government responded with a terrifying display of force, ordering "Polish soldiers to fire on Polish workers"—as the dark incidents were recalled afterward. Helicopters dropped tear gas on the crowds of surging demonstrators; tanks sprayed machine-gun fire. Dozens, perhaps hundreds, were killed; thousands were injured. No one knows the exact figures; the incidents themselves were quickly cloaked in official silence. Nevertheless, the rebellion did have substantive results: Gomulka was ousted, to be replaced by Gierek; and within a few months, after a decisive follow-up strike by the women textile workers of Lodz, the new government rescinded the price increases.

In 1976: The boom of Gierek's early years, financed largely by foreign loans, had gone bust. When Gierek tried once again to raise food prices in order to shore up his faltering economy, he, too, faced a workers' veto. This time, the disturbances were most pronounced at the Ursus tractor plant, outside Warsaw, and in Radom, a town about 60 miles south of the capital that was the site of an important armaments factory. The incidents were perhaps not as dramatic as some of the earlier confrontations, but their dénouement proved crucial, for it was in their aftermath that a small group of intellectuals formed KOR—the Committee for the Defense of the Workers (the group subsequently expanded its focus and changed its name to the Committee of Social Defense, KSS, although it would almost always be referred to by its original acronym, KOR). The activities of this group, which began monitoring various state campaigns of harassment against individual activist workers, publicizing trials, interceding wherever possible, and generally raising issues for public discussion, proved vital in at least two ways during the years to come. First, KOR at last transcended the separation between intellectuals and workers that had bedeviled the Polish dissident movement, to the detriment of both sides, since 1968 and, for that matter, through most of Polish history. Second, since many of those associated with KOR—including Jan Litynski, Adam Michnik, and Karol Modzelewski—were of Jewish origin, the organization likewise served to transcend the separation between Catholics and Jews, which might otherwise have been played upon by the authorities in the coming decade. As it happened, in 1980, when quasi-official groups tried to play the workers off against the "experts," and the Catholics against the Jews, their attempts failed dismally. "We remembered," a worker in Warsaw told me. "Those people had been with us and helping us for several years. The government couldn't fool us again as to who our true friends were."

In 1980: The summer of the Moscow Olympics. This time, the occasion was a rise in meat prices; many Poles felt that their meat was being shipped to Moscow for the festivities, a suspicion that only fueled their anger. The meat-price decree, issued on July 1st, provoked a rolling series of strikes: workers at one factory would lay down their tools, the government would quickly raise wages and rush in fresh supplies of meat, and the workers would return to work; when the workers at a factory a few dozen kilometers away heard about these results, they would go on strike, with a similar set of demands. Warsaw, Katowice, Lublin . . . And then, in mid-August, the Lenin Shipyard, in Gdansk. Sometime earlier, in somebody's idea of a brilliant preemptive move, the authorities at the shipyard had fired Anna Walentynowicz, a 51-year-old widow and crane operator who was an activist and a mother figure to the young workers in the crews. (They called her Pani Ania—Mrs. Ania.) That was stupid. You don't fire the crane operator. She's the most visible person around, and the workers know she's competent—after all, they trust their lives to that competence every day. In fury over such firings and the recent price increases, the shipyard workers put down their tools on August 14th and refused to be dislodged from the factory, their fortress: they had learned their lesson ten years earlier, witnessing the worst massacre in postwar Polish history, and they were not about to leave the plant or be appeased by a few extra slabs of meat. The next day, the strike began to spread throughout the region. (August 15th is one of the holiest days in the Polish Catholic calendar—the Feast of the Assumption, and a day particularly consecrated to the Black Madonna of Czestochowa. On August 15, 1920, in an action that Poles refer to as "The Miracle on the Vistula," Marshal Jozef Pilsudski, at the head of a Polish nationalist army, held off an invading Soviet Bolshevik force on the outskirts of Warsaw[3]—further increasing the stature of the Black Madonna in the Polish imagination.) The strike continued for 17 days, and the victorious workers returned to their machines on September 1st—the anniversary, of course, of the 1939 Nazi attack on the Polish garrison at Danzig (today, Gdansk) which set off the Second World War.

This was the history which that photo exhibition in Warsaw was attempting to document, and which its visitors were quaffing in draughts. The images themselves were interesting, sometimes even poignant, but to Western eyes they seemed if anything almost clichéd. Over the years we have become inured to photos of street demonstrations, banners, police phalanxes, hippie beatings; we have seen thousands of images of Selma, People's Park, Chicago, Northern Ireland, and so forth, and the power of such imagery has eroded for us. What was truly fascinating at this exhibition, therefore, was not so much the photos as the extreme intensity with which the Poles themselves were examining them. Never in all my years of visiting art and photo exhibitions have I seen images studied with such care and concentration. People would stand transfixed in front of a single image for two, three, five minutes before moving a few feet to the next image, upon which they would lavish similar attention. It was as if they'd never seen anything like it—and they hadn't. The entire exhibit seemed to say, "See, look, those weren't unfounded rumors; we told you this happened, here's proof."

Some of the official accounts had blossomed with spontaneous graffiti: over one article from the party newspaper concerning the 1956 disruptions, someone had scrawled, "Lies! Lies! Enough lies!" Across another official photo of the 1970 Party Central Committee appeared the word "Bandits!" Some of the dour images of individual officials had sprouted updates: "This murderer Kociolek," for example, "is still on the Secretariat of the Warsaw Party Committee."

A newspaper account of the 1976 troubles in Radom described them as "the work of hooligans." In the photo next to the article, a banner stretched above the throng, insisting "GLODNY ROBOTNIK TO NIE CHULIGAN" ("A hungry worker is not a hooligan"). Other posters read "CHLEB" and "WOLNOSC" ("Bread" and "Freedom"). The moral lesson was apparent: Don't believe everything you read.

Far and away the most powerful sequence of images was that depicting the events of December 1970. The photographs showed how the Gdansk strikers surged out of their factory and marched on the Old Town, where, stonewalled by bureaucrats, they set fire to the Communist Party's regional headquarters. (In one photo the building is ferociously ablaze, while across the street, on the roof of a nearby church, demonstrators are stamping out straying embers.) Then there were photos of the bullet-spraying helicopters, cordons of advancing militia men, tanks lumbering incongruously through the quaint cobblestone alleys of the Old Town. There were images of crowds fleeing and, in their wake, dead crumbled bodies. There was a surging crowd carrying a lifeless body atop a torn-off door frame. This last photo was draped with wilted flowers.

Standing before one of the images, a former resident of Gdansk held a group of Warsavites enthralled with his recollections. "Right over there"—he pointed to an intersection in one photograph—"I saw a policeman sneak up on a comrade and smash his skull in. Immediately the crowd surrounded the lone officer, disarmed him, and literally tore him to pieces. The officer was dead and virtually dismembered by the time reinforcements arrived. I saw that with my own eyes."

A few minutes later, outside the exhibition, I asked the man from Gdansk whether in the years between 1970 and 1980 he had felt free to tell his story. "Hardly ever," he replied. "If we spoke about such things at all, it was only among close friends. Once, it must have been in 1971, I had to travel to Krakow. Leaving the station, the taxi-driver asked me where I was from. When I said Gdansk, he turned off the meter and drove me around town for over an hour asking me for details of what happened. But in Gdansk, the townspeople seldom spoke of the events of 1970, except with our glances; when things began to pick up again last summer, it was clear everybody had been thinking about it all along."

A week after I visited the show, I happened to meet one of its organizers at Solidarity's national headquarters. He showed me some other photos, and then he prepared to play me a tape. Someone off the street had brought in the original cassette a few months before; this man had happened to be recording events in Gdansk at the very moment the shooting broke out. He'd kept the cassette hidden for years and never played it for anyone until that day in the Solidarity office.

Once again, the impact of the sounds on the tape—the crackle of bullets, the wail of sirens, the chanting of crowds, the scatter of people— was dulled for me by my Western familiarity with the aural vocabulary of violence. But as the tape continued—on and on, shooting, sirens, screams, more shooting and then *more* shooting—the horror began to bleed through. It occurred to me that our Western newscasts always offer us bite-size morsels, little digestible snippets that disguise the true horror of conflict—that is, that it just seems to go on and on and you have no idea when it's going to stop. The man playing the tape for me seemed no less moved, even though, surely, this was the hundredth time he'd heard it. After a while the tape ran out in mid-wail.

As I was getting ready to leave, the man reached into his cluttered desk and pulled out a file. It contained copies of some of the photos in the show, and he asked me to take about a dozen. "We want copies to exist in the West," he explained. "They need to be published everywhere, so that even if something goes wrong here in Poland, they'll never be able to say 1970 didn't happen."*

Two things seem to me important about the relationship of most Poles to this history—this rosary chain of dates. The first element perhaps applies more to activists and intellectuals. When you ask such people, "Why did '1980' happen in 1980, and not in 1976, say, or 1970, or 1968?" the answer you invariably get is "The moment wasn't right until 1980." This formulation is at once Marxist (the various elements of society had not achieved the appropriate configuration and consciousness until 1980) and Catholic (the Moment comes when It comes). In Poland today, these two categories are ineluctably intertwined.

The second, however, concerns just about everyone in Poland, and it has to do with the truly traumatic impact of some of the massacres that make up this litany of dates—to some extent, Poznan in 1956, but especially Gdansk in 1970. In America, by contrast, although we had our share of violence during the sixties (35 people died in Watts in 1965, at least 26 in Newark and 40 in Detroit in 1967, 4 at Kent State in 1970), we got over it. "That's history," we tend to say, meaning, "It happens, it's past, all you can do is look to the future." In Poland, when people talk about the massacre in Gdansk and say, *"That's history,"* the veins in their foreheads pulse and conversation stops dead cold. They *cannot* get over it. Poles, especially the residents of Gdansk, talk about 1970 the way Jews talk about Auschwitz: it's almost a transcendent category. This is partly because the memory of the incident was repressed for so long: virtually no official mention was made of it. The story persisted through word of mouth, turn of glance, and secretly passed photographs. (Over the years, an eerie, silent conspiracy of commemoration spread throughout the country. Whenever people had occasion to write "1970" they wrote it "19†0." This practice spread even to government documents reviewing the period.) But there's something more, and everyone in Poland seems to sense it: If these dates constitute the *via dolorosa* of the Polish people, then 1970 was the Crucifixion, and 1980, by implication, the Resurrection and the Life.

In Warsaw this spring, Woody Allen's *Manhattan* is the big American film. *Three Days of the Condor, Hair,* and *A Star Is Born* are also playing. People still talk about *Taxi Driver.* (One student tells me it was her favorite recent film, "because it portrayed a man who had the courage to be a nonconformist"—so much for what gets lost in translation.) Last year, *Star Wars* played briefly, without that much success (who needed science fiction?), but *One Flew Over the Cuckoo's Nest* is regularly packing them in. A few seasons back, the authorities heavily promoted *Norma*

* See page 232.

Rae, a film about union organizing in a textile mill in the American South; they were hoping to educate their countrymen to the horrific realities of capitalist exploitation, but, according to some Solidarity spokespeople, the message that most Poles came away with concerned the fundamental importance of trade unions. On television, Poles receive weekly transfusions of "The Streets of San Francisco," "Columbo," and —starting just recently—"Charlie's Angels" and "Starsky and Hutch." ("Oh, we love to see all those American cars," a Warsaw acquaintance tells me. "And I particularly love the way American phones ring.") But, for a change, the most talked-about movie in Warsaw this spring is not American but Polish, and you can't even find it listed in the paper.

Robotnicy '80 (Workers '80) is a documentary about the Gdansk shipyard strike of that year. Although it was grudgingly passed by the censors (the public would not have stood for its outright banning), it has not been allowed to receive regular distribution, and newspaper advertising is forbidden. On any given evening, it's playing somewhere in Warsaw, but to find out where you have to look in the paper for the theater where "All Seats Are Sold Out." That's the code. Go to that theater and you can most likely get yourself a seat for one of the most extraordinary films of recent years.

Before I saw *Robotnicy '80,* I had occasion to speak with one of its co-directors, Andrzej Chodakowski, a tall, gentle, soft-spoken man with an uncanny facial resemblance to Sid Caesar. "In August of last year, as the Gdansk strike began to develop, it took our unit ten days of intensive lobbying at Film Polski, the government film bureau, before we received reluctant permission to take our cameras up north," he told me. "As usual, the intercession of Andrzej Wajda proved crucial." Andrzej Wajda, Poland's foremost director, is a national hero and often wields his considerable authority to help realize progressive projects in the Polish film industry. "Once we got to the shipyards, it took still more time before the workers would let us in. They had the factory completely closed off and were exercising very strict security, trying to prevent the entry of secret-police provocateurs. They were also particularly suspicious of us because in the past photographs had been used, at the conclusion of a strike, to identify strike leaders, who then mysteriously disappeared. This had happened to hundreds of their comrades in the months after 1970. We finally reached an agreement—they could control the footage until after the successful conclusion of the strike, and destroy it if anything went wrong. Once we were let in, filming proved quite difficult. It was a tremendously emotional time, and there were moments when we ourselves were unable to continue—our own eyes became clouded over with tears. Beyond that, we had been able to secure only 13,000 meters of film stock, which we had to ration carefully without having any idea how long the strike would go on. During the final days, as tensions at the negotiating sessions mounted, we were particularly anxious,

because we were running out of film. But it all came to a happy conclusion, and a few weeks later, at a special midnight screening at the
Gdansk Film Festival, we were able to show some of the early rushes.
The auditorium was filled with veterans of the strike, and there in the
middle of it all was Lech Walesa, flanked on one side by the Archbishop
of Gdansk and on the other by the Deputy Minister of Culture. It was
incredible—six weeks earlier, this man had been an unemployed electrician."

In *Robotnicy '80*, the camera is scrunched right in there during the
most sensitive negotiations between the strike leaders and government
representatives—but then so was just about everyone else in the yard.
The government had asked for secret negotiations, but Walesa and his
colleagues insisted that everything be done in the open, and the negotiations were being piped live throughout the plant over the regular PA
system. Whenever Walesa made a particularly trenchant point, applause
swelled up from outside. When Mieczyslaw Jagielski, the shrewd government negotiator, suggested at one point that because of time constraints
they should hurry to sign the documents even though a few points remained to be resolved, jeers erupted outside and Walesa calmly declined.
"Time?" he said. "Don't worry, we have time."

Meanwhile, outside the negotiating hall the strikers had commandeered
the printing office and were hand-printing a daily newspaper, which they
were passing between the bars of the closed gates to the throngs of townspeople gathered on the other side. Coming in the opposite direction,
over the top of the wall, were vats of soup and loaves of bread. At night,
the workers slept by their machines, their families having passed them
blankets through the fence grille. The gate was slowly becoming festooned with flowers, crucifixes, and photos of the Pope. On Sunday
morning, when the negotiations had reached a critical stage, a priest
was brought in to say Mass. In the film, we watch a hush fall over the
throngs on both sides of the gate, and everyone falls to his knees in silent
prayer. Presently, they sing a religious hymn, and at this point a friend
who was translating for me began to cry. "That hymn has been banned
since the war," she whispered. "Look! Everyone still remembers the
words."

During the negotiations, which covered 21 points, Walesa and his
comrades were unmovable on the first two—the formation of an independent union and the right of that union to strike. When the government proved slow in acceding to another of the demands—the release
of KOR advisers and other activists who had been rounded up in recent
days—Walesa warned that the strikers would not go back to work until
the advisers were released, and that, once they were released, if any harm
should come to them "we have an independent union and we retain our
right to strike again."

The government negotiators were whipped; in the film they have the look of people who realize that the jig is up. In the large hall where the official signing ceremonies for the new covenant took place, a cross was conspicuously hanging on the wall between the Polish eagle and a sculpture of Lenin. Walesa signed the document with a huge souvenir pen commemorating the Pope's 1979 visit.

In Poland, the interpenetration of film and political reality is particularly fertile. Most Polish filmmakers start out as documentarians, even though many of their documentaries have been shelved by the censor and never released. One result of the recent political developments has been a loosening of the censor's authority. Among the most popular film series in Warsaw these days is a retrospective of once-banned documentaries at Non-Stop Kino, entitled *From the Shelves*. Looking at some of these films, you get the feeling that if the Party leaders had taken the time to look at the documentaries their minions were busy banning they might have seen the current upheaval coming a mile away.

The day I went to Non-Stop, two efforts in particular stood out. Irena Kamienska's bleak portrait of women textile workers, *Robotnice*, looked for all the world as if it had been shot in some Victorian hellhole amidst capitalist exploitation at its most savage: the relentless throb of the machinery, the dust-saturated air, the women wearing masks that both shield their lungs and muffle their voices. During one of their brief breaks, one particularly wrinkled and stooped old woman lets fall that she is in fact only 40 years old.

Marcel Lozinski's darkly sardonic semi-documentary, *Proba Mikrofonu (Microphone Test)*, is set inside a cosmetics factory where bored, alienated women run the endless assembly line. At one point the film's protagonist, the DJ who's in charge of stocking the factory's PA system with spunky Muzak, gets it into his head to fashion an aural portrait of the women at the plant. He lugs his tape recorder around, asking the workers if they feel responsible for what's happening in the plant. Some say no, but most don't even know what he means by "responsible." From their puzzled reactions, he weaves a collage that he then tries to get approved by the factory's Party Central Committee. In the film's wry epilogue, the Committee members angrily denounce the whole project, insisting that "the workers don't know what they're talking about" and scolding the DJ for asking the wrong questions ("If you had asked the proper questions, you would have known the answers in advance"). In the end the Committee votes to shelve the tape, just as upon Lozinski's completion of his project a few years ago, his own board of review voted to shelve the film.[4]

In a surprising number of Polish feature films, the fictional protagonist is a documentarian of some sort. In Krzysztof Kieslowski's *Amator (Camera Buff)*, a factory worker acquires an 8-millimeter camera and gradually goes haywire, filming everything in sight, documenting life at home, in his plant, in the surrounding community, and eventually running afoul of the censor. In Janusz Kijowski's *Kung Fu*, a Warsaw journalist pursues a tangled thread of corruption and coverup in a provincial manufacturing plant. In *Man of Marble*, Andrzej Wajda's 1977 masterpiece, and perhaps the most accomplished film in the genre, a young woman film student obsessively stalks the elusive trail of Birkut, a fictional "workers' hero" from the Stalinist fifties, a Stakhanovite brick mason whose awesome record at laying walls had catapulted him to national newsreel prominence, but who subsequently fell afoul of Stalinist purge trials and then disappeared. Through such documentarian protagonists, Polish directors during the late seventies seemed to be saying that in a corrupt and stagnant political situation it becomes a heroic task merely to discover and declare a true thing. As the years passed, that lucid insistence has recirculated through the Polish body politic, with sometimes surprising results.

When *Man of Marble* was released in 1977, it had clearly suffered a censor's slash. The last scenes, in which Agnieszka, the filmmaker, finally tracks down Birkut's son, Tomczyk, in the Gdansk shipyard, only to discover that Birkut himself died in the 1970 uprising, had been conspicuously mauled. Still, the film proved a tremendous success in Poland during 1978 and 1979; and in 1980, during the strike, when Wajda was visiting Gdansk, a shipworker shouted out to him, "Now you have to tell our story—*Man of Iron*."

Wajda accepted the challenge. Perhaps no filmmaker has been faced with this kind of national commission—this urgent mandate to fashion the onrush of lived and shared experience, as it is happening, into a mythic legacy—since the days of Sergei Eisenstein. Wajda hired Chodakowski (fresh from *Robotnicy '80*) as his assistant director, and in a mere nine months they and their co-workers scripted, shot, and edited the new story—this one set against the climactic backdrop of the August events in Gdansk. In the new film, release of which still pended review by the Culture Ministry as of mid-May ("Hell," one director told me, "this one's going to have to be reviewed by the entire Central Committee!"), Winkiel, a washed-up, jaded, alcoholic journalist, receives a mysterious assignment to go to Gdansk and dig up any dirt he can find on Tomczyk—Birkut's son—who is one of the strike's ringleaders. Through flashbacks, we see Tomczyk's life—his student rage in 1968 when his father wouldn't join him, his own hesitation to join his father in 1970, his grief at his father's massacre, his work in the shipyards, his meeting with Agnieszka, their marriage, their work together in the activist underground, and the birth of their child. Much of the historical footage derives from a restaging of some of the haunting photos now on exhibit in Warsaw (most strikingly, the photo from 1970 of the crowd surging forward, carrying the corpse on the door frame); much of the Gdansk 1980 footage is lifted straight out of *Robotnicy '80*. The soundtracks of the strikes are actual, including that secret tape someone managed to preserve from the violence of 1970. Lech Walesa and Anna Walentynowicz make cameo appearances. In Poland today, filmmakers can conceive of nothing more compellingly dramatic than what is actually happening before their eyes. Fiction and documentary are merging in a new epic form.

During the Gdansk strike in 1980, only one Party official emerged unscathed and if anything with higher stature in the eyes of most of the workers at the shipyard—Tadeusz Fiszbach, the Party boss in the Gdansk region. "He is the only one of those bastards who can sleep peacefully at night," a Solidarity leader told me in the yards. Indeed, this spring there was rumored to be an insurgent movement within the Party itself to place Fiszbach at the head of the national Party at its coming summer congress. Anyway, Wajda invited Fiszbach to repeat his historic role in a cameo appearance in *Man of Iron*, and Fiszbach accepted the honor.[5]

Polish cinema, which has had a good deal to do with generating the moral climate out of which the current political renewal has been emerging, is itself becoming one of that renewal's principal beneficiaries. During recent years, the Polish film industry reorganized itself into eight production units, each one headed by a world-class director (Wajda, for example, heads one unit, Zanussi another), who then represents his junior associates before the Culture Ministry in matters, for example, of funding and censorship. The Culture Ministry, however, retained the right to veto production on specific projects.

In the early spring of this year, thanks to the liberalizing atmosphere, the production units extracted a new concession—the right under specific circumstances to veto the Culture Ministry's veto. The first test case of this new policy involves a fascinating script by a young screenwriter-director, Ryszard Bugajski, entitled *Przesluchanie (The Interrogation")*. This is the story of a defiant young woman held prisoner during the Stalinist witch-hunts of the early fifties; her rape by her examining magistrate; her pregnancy; his growing concern, confusion, and disintegration; and their daughter's activism, 20 years later, in an underground KOR publishing house. The script was summarily vetoed by the Culture Ministry during the winter, but this spring, Wajda, the head of Bugajski's unit, vetoed the veto.

"However," Bugajski told me one afternoon over drinks at the Hotel Forum, "this go-ahead is merely provisional. The economic crisis is forcing the political crisis, but it's also rendering some of the political gains somewhat moot. Today, for example, there are only 35,000 meters of film stock in the entire country, for all the directors in Poland; and because of the foreign-exchange imbalance, we can't afford to buy any more."

Similarly, although censorship standards have eased on the importation of foreign films, Film Polski can't afford to bring any new films in. Roman Polanski, the Polish emigré director, was able to convince his producers to accept zlotys for their licensing of *Tess* in Poland, but nobody else in the world is going to accept Polish currency.

In publishing, likewise, new, more liberal standards have been formulated, but an extreme paper shortage means that it can take as long as three years for a book to get published in Poland. In Warsaw this May, you couldn't buy a Polish-English dictionary if your life depended on it; for that matter, Polish-Polish dictionaries were in short supply. "There's a sense in which the government and the Party are perfectly willing to extend us freedoms they know we can't use," a writer told me. "In a strange way, they have a vested interest in perpetuating the current economic constrictions."

In other fields, though, the economic crisis is abetting the spread of information. There may be a shortage of film stock, but there's also a shortage of videotape. Consequently the state television networks, which used to be the most zealously guarded and controlled media outlets, are having to turn more and more often to live coverage, with predictably spontaneous results. One afternoon, I joined a group of Poles outside a television store to watch live gavel-to-gavel coverage of the parliamentary debates over registration of the independent farmers' union—sessions whose results were by no means foregone. Few Poles used to take TV news seriously, but today most people watch—particularly the late-night broadcasts, where, like everyone else in Polish society, the TV newscasters seem to be testing the limits of their new situation. Details may surface late at night, disappear the next morning, but sometimes resurface several weeks later in prime time. Nobody quite knows the new rules. Poles watch TV partly for the news and partly for the news of what the news is allowed to say.

"It's crazy over there," a BBC reporter preparing a documentary on Polish television exclaimed to me over coffee one morning. "Television is supposed to be the Party's strongest bastion, but 4,000 of the 6,000 employees belong to Solidarity, admittedly mostly technicians and not the journalists—but *that* in itself presents interesting prospects. At some stage soon, Solidarity may be in a position to pull the plug on any coverage it finds offensive."

In some ways the most remarkable thing one finds in Poland these days is the breezy openness of political conversation. Indeed, Poland seems much more open politically today than does the United States— at least the Poles are *having* a political conversation. The constraints that until nine months ago limited all discourse appear to have melted

away. While hard-liners in the Communist Party rail against "antisocialist elements" in the Solidarity movement, the latest craze on campus is
a T-shirt emblazoned with the bold, Ben-Hur-like letters "EA," and underneath, in smaller typeface, the legend "ELEMENT ANTYSOCJALISTYCZNY."
"Socialist? Antisocialist? Who knows what anyone means by those categories?" explains the enterprising T-shirt salesman. "People buy the
shirts as a joke. If they want to call us that, fine—here, we'll wear it on
our chest."

One afternoon I was in a hotel bar having an unusually frank political
conversation with a screenwriter. At one point he nodded over his shoul-
der. "That guy over there," he whispered. "Police spy." I suggested that
maybe we should move outside. "No, no," he insisted. "It's all right.
Everything is open. Let him listen. Maybe he'll learn something."

Earlier this spring, in an exceptionally thoughtful passage in *The
New Yorker*'s "Talk of the Town" section (April 13, 1981), an anonymous
contributor noted that the real splendor of the current Polish renewal
was the way it had, in one sudden surge, completely transcended the
perennial revolutionary quandary about ends and means—about, for
example, whether violence is an acceptable route to peace, or dictatorship to democracy. This contributor felt that the Poles had contrived a
new strategy altogether:

> They appear to have discovered nothing less than a new principle
> of action. It is simply *to be what you want to become.* Thus, if you
> want to have free elections, begin by freely electing someone; if
> you want to have free speech, speak freely; if you want to have a
> trade union, found a trade union. The Poles have discovered that
> if enough people act in this way, the very foundations of the un-
> wanted government begin to dissolve, even while it retains a mo-
> nopoly on the means of violence.

And that has indeed been largely what has happened in the remarkable opening-out of Polish political discourse. Only, as I came to realize
during my weeks in Poland, it didn't "just happen."

The Polish national renewal was preceded, over a period of several
years, by countless acts of individual courage. This was particularly the
case with the participants in KOR. One afternoon a writer showed me
some back issues of KOR's *Biuletyn Informacyjny*, from the 1978–79 period, in which, on primitively mimeographed sheets, KOR had monitored
the various campaigns of police harassment against activist workers on
a case-by-case basis. In several issues, one can find accounts of the sporadic
arrests and detentions of a Gdansk electrician named Lech Walesa. The
thing that is particularly impressive about KOR's bulletin, however, is the
fact that at the back of each issue the names, addresses, and phone numbers of the members of the KOR steering committee are openly provided

(Jacek Kuron 39-39-64, Adam Michnik 28-43-55, etc.). It's as if KOR were calling to everyone else, "Come on out! Be open. What can they do to us if we all start taking responsibility for our true dreams?"

One day I am introduced to Jan Litynski, a fortyish (Jewish) KOR activist, who started out as a mathematician but presently found himself editing *Robotnik*, one of the most vital of the post-1976 dissident journals. His English is extraordinarily good, considering that he's never been to England or America, and I ask him where he picked it up. "In jail," he answers, smiling. "That's where most of us learned our English. We had a lot of free time during the seventies."

I ask him if the transition to activism was frightening for him.

"The worst is the first time they throw you in jail without giving you any idea how long they're going to keep you. I didn't know if I could stand that. It scared me. But I survived—one does—and afterward the fear was never so bad."

Because some people faced down that fear, the whole society today has opened out. And nowhere is that openness more breezy, more bracing than in Gdansk, the northern seaport where the repression initially started to come unravelled. The very first place the taxi-driver takes you when you arrive in the city provides the most bracing evidence of all. Just outside the gates of the Lenin Shipyard rises a towering, gleaming monument to the martyrs of December 16, 1970—a monument that nine months ago nobody would have thought possible, commemorating an event that nine months ago nobody official would even admit had happened. As part of the August 31, 1980 settlement, the shipworkers of Gdansk won the right to build a monument to their fallen comrades. For several years, each December 16th the plaza outside the shipyard entrance had become mysteriously strewn with commemorative wreaths. Now the shipworkers were intent on making sure that by December 16, 1980, the wreaths would adorn a proper altar. "And not some flat low slab of marble," the strikers insisted. "We want it to be visible from every place in the city!" And it is. The memorial was designed by Bogdan Pietruszka, one of the artisans in the shipyard; it was manufactured by the shipworkers themselves in a fever of activity in October and November, as if to mock the government's complaints about their low productivity. In early December, the three huge components were carried out of the shipyard into the plaza in an emotionally wrenching processional: each component was a cross. The memorial consists of three towering crosses joined back to back at their arms in a triangular configuration. They rise 140 feet above the plaza. On their bases are bas-reliefs of workers behind bars in jail, workers at table with their families, workers holding strike banners reading "SOLIDARNOSC," and even workers erecting the monument itself. Gradually, these bas-reliefs give way to strong beams, piercing skyward. Crucified at the top are three anchors, their arms twisted in allegorical suffering.[6] The image is simple and yet tremendously powerful: it seems to gather up all the themes of the recent Polish experience. Along a fronting wall has been engraved a quotation from a Psalm translated by Czeslaw Milosz. My taxi-driver tells me that Milosz, whose books were banned in Poland until recently, will visit the monument and the shipyards this June. While we are looking at the monument, the afternoon shift lets out. Workers file through the gate, as they do every afternoon, and past these crosses, at once a memorial to their fallen comrades and a monument to their own remarkable vengeance. Some of them, as they pass, cross themselves across the chest.

Later that evening, while walking through the quaint, exceptionally lovely old quarter of Gdansk, I begin to get a sense of another force that may have animated the 1980 rebellion. From almost anywhere in the city, the cranes of the shipyard dominate the skyline—huge, muscular limbs flexed toward heaven. These machines are absolutely mammoth: looming there, they suggest vast reserves of power, held in restraint through Olympian control. It's easy to see how a worker who spent his life around such machines might begin to have delusions of grandeur—how, when he lost patience with the pesky incompetent bureaucrats downtown, he just might begin to imagine he had the power to do something about them.

The next morning, I arrange an appointment with Stanislaw Bury, one of eleven members of the presidium of Solidarity's local chapter inside the Lenin Shipyard. On the way to the meeting (the Solidarity offices are just inside the main gate—workers pass them every day on their way in and out), I get a look at the bulletin board. On one poster, Article 19 of the Helsinki Agreements, dealing with human rights, is reproduced in full, and underneath it, in a broad scrawl, is written, "Poland ratified this in 1977!" A faded poster features photos of the bloody, battered faces of two of the Solidarity leaders who were wounded in the Bydgoszcz incident back in March, with updates on their conditions and Solidarity's response. Another poster declares simply, "Monday through Friday we work for the Country—Saturday and Sunday are for you and your children."

Stanislaw Bury, a strong, roguish man in his late thirties, escorts me into his office. During our interview, people keep barging in, usually without knocking. That's one thing I notice everywhere I go in Solidarity: nobody bothers about honoring a closed door.

Bury explains his position in the union. At the time of the strike, he worked in the yards, but today, as a member of the shipyard local's presidium, he works full time for Solidarity. Each of the 16,000 shipworkers (and, for that matter, each of the ten million members of the national Solidarity) commits one percent of his annual income to the union: 60 percent of that is kept by the local chapter, and 40 percent goes to the national organization. The administrative functions of the local chapter are handled by the presidium, two of whose eleven members—Lech Walesa and Anna Walentynowicz—in practice spend all their time across town, at the national headquarters. The presidium is elected from among a 94-member council of delegates, who, in turn, are elected by the membership through the local's subdivisions. The presidium meets as a body every day, the council once a week. The presidium is answerable to the council on all issues, and only the council can render final decisions. Each week, the 94 delegates pass along complaints and comments from their constituents, and at the beginning of each council meeting the presidium has to report on actions it has taken in response to the previous week's concerns. All delegates and presidium members are elected for two-year terms, with a maximum consecutive service of four years, and they are subject to immediate recall at any time.

Bury points out that a special regulation requires that at the end of their terms the presidium members must return to the yard with exactly the job they had upon joining the presidium, and they cannot then accept advancements for at least one year. "We are still young at this," Bury explains. "Nine months—hardly even a toddler yet. We are still trying to learn how to make democracy work. It's very hard, and we have no experience. But we are making improvements. For example, we now have a rule that final passage of any item by the council of delegates requires a three-fourths majority vote. We feel that if we haven't achieved that level of consensus we haven't considered the issue long enough."

Each of the nine active presidium members supervises a specifically apportioned territory besides handling general tasks. One supervises internal finances, one supervises elections, one attends to individual grievances, one is developing the groundwork for a workers' council with the collaboration of "experts," one does troubleshooting. . . . "Me," Bury says, smiling, "I'm in charge of propaganda."

I ask Bury if he sees any application at the national level of the lessons in democratic process they've acquired locally.

"Oh," he says, sighing. "You're asking too much. We are only just beginning to understand horizontal democracy. Vertical democracy will be a labor of many years."

At the conclusion of our interview, I ask Bury whether he could give me a tour of the shipyard itself. In the meantime, a few other Westerners have gathered in the hall—a Canadian historian, a Swedish student leader, an American lawyer—and they all join in the request.

An assistant starts to explain that the yard is a security installation, off limits to—

"Nonsense," Bury interrupts. "If they're with me, there's no problem."

We leave the office and head for the yard, walking right past the guards, who merely nod cheerfully toward Bury. It turns out that even the guards belong to Solidarity.

We pass all the places I'd seen a few days earlier in *Robotnicy '80*—

the entry plaza where Sunday Mass had been held, the hall where the delegations from other factories had listened in on the negotiations, and, off to the side, the small room where the negotiations themselves had worn on and on. Everywhere in the yard, we pass beneath the large speakers of the PA system, speakers that in August broadcast the negotiations live. Usually they confine themselves to upbeat pop melodies; today, however, they are offering somber, elegiac classical and religious music—the wounded Pope is still in very serious condition. Every few minutes an authoritative voice announces a special 6 P.M. Mass in the main cathedral.

I never really enjoyed the Socialist Realism that permeates so much of the old American left's depiction of the Pride of the Workers: the kind of thing you find a lot of in "socially conscious" movies from the thirties and forties—all that determined brawn and those broad smiles. I don't know: it just never seemed real to me. But that's what it actually feels like in the Gdansk shipyard. These workers are *proud*. They walk around as if they mattered: they've really proved themselves, and nobody'd better mess with them again. Especially Bury himself. He ambles with grand strides, greeting just about everyone, slowing down to listen to complaints or offer updates on grievances, to accept invitations to weddings or to jokingly chide one worker on his poor attendance at meetings—he struts around as if he *owned* the place. And in a way he does. He and his fellow-organizers, who just a year ago were having to meet in secret and endure endless harassment, are today clearly the authoritative force in the yard.

All around us, huge tankers and container ships are coming into being. At one point, we pass a puny little yacht, incongruously shackled to a dock. I ask Bury about it.

"Confiscated," he says. "Used to belong to the head of the state TV network."

I ask him if he thinks that he and his comrades have been building better ships since Aug—

"Yes!" He doesn't even let me finish the sentence.

It's all quite exhilarating, this walk among the workers. But it's also profoundly disheartening, because, for all their pride, these men and women are laboring at backbreaking jobs under horrible conditions (in one hangar, the brown air hangs suspended, it seems, almost in clots)—conditions that have not changed overnight and are not about to change significantly any time soon.

Poland is a poor, poor country, and this is going to have to be a long, slow revolution.

One "Western source" (as he preferred to have himself characterized, during a "deep background" session I'd had a few days earlier in Warsaw) noted, "There is, of course, an exhilaration in all this venting of anger, but at some point the economic reality of Poland's situation is going to require some extraordinary maturity on the part of Solidarity's leadership. They've shown they can take the nation out on strike, but can they put it back to work? Specifically, they are going to have to motivate workers to a much higher productivity while at the same time prevailing upon them to accept a sizable cut in their already low standard of living, at least over the short term. It took American unions 40 years to reach that level of maturity; it's asking a lot of a year-old organization."

My Western source's celebration of the relative maturity of American labor struck me as ironic. Two weeks earlier, back in the States, I had asked William Winpisinger, the head of the International Association of Machinists and Aerospace Workers, which is one of the leading industrial unions in America, what he felt American labor could teach Solidarity.

"Hell, it's the other way around," he replied. "It's what they can teach us. For instance, they can teach us balls. While American labor has been steadily backtracking on all fronts, Solidarity has reminded us what spine is all about. And they've done it by uniting: shipworkers, truckers, coal miners, secretaries, machinists—everyone uniting around a set of general principles. American labor today lacks principle as a movement. And until American labor and the American left generally learn to fashion that kind of solidarity on behalf of principle, we're going to continue to be the pathetic victims of our American bosses, just as much as, until recently, the Poles were the victims of theirs."

The question remains, however: Just what is Solidarity's plan for the nation? Sometimes Solidarity's aspirations seem very large indeed. According to a banner at the entrance to the Lenin Shipyard, "THE GOVERNMENT TAKES CARE OF LAWS, THE PARTY TAKES CARE OF POLITICS, AND SOLIDARITY TAKES CARE OF THE NATION." But when you talk to individual union officials the answers are often considerably more circumspect.

"Up to now, we've avoided taking economic responsibility," a staff member at the Warsaw Solidarity office explained to me. "The government has recently been trying to maneuver us into taking some form of co-responsibility in areas such as productivity, but we've declined to do so until we can fashion mechanisms whereby we can exert substantial leverage in formulating and carrying out economic policy."

Sometimes answers can get downright coy. "They got us into this mess, let them get us out," Bury said the day we spoke in his Gdansk office. "Besides, we're workers, not economists."

That abrupt response notwithstanding, Solidarity is intensely interested in the future of economic life in Poland—it's just that it is taking longer for an economic consensus to emerge than it did for the political consensus. Or, to phrase it more precisely, an overwhelming number of Poles have an astonishingly consistent idea of what they don't like in their lives—the distant and arbitrary central authority, the repression, the corruption. They also have a consensus, in general terms, on what they want to replace it with: some sort of democratic worker control in the workplace. But when you get to asking specific questions about what that democratic control will look like, what the workers will democratically choose to do with that control, and how the pieces will fit together, things get very hazy. It's just too soon to tell. And, in the absence of consensus on such precise issues, Solidarity is taking its time.

In a sparsely furnished office at the union's nondescript national headquarters, in Gdansk, I meet Bogdan Lis, the vice-chairman of Solidarity and Lech Walesa's first lieutenant. Lis looks tired, even haggard. He looks like he has been bearing the weight of the world on his shoulders for months, and in a way he has. His hair is thinning, maybe even beginning to gray. I ask him how old he is, and he replies, 28. (Walesa is 37. Andrzej Gwiazda, the old man of the union leadership, is 45. Zbigniew Bujak, the head of the union's Warsaw region branch, Solidarity's largest, is 26. Jerzy Borowczak, who was one of the main firebrands during the Gdansk strike and is now a leader on the shipyard-union presidium, has just turned 21.) As exhausted as Lis seems, he still clearly revels in the play of words and silences which so often characterizes an official Solidarity interview. The way some people have worry lines, Bogdan Lis has developed irony lines; they crinkle out from his eyes whenever he feels the need to turn delphic, and he's a master. When he's asked about the Soviet Union, for instance, his face opens into a wry smile that speaks volumes without leaving a quotable trace. "Are you kidding?" his eyes seem to say. "You think I'm going to jeopardize all this for some easy quip? Next question, please."

I ask Lis about the distinction between "political" and "social" realms that seems at the heart of so much of the ongoing wordplay between the government and the union. The government accuses the union of trying to become "political," while the union insists that it's continuing to be merely "social."

"That goes back to the August agreements," Lis explains. "Late in the bargaining, something very interesting happened. The Party has long considered itself to be the leading force in all political and social affairs in this country. In the early drafts of the agreement, there was language to that effect in the text—it basically echoed similar formulations in the state constitution—in which the union agreed that the Party would continue to play such a role. At one point, however, late in the negotiations, when all kinds of other things were going on, we merely deleted the words 'and social' from the formulation—and they never noticed! They signed a document in which all we conceded was the Party's leading role 'in political matters'—and, of course, we still concede that." The irony lines blossom across his face once again.

The game really comes into its own when you try to get a union official to specify which issues are "social" and which "political," and this is one of Bogdan Lis's specialties. "The media, for instance, are social institutions," he says. "And therefore Solidarity has every right to demand an end to state censorship. The improvement of working conditions is a social issue, as is the appropriate distribution of wealth throughout the society. For that matter, the liberation of political prisoners is also a social issue."

"Well, then, what's a political issue?"

"Why, the sort of thing the Party concerns itself with."[7]

Similarly, Solidarity spokesmen often contrast legal authority, which they admit they lack, with moral authority, which they insist they have —the implication being, of course, that the legal authorities lack moral authority and are, indeed, immoral.

A few days later, back in Warsaw, I happen to be watching television with a Polish friend. A Communist Party official is complaining that Solidarity wants to reduce the Party's role to that of a discussion club. "No," my friend says. "He's got it all wrong. The role we have in mind for the Party is something a bit more like that of the British queen."

In Poland today, Solidarity officials insist that they speak on behalf of "society." Over and over, one hears such phrases as "The society wants this" and "The society won't stand for that." And most of the people one talks to in the street concur: not only is Solidarity their representative, it is the expression of Polish society. I have heard several Solidarity spokesmen scoff at the government's accusations that they are antisocialist. "On the contrary," they insist, "socialism consists in the *social* ownership of the means of production, which is *precisely* what we advocate."

This last word game yields a kernel of substantive significance—because although Solidarity (and society) may not yet have arrived at a consensus on how to proceed from here, there is virtually no one in Poland who advocates the restitution of a capitalist free market. "There is a profound egalitarian impulse at the heart of the Solidarity movement," explains a Warsaw sociologist who has spent time in the West. "Maybe that's one valuable legacy of the 35 years of Communist rule here: people have been exposed to those slogans for so long that now they want to make them real. There has thus far been relatively little individual opportunism. The movement's first concern has been for its poorest members. Wage demands, for instance, have always been on an across-the-board rather than a percentage basis. Everybody, no matter what his current salary, gets an extra thousand zlotys rather than an extra five percent.[8] As a researcher, I have no objection to seeing a factory worker get paid more than I do; after all, I enjoy my work, while his is often drudgery. And I think my attitude is fairly common among professionals here in Poland. I think I'd be hard pressed, though, to find a similar attitude among professionals in the West."

During my last few days in Poland, the cigarette shortage gets serious. Everybody in Poland seems to smoke. "You would, too, if you'd been living here the last nine months," an acquaintance tells me teasingly. By the end of the week, you can't buy a pack anywhere. Even the PEWEX shops have run out. And yet, on innumerable occasions, I see people go up to complete strangers, ask for a cigarette, and get one. I see people with two cigarettes left in their last pack not hesitate for a moment to offer one of them to the most casual of acquaintances. It seems each person knows that when his pack runs out he'll be able to borrow from the next, and that there will be no hoarding. The country will just share until the shortage has exhausted itself. The only trouble is, nobody has any matches.

In *The Road to Gdansk*, a remarkable book on recent Polish history that was completed a mere six weeks before the onset of the August 1980 strike in Gdansk, Daniel Singer, one of the most insightful chroniclers of the situation in Eastern Europe, concluded:

> The tensions are such that nobody in Warsaw asks whether everything will blow up once again, but when it will happen. The crucial question is whether the explosion can be put off sufficiently to allow for the emergence of a political movement, resting on real social forces, strong enough to move beyond veto power to impose changes in policies and institutions, but also cohesive enough and sufficiently in charge of the situation to dissuade the Russians from taking the plunge. It is difficult to be very optimistic about this race against the clock.

Singer's trepidation notwithstanding, the Solidarity movement during its first nine months has performed extraordinarily well precisely with regard to the criteria that Singer set. Most Poles I have spoken with were as pleasantly surprised by the movement's cohesion, strength, and maturity as Singer must be.[9] But now the questions are beginning to change. It seems to me that today they fall into three general areas: (1) How, specifically, even under ideal conditions, does a body politic begin to mesh its desire for a decentralized system of democratic worker control of the workplace with its need for some kind of integrated national planning? (There are no models here. No one in modern history has succeeded in mastering this challenge.) (2) How, specifically, given the realities of Polish political life today but for the moment excluding the question of the country's economic situation, can Solidarity move to carry out some of its policies while avoiding any direct confrontation with the Communist Party, on the one hand, and the huge, entrenched bureaucracy, on the other? What will the distribution of power in Poland look like two years from now? And, finally (3), given Poland's actual economic situation, are any of these reforms happening in time? Is it already too late to salvage the foundering Polish economy? Will economic realities allow the Poles any room to maneuver? Or to phrase the question more darkly, are all the things that are happening in Poland today merely epiphenomena—lots of dazzle and firecrackers that blind us to the essential reality, which is that the country is going bankrupt and all forms of authority are therefore melting away? Do we have any idea what it means for a semi-developed country to go bankrupt in 1981?—what happens next? While almost all the Poles I spoke with expressed enthusiastic support for the Solidarity movement, many were quietly skeptical of the movement's long-term chances. Their misgivings almost always centered on this third area.

One thing that most Poles I spoke with were *not* worrying about in May 1981 was the possibility of a Soviet invasion. Over and over Poles asked me about "the hysterical concern of the Western media over this question of whether the Soviets will invade."

"Some of the American reporters here in Gdansk have been so busy looking out to sea waiting for the Soviet armada," one Solidarity staffer complained, "that they've hardly even noticed what we've been doing in the yards."

"Well," another corrected him, "actually, most of the really hysterical stories have been datelined Washington or New York or Paris. The reporting out of here has usually been fairly decent."

"It's almost as if the Western media and the U.S. State Department *wanted* the Soviets to invade," one screenwriter commented. "As if what we are trying to do here were in some ways as threatening to corporate capitalism as it is to Soviet-style Communism."[10]

Have the Poles themselves worried at any point about a Soviet invasion?

"That was not one of our main concerns," another writer told me. "There were maybe four days last March, at the height of the Bydgoszcz crisis"—when Solidarity brought the nation to the brink of a general strike by protesting a brutal police attack on three of its regional leaders —"when the Warsaw Pact forces were dragging their maneuvers on and on. For a few days there, yes, it was very tense, there were even rumors that the Soviets had streaked a few of their jets over Warsaw as part of the maneuvers, and that rattled our nerves pretty good. But at a certain point, after they kept threatening and threatening and threatening and *not* acting—well, the threat began to wear thin. Each new threat proved that they were even more scared than we were."

When I asked Poles what they would do if the Soviets did invade, I got a variety of answers. Some said they would fight, some said they would fight if others fought (when I asked where they would get the arms, they assured me that the Army would provide them, the Army, after all, being made up largely of conscripts, which is to say, of their brothers and their friends), some said they would simply refuse to work, and some said that there were ways of causing damage without specifically resorting to arms. But perhaps the most trenchant reply came from a man in a Gdansk bar: "O.K., so they invade. So what? We will simply go on doing what we're doing. To stop us, they'd have to send in one Soviet soldier for every Pole, and if they did that, one by one, one on one, we'd convert their entire Army."

"Look," another man at the bar said. "The Russians are no longer allowing any of their citizens to get tourist visas to visit Poland, or Poles to get visas to visit Russia. You think they're going to go and expose 400,000 of their young, impressionable future workers to what's going on here?"

The more time you spend in Poland, the more irrelevant the Soviet Army seems. After a while, the question of a Soviet invasion just seems beside the point. As you line up the arguments for and against such an invasion from the Soviet point of view, such a strategy appears transparently counterproductive. Having said that, one should also note that recent history provides no particular ground for deeming temperate consideration one of the principal characteristics of top-level planning in either of the superpowers. Still, it should be clear that, given the extremely constricted economic situation in Poland today, the Soviet Union finds itself with all kinds of opportunities for leverage without having to resort to outright invasion. To say that an invasion is unlikely is not to dismiss the significance of the Soviet factor.

Thus the Poles come hurtling back toward summer, the first anniversary of their remarkable resurgence. All over Poland, people are looking toward the immediate future, toward what promises to be an extremely eventful few months: the Communist Party convocation has been set for July and will be preceded by a wide-open round of grass-roots balloting. By late August or early September, if it has the time to pull it together, Solidarity hopes to hold its first national convention, with delegates elected from all over the country in balloting that will in one way or another involve all ten million members. With the Polish primate, Cardinal Wyszynski, lying near death, the Catholic Church may likewise be experiencing a major period of transition. Czeslaw Milosz will be returning from exile in June to accept an honorary doctorate from the Catholic University in Lublin, and then he will visit the shipyard in Gdansk. In one form or another, Wajda's film *Man of Iron* should be opening. Meanwhile, on the stage, another returning exile, Roman Polanski, will be appearing as the naughty-boy genius Mozart in his own production of Peter Shaffer's *Amadeus.*

"You have no idea how things have changed," the filmmaker Ryszard Bugajski tells me one afternoon in Warsaw. "Today, you see all this activity, all this energy. At the beginning of last summer, there was so much depression, so much hopelessness. It wasn't even like hitting your head against a brick wall. Rather, it was like running up against a wall of butter—it gave a little, but never enough, and in the meantime you got all sticky and soiled. Now, at least, things are tangible—the challenge is solid."

At a coffee-shop in Warsaw, on the eve of my departure from Poland, I ask a staff member from the regional Solidarity office, how long can the reforms continue, how far can they reach, is there a line that the Poles will not possibly be allowed to cross?

"We crossed that line," she replies, without a moment's hesitation, "back in August 1980."

The Polish Airlines morning flight for East Berlin, scheduled to leave at 11:45, in fact leaves at 9:45. If you happen to be at the airport, you've got yourself a ride.

The Polish customs officials in Warsaw clear my luggage without even a cursory inspection. An hour and a half later, my plane lands at East Berlin's Schoenfeld International; I am intending, following customs, to bus the mere quarter-mile into West Berlin. The East German customs officials, however, noting my American passport and Warsaw point of origin, escort me into a small, bare, fluorescent-lit room. There they empty my bags and in no time uncover some Solidarnosc posters, pins, and, presently, the photos of the 1970 massacre that the young man in Gdansk gave me for safekeeping. The junior agents quickly summon their superiors, and over the next 45 minutes, virtually all the customs people at Schoenfeld parade in to examine the material. They grill me with questions, to which I feign naive incomprehension. After an hour my predicament begins to feel fairly serious; but just as I am beginning to wonder about the applicability of my Miranda rights and whether *they* supply the dime, it becomes evident that my interrogators aren't so much officially angry as personally curious. They, too, want to know what is going on in Poland.

Interlude

A FEW WEEKS LATER, back in the United States, I happen to recall an old Polish joke, vintage early seventies. "What nationality were Adam and Eve?" the wag would ask you, and you'd say you didn't know, and he'd say, "Polish," and you'd ask, "Why?"

"Well," he'd say thoughtfully, "for three reasons." And then he'd list them. "First off, they were so poor they couldn't afford any clothes and had to run around naked. Second, between them, all they had to eat was one apple. And third, *they thought they were in paradise!*"

And you'd laugh, or you wouldn't. But the point is that that joke, which used to be merely derogatory—one more swipe at the supposed stupidity of "the Polacks"—has in the meantime undergone an extraordinary transformation: it has become purely descriptive.

September 1981: Solidarity is one year old, and this poster announces the convening of the union's "First Annual Congress of Delegates" in Gdansk. This convention would also prove to be the union's last.

September—October 1981

Four months have passed and I am back in Warsaw. Poland in September 1981. Paradise in fall. Paradise fallen.

One of the first things I come upon here in Warsaw is a slightly defaced wall poster advertising the new season of Poland's famous national circus, Cyrk. The poster reads:

CYRK
PRESENTS
A NEW, ACTION-PACKED 1981 SEASON
FEATURING
TRAINED ANIMALS, DOGS, HORSES,
ACROBATS, JUGGLERS, CLOWNS AND
COUNTLESS OTHER ATTRACTIONS

Beside the "CYRK" someone has scrawled, in plain black letters, "POLSKA."
Circus Poland.

But no one is laughing, and the vitality has gone out of life in Poland this sorry autumn.

Elsewhere, the city is plastered with posters for Andrzej Wajda's film *Man of Iron*, which opened, uncensored, during the summer and is playing to packed houses. (Virtually everyone I speak with has seen the film at least once.) There are two posters. In one, a blood-smeared long-sleeved white shirt is spread-eagled against a plain white backdrop—a reference to the crucifixion of Poland's red-and-white flag during the events of 1970. The other poster alludes to the events of 1980, and shows the head of a large, powerful worker. An oversize metal industrial nut has been wedged around his temples, and as his facial muscles strain in grim determination the nut is splitting apart. (Wajda himself has been down in Krakow directing a stage production of *Hamlet*, what one might call Shakespeare's version of *Man of Iron*—another tale about legitimacy and false succession, in which the hero avenges the murder, by a counterfeit pretender, of his father, the state's rightful ruler.)

There are other posters, of course. One shows a skull and crossbones—or, more accurately, a skull and crossed fork and knife. It's captioned "THE FIRST RESULT OF THE COMMUNIST PARTY'S NINTH CONGRESS: LOWER FOOD RATIONS." The poster is often taped on shopwindows; its vacant eye sockets stare back at the vacant faces in the lines.[11]

The shelves in the shops are even emptier than they were during my last visit, in May, the lines much longer. Sporadic shortages have given way to pervasive insufficiencies in almost every sector of the economy. One of the most extreme shortages on the list—and one that is causing particular consternation and anxiety among the Poles—is soap. Only fresh vegetables and certain fruits seem plentiful; September, after all, is the peak of a rather good harvest season. The produce is brought in privately by farmers from the surrounding countryside—they bypass the official government purchasing centers and sell in outdoor public markets, at several times the official price. Jan Kulaj, the head of Rural Solidarity—the agricultural union—recently told an interviewer from Solidarity's *Glos Wolny*, "Except for meat and citrus fruit, there shouldn't be any shortages of food in Poland now. I want to tell you that in my district alone hundreds of thousands of tons of cucumbers, cabbage, and other products were squandered because of the inefficiency of purchasing centers."

Although per-capita income has gone up 27% during the last year, thanks mostly to Solidarity's agitation, the cost of living has risen much faster. Just how much faster is difficult to determine, because so much of the inflation is hidden. There are the official price increases—cigarettes, for example, up almost 100%; a loaf of bread up 200%—but these provoke such resistance that the government tends to just leave prices as they are and let supplies lapse. To put it charitably, the government cannot afford to deliver products at the price that people demand and lacks the legitimacy to raise prices to a more realistic level; therefore, it simply stops attempting to meet the demand. People are left to scramble for themselves, outside official channels—in a market where their ration cards are useless and prices are seemingly without limit. Indeed, some farmers have stopped selling their produce altogether: The zloty being worthless, they prefer to deal exclusively by barter—and few city dwellers have anything for which the farmers would be willing to trade.

The situation is made for profiteering. In one increasingly common practice, a trucker bringing, say, 20,000 zlotys' worth of meat to market gives the storekeeper 20,000 zlotys (perhaps a bit more) in cash and then sells the meat on the black market at a 500% markup. "The government's not satisfied with having wrecked our economy," a disgusted shopper tells me. "Now it has to give us a Mafia, too."

Rationing, far from stabilizing the economy, as Solidarity had hoped it would early in the crisis when the union demanded its imposition, has introduced some destabilizing elements of its own. The rationing system is administered on a regional basis, with the result that neighboring districts may have wildly different allocations: places that have plentiful milk coupons may not have milk, whereas the next village may face the opposite situation. There seems to be little relationship between the number of coupons issued and the anticipated supply of a given product. Meanwhile, many people who have been denied government-sanctioned employment aren't allotted any coupons at all for such basics as sugar, butter, and meat. Once again, the result is a highly inflationary black market—this time in the coupons for regular food.

"Rationing *or* lines," a woman standing outside a grocery store comments. "You expect one or the other, but not both at the same time. And then to have the price increases on top of that. It's really too much."

Over and over, older Poles offer the same eerie comparison: "Take a look," they say, showing you their ration cards. "Now go look up the figures. These allotments are even lower than in Nazi times!"

A particularly hard situation is faced by families with alcoholic members—of which there are distressingly many. The standard ration for vodka is now only a half a liter a month. With two coupons, you can buy a standard liter bottle for a few hundred zlotys—if you can find the bottle. People intent on getting more must either go to a restaurant or bar, where a liter bottle can cost upward of a thousand zlotys, or trade the meat, milk, bread, and other portions of their family's coupon cards for vodka stamps. "Either way," someone tells me, "those families are beginning to starve."

Long before 1980, you could get certain goods only at government-run PEWEX stores, and only for dollars or other hard currencies. But as the value of the zloty plummets, it takes more and more zlotys to buy the same number of dollars, and hence the same items at the PEWEX stores. Just how many more can be seen any day of the week outside the Hotel Forum, where the black-market rate of exchange for a single dollar (the official rate is now around 34 zlotys to the dollar)[12] has leapt from 160 zlotys in May to between 300 and 340 zlotys four months later. (Black market computations are therefore a bit easier on this trip: factors of ten. The street value of the dollar has ballooned to approximately ten times the official rate!)

You want to know how bad the economic situation is in Poland today? Well, there is a coin, an actual piece of metal, called the grosz, 100 of which equal one zloty. It would take you 300 of these coins—a treasure trove—to buy one American penny.

The 1973 and 1979 oil crises in the United States forced Americans to smolder through some moderately long lines, but those crises lapsed within a few weeks, and the lines quickly disappeared. Imagine a situation in which you have to queue up not only for gasoline (for which the average wait in Warsaw is now two hours) but also for food, appliances, clothes, soap—just about everything—and that you have been doing so for months: imagine that, and you begin to sense what daily life is like in Poland today. Now imagine supplies are clearly dwindling and winter is coming on.

Perhaps the biggest difference between September and May isn't the size and length of the lines but the spirit of the people in them. Back in May, the lines were friendly places where neighbors gathered, at the beginning or end of their day, to share gossip or trade opinions about political developments. People aren't talking in the lines anymore: the faces are grim, and fistfights are not infrequent. During this visit, I notice, as I perhaps failed to last time, the high number of young children in the lines—two- and three-years-olds. Most young women seem to have toddlers in tow. (More than half the population of Poland today is under 30, and three million Poles, out of a total population of 35 million, are less than four years old.) It isn't so much that the Poles have large families; their Catholicism notwithstanding, most families seem limited to two or three children. Rather, in Poland, as opposed to America, the postwar baby-boom generation had been getting married fairly young and having a baby boom of its own—or was having one until recently. On this trip, I haven't noticed many pregnant women or many infants under six months of age. "Women who have babies today are the heroes of this country," a friend tells me. There is an extreme shortage of milk.

Even the luxury restaurants catering to tourists and the upper levels of Poland's bureaucratic bourgeoisie are noticeably straining now. At the Bazyliszek, perhaps the poshest restaurant in Warsaw, the offerings are confined to wild game—boar, stag, wild duck. There's no beef available. At most restaurants, if you ask for chicken they'll say, "No, you're having pork"—or vice versa, depending on the vagaries of available supply. At my hotel restaurant in Gdansk, my waiter and I play this game for about a week, but no matter what he claims to be bringing—"chicken," "pork," "veal," "lamb"—he always ends up delivering the same patty of nondescript ground-up flesh; only the sauces vary. Toward the end of my stay in Warsaw, access to the restaurant at the Hotel Forum, which somehow manages to keep up its "intercontinental" standard, is suddenly restricted to hotel guests.

"It's really tragic," one American tourist, a veteran of many Polish vacations in better times, says to me. "Poland has an exceptional national cuisine, and there are some extraordinary chefs in this country. You know how they've set up preserves for wild African animals in the United States, for instance, to protect them from the political chaos in their home countries, with the hope that someday they'll be able to return them to their natural habitats? Well, somebody ought to do the same thing with Polish chefs."

Many things that were available only for hard currency back in May are no longer available at all. A moderately well-off friend tells me that he has been trying to procure motor oil for two months and hasn't seen any anywhere—not even at the PEWEX shops. He's worried that he'll soon run his car into the ground and then be forced to rely on public transport. For that matter, buses have been breaking down at an alarming rate for lack of proper maintenance and spare parts—in other words, for lack of hard currency. Routes which used to be serviced every ten minutes are now lucky to see a bus once an hour; when the buses do arrive, they're often too packed to take on new passengers. Most queues seem to be attached to buildings or shops; when you see an apparently free-floating line milling by the roadside, it generally means that a bus is long overdue. "Millions of zlotys went into transportation during the past ten years," a man standing in one such line tells me. "But most of it went into highway construction. Gierek didn't care about anyone who couldn't afford a car."

Some of the longest lines in Warsaw these days spill out of the visa sections of the Western embassies. You think it's hard getting into Poland from the United States, you should try going the other way around. "We get about 200 applications for tourist visas every day," an American embassy official tells me, "about 60% of which we reject right off because the applicants clearly cannot demonstrate touristic intent." (Among Poles, the West German embassy has a reputation for being somewhat more lenient.)

"That does it," an American businessman friend of mine says one afternoon when the driver of the taxi we are sharing parks his car by the roadside, opens his trunk, pulls out three jerry cans of gasoline, and begins filling his tank. "That does it. Now I have seen *every* image of life the way it was being lived in Europe when I was a soldier stationed in Germany right after the war. The jerry cans, the lines, the black market in currency, the ration cards, the desperation for chocolates and nylons, the prostitutes, the crowds milling around the embassies trying to get visas—it's as if the war ended here just six months ago."

Although Bob Dylan has been replaced in the Muzak at the Hotel Forum by Gloria Gaynor singing her gutsy disco paean, "I Will Survive" (it's a song you hear everywhere in Poland this fall, coming in over taxicab radios or hummed at nearby tables in student cafés), survival seems a decidedly open question. Indeed, the three questions with which I left Poland back in May now seem to have been superseded by a fourth, far more urgent one: How the hell is this country going to make it at all through the coming winter?

One evening in early September, rumors spread throughout Poland—rumors that were presently corroborated by hastily printed Solidarnosc fact sheets slapped onto public walls—concerning a prison takeover in Bydgoszcz, a town about 80 miles south of Gdansk. The prisoners, protesting conditions in the jail, had taken over the yard; the guards and city police were surrounding the prison; the people of Bydgoszcz were surrounding the guards; the power of the Polish state was surrounding the people of Bydgoszcz; the eyes of the Polish nation were constraining the power of the Polish state; the military might of the Soviet Union and the Warsaw Pact was threatening the vigilance of the Polish nation; and the concern of the West was limiting the options for exercise of Soviet might.

It was another instance of what was becoming a classic pattern in post-1980 Poland. For a few hours we all held our breath: Don't Anybody Move.

Eventually the prisoners surrendered—but to Solidarity, not to their guards.

The next day, I spoke about the incident with John Darnton, the *New York Times* correspondent. He recounted a conversation he'd had several months earlier with a man who has since become a high government and Party official. "What you have to remember about this country," the man had said, "is that the whole society hates the authorities, the society wants to overthrow the authorities, the society has the power to overthrow the authorities—*and the society cannot overthrow the authorities*."

Darnton's wife, Nina, who is a correspondent for National Public Radio, told me a similar story from another angle. "A few months back," she recalled, "I was present when Adam Michnik, one of the leaders of KOR, went to a factory where he was going to address the workers. It was during a stage when a lot of emphasis was being put on the workers' political education. Some of them started complaining about the incompetence and corruption of the plant's managers, and Michnik very thoughtfully and carefully tried to raise the discussion to a higher level —'to raise their consciousness,' as it were. He explained that it wasn't merely a problem of individual personalities—that the system itself bred such distortions, that they could replace those managers with other people, but that because of the system, those new people would behave similarly. . . . Suddenly, one of the workers shouted, 'Right! So let's get rid of the whole system!' Michnik immediately had to double back and explain that—well, there were certain geopolitical realities that had to be taken into account, and you couldn't just . . . And so on."

In many ways, the situation in Poland seems constantly on the verge of stalemate: each of the sides—Solidarity, the Party, the Soviet Union— has the power to veto the initiatives of any of the others but lacks the power to push its own program through. (I include the Soviet Union in this formulation because perhaps the most fundamental element in the whole remarkable situation is that the Soviet Union, for all its military and economic leverage, has not been able to impose its will, and doesn't seem likely to be able to any time soon.) The result is that periods of intense, often perverse, and sometimes terrifying bickering are occasionally suspended for moments of wary, and often short-lived, compromise.

In Poland today, the institution with power lacks legitimacy, while the institution with legitimacy lacks power. Or, as Jan Litynski, a veteran KOR activist, put it to me, "In this country today, there are two powers and no power."

There had been some hope back in July that the Communist Party could transcend this near-deadlock by renewing itself in the public's estimation. There was at the time much emphasis—perhaps more in the West than in Poland itself—on the supposedly democratic character of the delegate-selection process for the Party's national congress and the surprisingly open character of the floor debate. "I guess it was after the Party congress that my gloom really bottomed out," a Western diplomat in Warsaw told me in early September. "I mean, the only way I can see this logjam breaking is if both sides, Solidarity and the Communist Party, develop strong, authentic leadership—two leadership bodies capable of sitting down for some hard, solid negotiating and then of delivering on the terms of those negotiations. We have yet to see if Solidarity itself will come up with that kind of leadership, but it's pretty much a moot point, because the Party didn't. Some of the faces changed—surprisingly few—but the leadership that emerged can hardly be considered strong, either in authenticity or in imagination. The few strong, imaginative people (people like Tadeusz Fiszbach of Gdansk) didn't make the final cut, because the two extremes at the congress tended to cancel each other out, leaving only this fairly mediocre middle."

"Oh, the Party congress was very democratic," a Gdansk taxi-driver assured me. "It's a party of idiots, and they elected the biggest idiots as their leaders."

At the time of the Gdansk strike, in August of 1980, one of the most succinct bits of graffiti, in a reference to the strikers' 21 demands, said simply, "21 × TAK," meaning "21 TIMES YES." A year later, a ubiquitous poster sums up the national frustration: "STILL, AFTER A FULL YEAR, ONLY 2 × YES AND 19 × NO." The only demands that have in fact been honored, according to this slogan, concern (1) the registration of an independent, self-governing trade union and (2) the radio broadcast of Sunday masses. Most of the government's other concessions, in areas such as health and working conditions, have gone largely unfulfilled.

Some commentators think that in the heat of the moment, in order to end the strike, the government made concessions that, given economic and geopolitical realities, it knew it could never honor and that it secretly hoped it would never have to honor: there was a vague sense that this revolution couldn't possibly last, that no one would be held accountable in the long run. "Even today," a prominent documentary filmmaker told me in Warsaw, "the Party behaves as if this were all just some bad dream from which any moment now it will awaken."

The perversity of the situation lies in the fact that while the country's economy spirals downward, the various leaders who ought to be addressing the crisis are instead expending huge amounts of intellectual, political, psychological, and spiritual energy sparring with each other. The most visible result of the Party congress was not some new economic program but rather the launching of a withering media attack on Solidarity. For several weeks preceding the convening of Solidarity's own First National Congress, in September, the media truce that had been so precariously sustained during the spring was completely suspended, and the airwaves—especially television—bristled with angry, almost hysterical attacks on the union's leadership and its aspirations.

The state media during this period took particular delight in pointing to the Reagan administration's handling of the air-traffic controllers' strike in America. In essence, the editorial line boiled down to: "See, strikes by government employees are not allowed even in the United States! How dare all of you state-employed workers threaten to strike here?" When I brought this issue up with a union delegate in Warsaw, he said, "The failure of American labor to stand together is a reflection of its inadequacy, not our impertinence. Apart from a few flimsy resolutions and token gestures, the American air controllers' colleagues in labor stood idly by while Reagan gutted the isolated union." He pointed to a badge he was wearing on his chest. "Look, see this badge? What does it tell you? My name and region—not my trade. From this badge, you can't tell if I'm a coal miner, an editor, or an air-traffic controller. We are organized by region, in solidarity—not by trade, in isolation. If American labor had been similarly organized this summer, Reagan would never have been able to emasculate your air-traffic controllers."

As the date of the Solidarity congress approached, labor unrest spread from factories and transportation networks into newsrooms and printing plants; workers belonging to Solidarity refused to publish the increasingly high-strung government tirades. As the economy lay reeling, Solidarity and the government entered into negotiations on access to the media— among other things, on whether Solidarity could have its own columns in the Party-controlled daily papers and its own time slots on television, especially during the congress. Solidarity did achieve a few uncensored moments on television just before the opening of the first session, but then the negotiations broke down completely. As one of the first orders of business, the 890-odd delegates to the Solidarity congress voted to ban Polish television cameras from the hall altogether.

Typical of the energy being lavished by both sides on these skirmishes was the Ongoing Incident of the Wall at the Gdansk train station. Along the far wall of the station, parallel with and fronting all the incoming tracks, some of Solidarity's midnight commandos had scrawled in huge, bright white letters, "DON'T BELIEVE WHAT THEY SAY ON TELEVISION—TV IS LYING!" The next day, the rail-yard administrators managed to put together a 25-car empty train, which they parked in front of the offending message, blocking it from everyone's view. That night, the Solidarity people scrawled the same message on the train cars. The next afternoon, as I was passing the station on the way to the congress, I could see several rail-yard officials out on the tracks uncoupling the cars and rearranging the train. "Great," an American reporter sharing the taxi with me said. "Real good use of energy and time."

Olivia Sports Arena, a few miles north of the Gdansk shipyards, is a sleek, modern facility with a soaring roof. For six days beginning on September 5th, and another twelve days beginning on September 26th, it was the site for the two sessions of the First National Congress of Solidarity Delegates. (During the two-week break, delegates returned home to consult with their constituents.) Outside, townspeople milled around at all hours, listening to the deliberations piped through loudspeakers, exchanging hunches, and trading—not selling—Solidarity pins and memorabilia from the various regions. Reporters from Polish television sulked, trying vainly to snag anyone they could find into talking before their cameras. Dozens of buses from all over Poland were ranged in the arena's large parking lot, festooned with all sorts of art and posters. One popular broadside proclaimed, simply, "SOLIDARNOSC: 10,000,000 SOLID"; another, the congress's official announcement, featured a large photograph of a toddler—a plump little kid in a Solidarity T-shirt launching into his first confident steps. The two posters summed up what was perhaps the most awesome achievement of the congress—the fact that it was taking place at all. Barely a year old, Solidarity not only had acquired a membership of approximately ten million but, through an elaborate, decentralized process, had even managed to include all ten million in the sequence of grass-roots balloting, local caucuses, and regional congresses that finally selected the representatives who were gathering in the hall.

Inside the arena, beneath large, colorful banners, the delegates sat in rows of chairs arranged by region. Only 6% were women.[13] The average age was 36. Half the delegates were university graduates—a figure that some observers found surprisingly, disquietingly high. Every twentieth delegate belonged to the Polish Communist Party. (Of the Party's three million members, one million belong to Solidarity.)

In tiers of seats angled high above the floor, the journalists, many of them Western, struggled with the appallingly primitive and static-ridden simultaneous-translation headsets. ("I'm sure these things are giving my ears cancer," muttered one British reporter as he jammed the devilish devices deeper into his ears and cocked his neck into the best, if least comfortable, receiving position.) A curious double flow of condescension seemed to develop: The Western reporters smiled expansively at the delegates ("Oh, isn't it cute how they're trying to master this democratic process"), and the delegates indulged in their own smug estimation of the reporters ("Oh, isn't it cute how they're straining to fathom the unique Polish soul").

At the front of the auditorium, an elaborate scoreboard—a computer-controlled pattern of lights—was emblazoned almost the entire time with a huge pointillist rendition of a cross. The congress opened with an emotional Solemn Mass, celebrated in the nearby Oliwa Cathedral by Jozef Glemp, the new primate of Poland (heir to Cardinal Wyszynski, who had died early in the summer). No one missed the symbolism: Unlike the Communist Party congress in July, this meeting had the imprimatur of all of Polish history.

As if to hammer the point home, Lech Walesa, in his opening address, singled out the observers from the government: "I welcome first of all the representatives of the government. We are independent and self-governing"—the phrase set off an outburst of applause—"but we are active within the state, and as hosts of the present congress we respectfully welcome the arrival of the government delegation." He paused—there was no applause—and then continued, "I am not a diplomat, so I will be frank. Up to the very last minute before the opening of the present congress, a number of actions were being launched and a number of words were being spoken that might have been avoided. We are expected to answer various questions. We shall debate them. But it is also we who are expecting an answer to the basic question. A year ago, we said that we are talking 'like a Pole to a Pole.' Now, 12 months of many conflicts later, we want to know whether we shall continue to talk like that." These remarks—so characteristic of Walesan rhetoric—were at once passionately earnest and dripping with irony. Twelve months earlier, after the exhausting negotiations between the strikers and Mieczyslaw Jagielski, the government's chief negotiator, which concluded the shipyard strike, Walesa had graciously agreed with Jagielski's statement that they had spoken "like a Pole to a Pole." Jagielski had since been purged, wiped out in the balloting at the Party congress in July—presumably for his part in the Gdansk capitulation—and now Walesa was asking the new officials if Solidarity would be able to talk to them "like a Pole to a Pole." There was no question that Solidarity was Polish (after all, just hours earlier they had celebrated Mass with the very embodiment of Polish history)—the only question was whether this government and the Party that controlled it were Polish. The crowd went wild.

It was the last sign of life from the delegates for several days. The congress quickly lapsed into a morass of procedural wrangling, parliamentary maneuvering, and ceremonial greeting. (In one strange moment, the emissary from the West German federation of trade unions, Ervin Kristoffersen, offered the delegates his opinion that "order without freedom cannot last long, but freedom also calls for order." Some of the delegates wondered what business a German emissary had offering Poles advice of any kind.) For hour after hour, the delegates sat, pasty-faced, absorbing the miasma. ("Banning television from the congress was the smartest thing Solidarity could have done," a friend remarked to me. "The coverage so far would have been embarrassingly dull. Instead, we get to watch the spectacle of the TV people, banned from the hall, having to report each night from their pathetic stations outside the auditorium. The look on their faces—it's great!") At one point, one of the delegates met me outside for a smoke. "Boy, this democracy may be worth dying for, but it can kill you with boredom once you've got it," he said. At another point, I asked Jan Litynski if people were getting disappointed at the slow pace of the proceedings. "Yes," he replied. "People are even getting angry, but the trouble is they're getting angry in different directions." Jan Rulewski, one of the leaders of the Bydgoszcz delegation, and considered by some delegates one of the most hotheaded figures at the convention, was surprisingly understanding. "Keep in mind," he told me, "that we are trying to coordinate the thinking of ten million people here. This is our first meeting. Of course it takes time." One of the townspeople listening to the proceedings over the loudspeakers was even more indulgent. "Hell," he exclaimed, "the Communist Party congress took *seven* days, and they weren't talking about anything! These people are trying to save the nation."

Beneath the deadly dull surface, however, powerful forces were already at work, as would presently become clear. For as the speeches and motions dragged on, the delegates were gradually orienting themselves with regard to the three principal issues that would come to dominate the congress: the problem of democratic process within the union; the question of how hard the union should push the Polish state and the Communist Party in demanding decentralized self-management at the workplace; and—somewhat more amorphous but perhaps most crucial of all—the question of whether the delegates, mindful of the history of Polish rebellion, could overcome a centuries-old tradition of romantic, doomed grand gestures.

The dilemma Solidarity faces concerning internal democratic process is this: its principal claim to legitimacy lies in the democratic contrast it offers to the arbitrary, authoritarian alternative embodied in the Party; Solidarity's principal chance for survival, however, derives precisely from its *solidarity*—the fundamental unity of some ten million workers. Ten million people belong to Solidarity because it is democratic and participatory—but if ten million people (or their 890-odd representatives in Gdansk) were really to start behaving democratically, if differences over fundamental issues were allowed to lead to the formation of hardened factions, then the union's very existence could come into jeopardy. Conversely, in a situation that requires ten million members to speak as one, there is a perennial danger that an individual spokesman for the ten million may begin speaking on their behalf without their authorization. Authenticity, authority, authorization—these are the crucial but evanescent components of Solidarity's fragile achievement.

Even before the congress convened, Adam Michnik, the KOR activist, in an anniversary essay published in the journal *Niezaleznosc*, marvelled at the paradoxical nature of Solidarity: "a movement . . . that combines a cult of the leader with an insistence on democracy verging on pathology, and surprising wisdom with rarely encountered naiveté."

Although his name was seldom mentioned, much of the procedural debate during the first several days of Solidarity's congress could be summarized under the simple rubric: what to do with Lech Walesa. Veterans of populist and radical conventions in the United States and Western Europe could recognize a familiar pattern in the proceedings: humiliate the leadership and then reelect it.

Walesa is almost the same age as the Communist system he is attempting to transform; he is very much the product of the postwar Polish order. Born in 1943 near Lipno, a farming community about halfway between Warsaw and Gdansk, Walesa never really knew his father, a peasant carpenter; two years after the son's birth, the father died of privations he had suffered in a Nazi prison camp. Lech's mother presently married her late husband's brother, and some years afterward mother and step-father left for the United States. Lech, for his part, attended technical school, served his mandatory term in the Polish Army (he achieved the rank of corporal), and then joined hundreds of thousands of Polish peasant youths in abandoning rural life for jobs in the newly expanding industrial centers. Walesa became an electrical technician in the Gdansk shipyards. (Many of the eventual leaders of Solidarity, including Andrzej Gwiazda, from Gdansk, and Zbigniew Bujak, the head of the Warsaw region, began as electrical or heating technicians—jobs that allowed them to circulate freely through their plants, to converse with workers at all levels, and, as one of them told me, "to get to know how the place was put together.") Walesa was only 27 in 1970, but he was active in the December events, was elected to the strike committee, and represented strikers at a meeting with Edward Gierek, the new Party chief, in January 1971. His activities, like virtually everyone else's, were subdued during the early seventies (partly out of a sense of defeat and partly, perhaps, out of a cautious hope that things might actually improve under Gierek), but in the mid-seventies he again became active. Following a fiery speech in April 1976, he was sacked from his job at the shipyard, and during the next four years he endured a succession of odd jobs and frequent 48-hour arrests. (The final arrest occurred on July 31, 1980, when he was picked up outside his apartment as his wife was on the verge of entering the labor which would culminate, while Walesa was still in jail, in the birth of their sixth child.) Between 1976 and 1980, Walesa developed close relations with members of KOR and participated in the formation of the minuscule Baltic Free Trade Union, the seed from which Solidarity presently sprang.

Walesa's August 1980 exploits, which began during the strike's first hours, as he scaled the shipyard's walls to get inside, have already achieved the status of legend in Poland, and his own accounts have become subsumed to the requirements of myth. It is clear that almost from the start Walesa served as a charismatic leader, calm but firm in negotiations, flamboyant and inspirational in public speeches; that he had a particularly fine sense of the mood of the crowd and a conviction that it was necessary for the leadership never to vault too far ahead of that mood; and that his abrupt, ironic personal style utterly captivated both the Poles and the Western press.

A year later, that charisma still persists. As he enters the hall, the delegates seem to stir. Everyone is aware of his presence—where he is, what he is doing, how he is reacting—at all times, no matter what else is going on. Lech Walesa has tremendous authority—or, rather, he has been vested with tremendous authority. When you talk to Poles individually, they will list his shortcomings—he is not very well educated, he is sometimes arrogant, he is perhaps too strongly influenced by the moderates in the Church, his Polish is less than elegant. "But," they will invariably conclude, "we need someone like him—the movement needs the kind of focus he provides."

This sense of authenticity, of legitimacy, of authority, is perhaps the key element in Polish political life today. Some people have it; they can transmit it to others or confirm it in each other. Much of this circulation and recirculation of authenticity takes place across a series of images —photographs that recur on the walls of thousands of Polish homes and factories. There is the cherished image of Cardinal Wyszynski, the old man, the beloved grandfather figure, the embodiment of the persistence of the Polish spirit despite years of foreign domination. Then, there is a photograph you see everywhere: Wyszynski bowing and kissing the hand of his onetime protégé, the former archbishop of Krakow, now suddenly the Pope, John Paul II. In that image you can just see the authority coursing from one to the other. (An oil painting of that photograph has already joined the baroque succession of images of kings and saints gracing the alcoves at the national shrine in Czestochowa.) Often next to that photograph you will see another: John Paul II greeting Lech Walesa at the Vatican. In this picture, authority flows, clearly, from father to son. "We have a new trinity here in Poland," a taxi-driver in Gdansk told me, half seriously. "John Paul II is our father, Walesa is his son, and the 1970 martyrs are the Holy Spirit."

There are other images as well. For example, in the new documentary *Farmers '81*, which is a chronicle of the negotiations that culminated in the registration of Rural Solidarity, the agricultural union, one can see how the talks were floundering until Walesa personally intervened, leading a delegation from Solidarity headquarters in Gdansk. He hardly says anything—just sits there, puffing his pipe thoughtfully—but things begin to happen. Higher government officials arrive to advance the negotiations, the pace quickens, and then, suddenly, there is agreement. At the victory celebration, Walesa joins his hand high in the air with that of Jan Kulaj, the young leader of Rural Solidarity. Kulaj is huge, a towering, robust figure, and Walesa seems to dangle limply by his side. Even so, it is clear which way the authority is flowing.

And there is another, somewhat more curious instance of the phenomenon in Wajda's *Man of Iron*. In one of the film's most touching scenes, Agnieszka, the onetime film chronicler of the 1970 martyr Birkut, is marrying Birkut's son, Tomczyk, who will go on to become a leader of the 1980 strike. The year is perhaps 1978, the scene a Gdansk church. Within the context of the film's fictive reality, this is the marriage of the New Polish Woman and the New Polish Man. There are only two witnesses, friends from the shipyard and its as yet underground dissident movement: Anna Walentynowicz, the crane-operator heroine whose dismissal was partly responsible for setting off the 1980 strike, and Lech Walesa. Playing themselves: offering flowers and soft teasing. It's a very strange moment—you don't know who is conferring authenticity on whom. But the audiences love it, and there's not a dry eye in the house.

Recently a new image has been added to this rosary chain of legitimization. Solidarity offices all over the country are selling photographs of Marshal Josef Pilsudski, Poland's leader between the wars. Historians rate Pilsudski an ambiguous figure at best: he was something of a populist, but also something of a Fascist. Poles today celebrate him partly because he headed the nation during much of the only period in recent centuries when Poland can be said to have been truly free and independent, but especially because he headed the Polish nationalist army that triumphantly routed the invading Bolshevik Russian force in August 1920. The thing you notice about this picture, however, is that with his heavy, dark, droopy mustache, the marshal looks uncannily like Lech Walesa.

"Walesa isn't antidemocratic, he's ademocratic," Jan Litynski, the KOR activist, tells me one afternoon. The situation in which Walesa and the rest of the Solidarity leadership have had to work during the past year has often rendered consideration of the finer points of democratic process something of a luxury. Crises arise and have to be addressed immediately. Afterward, however, there is often a residue of resentment at how decisions were reached. The resentment is particularly pronounced among those who feel that the concessions were too large, the compromises too harsh. Thus, it is usually the union's more radical and adventuresome elements who, when objecting to the content of decisions, prefer to phrase their objections in terms of the method by which the decisions were reached. There's no particular reason to believe that the majority of the union's members didn't agree with a particular compromise, but since they weren't consulted anyway, it's fairly easy to cast the concessions as a failure of democratic process.

The debate drags on. Leszek Szaruga, an intellectual who works for the Solidarity press agency, walks outside for a breather and speaks of the union's need to defer certain aspects of the democratic process for the time being. "The government's attack on us is highly centralized and coordinated. We need a leadership with the authority to respond in kind. We have to be able to counter their propaganda attacks and to strategize our own campaigns, and we can't be expected to go back to the membership for consultations every time."

A few minutes later, Litynski comments, "It's very hard. We are trying to find an authentic way of conducting internal politics—one that will allow us to consider positions and alternatives without factionalizing into categories like 'radicals' and 'moderates,' which is precisely what the Party would like us to do."

One morning near the mid-point of the first session of the congress, things get out of hand. A proposal is made to separate the functions of the regional leader from those of the regional delegate to the national coordinating committee, which Walesa heads. According to the proposal, no one will be allowed to hold both posts simultaneously. In effect, Walesa's committee would be reduced to a discussion club, since all power would rest with the regional heads, none of whom would be on the committee. The debate takes the form of "dictatorship versus democracy"; the votes are cast, they are being tallied, the proposal seems on the verge of victory, when suddenly Walesa bounds furiously up to the rostrum. Any semblance of parliamentary procedure evaporates. Walesa is, of course, allowed to speak. He orders a ten-minute recess, and when the delegates return, he tells them that he's tired of this nonsense, the country is in the grip of a terrible economic crisis, that's what the nation is waiting for this congress to confront, and if it's not willing to do so then he's going to have to do things himself, dictator or no. He finishes by demanding that the vote be taken over again. It is, and he wins.

But the cost is high. Walesa's stature is lessened by the whole episode. He has lost—he has spent—some of his authority. Karol Modzelewski, one of Solidarity's leading theorists, remarks later in the afternoon, "It was not a very fortunate thing for the political education and evolution of the union as a whole. The debate was phrased all wrong—between dictatorship and democracy—when it should have been seen as a choice between two ways of doing things, each with certain advantages and certain disadvantages." The union moves on to other business, but the dilemmas concerning authority and internal democratic process remain.

Each morning, as the buses converge on the arena from the various schools and halls and church basements where the representatives are spending their nights, they pass the ever-lengthening lines in front of the ever-emptying shops. It isn't as if the delegates need the reminder, but there it is anyway: Poland's economic situation is dire.

Poland's economy has become entangled in a series of double binds. The situation in Silesia, the coal-rich region to the south, is typical. Coal production is perhaps the most crucial element in Poland's national economy. Coal does more than provide for the bulk of Poland's own energy requirements—when production is going well, it also becomes one of the country's major exports and a principal source of hard currency. In 1979, coal production reached an all-time high of 204 million tons, but production has since fallen by almost 20 percent, and the grim anticipation for 1981 is a mere 168 million tons. In 1979, Poland was able to export 40 million tons, yielding a hard-currency profit of three billion dollars. In 1981, Poland will be lucky to export 10 million tons. The pattern recurs in other industries. For lack of hard currency, Poland cannot buy the spare parts to repair its failing machinery or the raw materials to supply its manufacturing sector, and productivity declines further.

In the coal region, as elsewhere, one of the major causes of the drop in productivity is that, thanks to the success of their movement, the workers—the miners—now get Saturdays off. The government has tried to entice the miners back to work on Saturdays with offers of triple pay, but they tend to ignore the offer, since the money is worthless and there's nothing to buy in the shops anyway. Thus, the vicious circle: there's nothing to buy because, for lack of hard currency, the state can import neither consumer goods and food nor the spare parts and equipment that could help Poland to produce its own; the only way to generate the hard currency is to get the workers to work harder, but they have no incentive to work harder, because there's nothing they could buy with any extra money they might earn. Solidarity spokespeople point to that vicious circle, and to the atrocious record of administrative mismanagement that characterized the Gierek years, in offering their own solution to the economic crisis: *samorzad*, or worker self-management. It is their answer to almost every economic question. Sometimes it's an answer that provokes more questions than it resolves.

Back in August 1980, Solidarity was reluctant to press the issue of *samorzad*, partly because of a prior history of disappointments. In 1956 and 1970, the authorities had responded to crises by drafting supposed reforms, instituting "worker self-management" arrangements of various kinds, but in the long run nothing changed: beneath the wordplay, power remained vested in the Party bureaucrats. Solidarity was also reluctant to take on the management of an economy that was clearly in a lot of trouble, particularly within the framework of the kind of partial participation the goverment seemed to be offering: not enough authority to make the necessary reforms but just enough so that Solidarity could end up catching most of the blame for the coming collapse. Finally, Solidarity still saw itself as a trade union—a vigilant protector of its workers' interests but not the kind of organization that wanted to become a quasi-authority in its own right. Solidarity preferred to respond to the government's initiatives.

As time passed, however, the economic situation worsened, and the Party and the government seemed paralyzed. "Vigilance alone was not enough," Solidarity decided, according to an official in its press office. "What were we to be vigilant about if the government rendered no decisions?" By early spring of 1981, many Solidarity chapters were beginning to frame proposals for worker self-management. These proposals invariably grew out of a consistent double critique of the current arrangement. Solidarity's theorists argued that one principal cause of the economic debacle was the overcentralized character of state planning: the system was top-heavy, inflexible, barely responsive. It wasn't difficult to come up with a parade of ludicrous examples to prove that point. But Solidarity also attacked the way in which the upper- and middle-level bureaucratic slots were filled; Solidarity began to confront *nomenklatura*.

Nomenklatura is an elaborate system whereby the Communist Party exercises the right to appoint the top 100,000 bureaucrats and administrators in Poland. Whatever the internal structure of an organization, the Party selects, usually from within its own ranks, the heads of all the important sectors. There's a list—*nomenklatura*—which is continually being refined, and if a person is not on that list he's not eligible for a given administrative post. Whatever can be said about the idealistic intentions with which this system was originally devised (a vanguard Party's way of coordinating the tremendously complex and interconnected aspects of a ravaged country's postwar reconstruction, for example), *nomenklatura* has for the most part degenerated into a lunatic collage of incompetence, privilege mongering, and outright corruption. "The administrative overseer of our unit," a filmmaker tells me, "got the job because, having failed as a diplomat, he was brought back to Warsaw and he requested job placement within walking distance of his home. Our studio happens to be three blocks away. I don't think he'd ever seen a film."

"Of course, *nomenklatura* has produced some good managers," a delegate to the convention conceded to me one day, "but they are the exception, and in this crisis, good management must become the rule."

Solidarity's insistence on worker self-management is, therefore, a double demand, both for decentralization of decision-making and for greater worker participation in the making of those decisions.

There are various schemes for *samorzad*, but the basic idea goes something like this: the enterprise (factory, publishing house, airline, or whatever) would be the communal property of the workers who run it. ("Today, it belongs to the state, which, in turn, supposedly—but only supposedly—belongs to the workers.) The workers would elect a representative council, subject to continuing review as well as recall, and the council would appoint a manager, who would be responsible to the council alone. The state would exercise its influence through economic instruments (taxes, duties, investment credits, etc.) or normative laws (regulations, pollution standards, etc.), but otherwise it would stay out and allow the free play of the market to rationalize the economy. Workers' councils at various large enterprises—some factories have already elected such councils, which have been exerting varying degrees of influence, though nothing near what they eventually hope to achieve—would form interconnecting bodies. Already, an entity called Network joins representatives from Solidarity branches at the Gdansk shipyards, the Katowice coal mines, the Ursus tractor plant near Warsaw, the steel mills outside Krakow, and several other large enterprises in a kind of self-management study group.

Eventually, according to several theorists, each factory might contain two parallel organizations—a trade union and a workers' council. Many Solidarity officials have noted that the union cannot be expected to represent all its members as workers and at the same time develop managerial and marketing strategies that might prove detrimental to individual subgroups of its membership. Earlier this year, Zbigniew Bujak, the Solidarity leader for the Warsaw region, who has all along been one of the more farsighted strategists in this area, theorized that a workers' council might earmark a certain share of the profits for, say, capital investment and expansion, while the trade union might insist that the money go instead into safety improvements and workers' pensions. Negotiations would then occur between the council and the union.

It is difficult to imagine how such a theory would work in practice, and Western reporters tend to besiege Solidarity's theorists with their misgivings. How can the same body of workers act as both management and labor in any given negotiation? What of the lack of managerial experience and skills on the part of workers who are suddenly asked to map out—or, at least, decide on—strategies of investment, planning, marketing, and so forth? What of the need for central planning—for a centralized co-ordination of response to what is, after all, a nationwide crisis? Isn't it conceivable that, for example, profits from coal should go into agriculture? Then how is that transfer to be effected in a decentralized system of self-managing units? What if a shipyard democratically chose to build a certain kind of tanker, and the workers at the relevant steel mill simultaneously decided that they no longer wanted to make the required kind of steel? What if the workers in a shipyard decided they didn't want to fill an order from, say, the Soviet Union, because they could get more hard currency from the West? (Is the Soviet response going to be decentralized?) Is is fair to expect steelworkers at a 30-year-old plant to compete with those at a plant that has just been opened, as if the two were setting out on an equal footing? And isn't Solidarity's own experience of democratic process—the convoluted movement and the agonizingly slow pace of the process—cause for concern when Solidarity is advocating its transposition into the economic realm, where decisions have to be made within the context of a world market that is constantly changing at the speed of a computer printout?

Unfortunately, the answers one gets to such questions are usually fairly glib. Generally, they fall into three categories: (1) "You can't understand, because you're not Polish. We Poles have a special history—of nationalism (even though it's been thwarted) and socialism (even though it's become deformed)—that has prepared us for the task of transcending such problems." (2) "What do you expect? We're only one year old. It takes time to develop all those details. You're asking way too much of us." (3) "That's not our problem—that's the government's problem."

My favorite conversation along these lines occurred with Stanislaw Fudakowski, an industrial psychologist and a member of the Gdansk delegation to the congress. It was late in the day, and the condescension, I'm afraid, was flowing hot and heavy in both directions. "Look," he finally said, "you're American, so perhaps these questions make sense to you, but they have little relevance to us. One of the main things to understand is that the strategy of insisting on self-management allows us to confront the centralized power of the state without ever having to confront it directly. Little by little, authority will be transferred to the local level, until in the end the state will have lost most of its power."

"Fine," I said, "but Poland owes the Western banks and governments around 25 billion dollars. Who's going to be responsible for paying that debt?"

"That," he said, smiling, "is the government's problem."

"Of course there are contradictions," the filmmaker Andrzej Chodakowski sighed one afternoon after I paraded my cavalcade of misgivings. "The situation is so tremendously botched up at this point—the status quo itself is so loaded with contradictions—that any response will also have certain contradictions. Basically, we are struggling to find some way of introducing competition without private ownership, in such a way that the losers in the competition will still be somehow protected. It's not easy—there are no models. But, seriously, it can't get any worse than what we've got. Anything would be an improvement over *nomenklatura*."

"Self-management may not solve everything," Karol Modzelewski explained to a group of reporters outside the hall. "But we've got to find some way of *institutionalizing* the integration of the workers' wishes into the decision-making process, without always having to have recourse to strikes, with the tremendous tension and danger they arouse."

"Self-management may not solve everything," Tadeusz Mazowiecki, the editor of Solidarity's national weekly paper, told another group of reporters, a few feet away. "But we expect it to increase worker interest and therefore productivity. If workers are working for themselves, they will be willing to make the sacrifices the situation demands. They won't do it for worthless pay increases or if they feel that their labor only enriches their bosses, but they may do it for themselves."

Sitting in the gallery, watching the debate, I was reminded of something that Ludwig Wittgenstein once wrote: "Philosophy unties knots in our thinking; hence its results must be simple; but philosophizing has to be as complicated as the knots it unties." The same could be said of the possibilities for political renewal in Poland today.

Actually, many of the contradictions that Western reporters point to in Solidarity's proposals are more apparent than real. When you really press the issue, it turns out that the debate isn't finally about ongoing democratic process in the workplace. Solidarity's membership by and large understands the need for strong and decisive management at the factory level. What it is trying to confront is the way that that management is chosen, the system of *nomenklatura*. It is trying to save the Polish economy by replacing incompetent, corrupt, and aloof administrators with competent, honest, and responsive ones, and by making them responsible to the workers. The frightening thing, as the first session nears its climax, is that while Solidarity seems willing to go to the wall on this point, it is the one issue on which the Polish Communist Party seems unwilling to budge. The Party can change faces at the top so easily precisely because its true control of the nation lies in its hold on the middle bureaucracy. A compromise had seemed possible back in March—there were promising signs from both sides—but then the first Bydgoszcz crisis erupted: three Solidarity members (Jan Rulewski was one of them) were savagely beaten by local police officers. Some people think that this incident was orchestrated by frightened middle-level bureaucrats intent on polarizing the situation and scuttling any compromise. That, at any rate, was the outcome. During the summer, the government drafted its own new law on worker self-management—a patently obvious attempt at cooperation that seemed even more transparent than the 1956 and 1970 reformist charades —and quickly began moving it through the Party-controlled national parliament. Solidarity's Network countered with its own "Draft of a Bill on Social Enterprises." On September 8th, as the parliament's vote neared, the Solidarity congress voted an ultimatum. The parliament had three options: (1) scuttle the government version and enact Solidarity's plan; (2) hold a national referendum and let the people decide between the two plans; or (3) Solidarity itself would hold the referendum. There was little doubt about how the people would vote in such a referendum. The implication was that if the government failed to honor its results, Solidarity might have recourse to a general strike.

"This is it," one heard over and over in the halls outside the auditorium. "We are nearing confrontation." A new mood was emerging at the congress: a combination of elation and gloom, a double sense of dynamic vitality and impending disaster.

One afternoon, John Darnton and I were catching a bite outside the hall, and he commented, "This congress is just like the New York City Council, which I used to cover. Things seem to be going along at a crawl, but you can't turn your back on them for a minute—they're likely to do just about anything while you're not looking."

A few days later, near the conclusion of the first session of the congress, I got a chance to see what he meant. I was out by the headset table, trying to contrive a combination of earplugs, batteries, and receivers that might in fact deliver something other than inchoate electricity to my sorry ears, when a huge ovation burst out from inside the hall. Jamming the plugs back into my tender head, I raced back to the bleachers and sought out the group of reporters with whom I'd taken to sitting. Their faces were incredulous. "What on earth are they doing that for?" one of them muttered. "They need this headache?" "Tell you one thing," put in another, "they're sure going out with a bang."

Solidarity had just voted to send a letter of greeting "to the working people of Albania, Bulgaria, Czechoslovakia, the German Democratic Republic, Rumania, Hungary, and all the nations of the Soviet Union." The letter read, in part, "We assure you that despite the lies spread all over your countries, we are an authentic organization of ten million workers. . . . We support those of you who have embarked upon the difficult road of struggle for the free trade-union movement. We believe that it shall not be long before our representatives meet yours to exchange experiences."

The next morning, *Trybuna Ludu*, the Polish Communist Party paper, published the entire text of the letter in the course of attacking it, paragraph by paragraph. For the first time in a long while, the paper sold out almost immediately.

Now, as the first session of the congress rushed toward adjournment for its two-week break, the predictable fire storm erupted. In Moscow, the reaction was furious. On the evening news, workers at the Zil truck plant outside Moscow were shown approving a reply to Solidarity's insolent note. As the Manchester *Guardian* reported the next day, the Zil letter "told the Poles that their country owed its existence to the Soviet Union, and that they should get back to work rather than follow the 'demagogues' of Solidarity." Throughout Eastern Europe—even in Hungary, which up to that point had been relatively tolerant—government spokespeople and journalists joined in the condemnation. The Polish Party's Politburo held an emergency meeting and within a few days released its most fiercely worded attack yet on antisocialist elements and tendencies in Solidarity. A few days later, it became clear that the Polish Politburo was acting in response to a harrowing ultimatum it had received from its Soviet counterpart. For the first time, it appeared—and various rumors heightened the sense of impending calamity—that the Soviet Union had threatened crippling cutbacks in its delivery of vital resources, including oil, if the Polish Party did not quickly reassert its authority. (Poland gets 95% of its oil from the Soviet Union.)

This sudden flareup of tension highlighted the misperceptions prevailing on all sides. On the one hand, Soviet commentators tend to blame Solidarity for Poland's current economic crisis: they blame the union for disastrous declines in productivity as a result of time wasted in anarchistic politicking and pointless strikes. Jan Litynski of KOR counters that the country was headed for an economic catastrophe in any case, owing to mismanagement and the disastrous foreign debt. "As the food lines lengthen, as shortages spread, Solidarity is the only thing keeping this country from ripping itself apart, from descending into wholesale food riots and anarchy," Litynski argues. "People are still channeling their anger into constructive criticism, but only because such a channel exists."

On the other hand, many Solidarity members put the blame for the economic crisis entirely on the Soviet Union. Each time a train leaves Poland heading east, freighted with coal or sulfur or grain, Poles begrudge what they perceive to be their colonial fate, their status as continuing victims of the Soviet leech. "But that's one perception they've got all wrong," insists the otherwise sympathetic Daniel Singer. "Sure, the Poles send the Russians various quantities of goods, but they are receiving much more than they're giving. [Poland gets 95% of its natural gas and 90% of its iron ore from the Soviet Union.] The Russians have been willing to go along with the situation for fear of the consequences of the complete collapse that might otherwise take place. But the Russian patience may not last forever. Indeed, the current crisis is occurring because the Russians are threatening to cut back their oil shipments not to some arbitrary level but, rather, to the precise amount that the Poles can pay for, in cash or barter—which is to say virtually nothing. That, of course, would be a disaster."

In any event, the question remains: Why has Solidarity done it? Why, after carefully avoiding provocations of any kind—especially cheap ones, especially anti-Soviet ones—has the union suddenly thrown just about the biggest, most gratuitous Soviet-baiting provocation one could imagine?

"Was this," as Daniel Singer wondered by telephone from Paris, "some aberration, or is it rather the first sign of some budding death wish."

As the days passed—in the meantime, I'd come back to Warsaw—and the prospects indeed seemed to be turning more and more deadly, I couldn't get the question out of my head: Why had they done it?

I remembered an interlude a few days before the resolution to send the letter to the Eastern European countries was passed. The delegates were debating the general economic crisis that day when they suddenly adjourned for an exceptionally long lunch break. The reason, it turned out, was that several delegations needed time to pile into their buses and take the half-hour drive out to Westerplatte, on the narrow spit of land at the head of the Gdansk harbor where, 42 years earlier, an overwhelmingly outnumbered group of Polish soldiers had held off an invading Nazi landing force for a few days at the outset of the Second World War. The cratered bunker has been left untouched ever since, as a memorial to the fierce but futile defense of the peninsula. An empty tank stands at the entrance to the memorial park in commemoration, and Solidarity had recently erected a simple cross by its side. The delegates were shuttling over to lay a wreath at the foot of the cross.

The country's economy is in complete collapse, I remember thinking as my taxi dogged the outbound buses. The congress is supposed to be deliberating the issue, and instead here we go on yet another memorial excursion to grieve over yet another martyrdom that happened some 40-odd years ago.

I was sharing the taxi with Henry Feiwel, an American textile whole-saler who was in Poland pricing fabric and had decided to pay a day's visit to the congress. (Feiwel, a Viennese Jew, had himself narrowly escaped the Holocaust.) As we drove out, the taxi-driver was telling us how we had to understand Polish history, the way the Polish nation had struggled, and so forth.

"This country is obsessed with that sense of history," Feiwel said as we left the taxi and approached the memorial ceremony. "With 1939 and 1944 and 1956 and 1970. They're always telling you how you have to understand their history. But the thing that you have to understand—that *they* have to understand—is the world today, a world in which things move so much faster than they ever have before. In a world like that, in a business climate like that, you don't have time to dwell on things that happened 50 years ago, 10 years ago. They shouldn't even spend so much time dwelling on August 1980. The world is passing them by."

A few days later, I mentioned Feiwel's comment to a Warsaw psychol-ogist.

"I understand what he is saying," the psychologist told me, "but you have to understand that when we speak of 1939, for example, we are not just talking about the past, we are talking about an attitude toward the future. Take that Westerplatte ceremony. At the very moment the dele-gates were laying those wreaths by the cross, less than 100 kilometers out at sea the Soviets were holding naval maneuvers, trying to frighten the congress into taking a softer line. On some evenings, I'm told, you could see their battleships from the shore. That ceremony concerned things that happened more than 40 years ago, but it was also about what could happen tomorrow. That's what you have to understand about the Eastern European resolution. You see, we Poles live on two parallel time tracks—especially these days. One is rational: If we do this, they will do that, and then we can do such-and-such. But the other is metahistorical. It springs from a long history of defeat and desolation. And it has to do with a sense that a sort of victory can be sprung from defeat. You see, we are always preparing for the worst. There is a conviction that we should behave in such a way that if worst comes to worst, at least our children will have the knowledge that we were a glimmer, that for a brief moment we lit a spark of hope. They will have that knowledge as they sit in their prison cells."

He continued, "We're doomed. Geography dooms us. If Poles had be-haved rationally in the past, the Polish nation would not exist today. We would have been absorbed into the Ukraine and Germany; our language, our culture would have long ago disappeared. Poland survives *because* Poles are irrational. It would probably take a tremendous amount of vodka to get them to admit it, but I think that deep down most people have a sense that disaster may well come. That's why the Eastern Euro-pean resolution was so vital. If disaster comes, at least they'll have something bright and burning to look back to, and therefore to look forward to." (This psychologist, incidentally, was Jewish—one of the group of young Jewish Poles I had met on my May visit. As I listened to him, his every phrase seemed equally charged with Jewish significance.)

The Grand Prize winner at this year's Gdansk Film Festival was *Goraczka (Fever)*, Agnieszka Holland's extraordinary portrayal of the tragic fate of a group of Polish-nationalist terrorists during the stillborn 1905 rebellion against the Russian occupying authorities. The tale, replete with police spies, corrupt Polish collaborators, and valiant young patriots, ends almost farcically: everything is botched. Surprisingly, the film was made before August 1980. The filming was allowed because the nationalists were also socialists, and the Russians were, after all, representatives of the czar. But everybody in the audience knew what the film was really about.

Or another example of the pervasive double entendre which is Polish history: When Poles include 1944 in their rosary of dates, they're not referring to their "liberation" by the Soviet army. It only seems that way. One of Solidarity's newest posters features the date 1944 and a modernist rendition of the heroic wall graffiti,

P for Poland, with an anchor, a longtime token of Polish Catholic nationalism. But also PW—*"Polska Walczaca,"* "Poland is still fighting!"— the motto of the Polish Home Army, the *Armia Krajowa*, which led the indigenous resistance to Hitler's occupation. PW, the symbol of the Warsaw Uprising, the valiant, futile battle waged by Warsaw's home resistance starting August 1, 1944, and then continuing for 63 days—while the Soviet army (or so the Poles insist) stalled in its advance, waiting for the Nazis to clean out the nationalists for them. (Of course, this symbolic lineage lent added weight to the crucified anchors in the Gdansk 1970 memorial.)

Or yet another example: In cemeteries throughout Poland, you are likely to happen upon individual plaques almost buried under flowers and student badges. Spread apart the wilting blossoms and you will find the date 1940 and the place of death: Katyn. Several thousand Polish officers were killed in three places that have come to be known collectively as Katyn—a village in western Russia. Officially, according to Soviet and Polish state versions, the massacre took place in 1941, as Hitler's armies barrelled toward Moscow, and the victims were martyrs to Nazism. But most Poles know better: they'll tell you that the massacres took place in

1940, when Soviet forces occupied eastern Poland in the aftermath of the Hitler-Stalin non-aggression pact.

There's no official memorial to Katyn, but every year, on All Saints' Day (November 1st), a particular corner of the huge Powazki Cemetery in Warsaw seems to overflow with a spontaneous laying of wreaths and flowers. Earlier this year (on August 1st, the thirty-sixth anniversary of the launching of the Warsaw Uprising), the local Solidarity chapter erected a simple wooden cross at the site, with the date 1940. It was removed within a single night by the police, but Solidarity is now going ahead with plans for a permanent Katyn memorial at the site. The government is trying to head off the project with a fancy memorial of its own: "Katyn 1941." But Solidarity is not likely to stand for the substitute, and sometime in the months ahead the issue may boil over into an extraordinary crisis.

In Poland today, commemoration is rehearsal. A Pole who lays a wreath in honor of a long-past martyrdom reconfirms the knowledge in his blood that if martyrdom should ever be required of him, future generations of Poles will likewise honor his sacrifice. There are no empty gestures.

"Confrontation." During the week after the Eastern European resolution, it's the word on everybody's lips. A taxi-driver in Warsaw tells me about the closet in his friend's eighth-floor apartment stocked with dozens of bottles of benzine to be hurled at oncoming tanks—an archetypically Polish romantic gesture. The government issues statement after statement, each more shrill than the one before. A poll appearing in a Warsaw journal this week (the Poles love taking and analyzing polls) reveals that fully 40% of those interviewed expect a bloody resolution to the crisis sometime in the near future. Everybody is jumpy: I see people in the middle of the street, in the middle of their day, suddenly break down crying. Many suspect that the government may try to cancel the second session of the congress. Bogdan Lis, Solidarity's deputy chairman, promises in an interview that the second session will take place no matter what—inside the Gdansk shipyards, if necessary, under the protection of the workers. In bars, people talk openly about Solidarity's "welcoming committee" and its plans in case of an invasion or a military takeover— how people are to avoid fighting in the street but instead report to factories; Polish workers will command the seats of industry, and the Russians will not dare fire on factories so important to their own economy.

Is this all a presentiment of disaster, one wonders, or simply sentiment? Premonition, or predisposition?

There are medical studies that suggest that some New York City executives have become addicted to the adrenaline rushes that their high-pressure jobs provoke. They come physically to require the high risks their jobs entail. Similarly, Poles sometimes seem addicted to the poignancy that their history has engendered in them. Repetition compulsion: they crave another fix.

The Eastern European resolution, at any rate, and the crisis it provokes provide some utterly poignant moments, moments just waiting to be memorialized.

But there is something else going on here, this first week after the first session. Remarkably, for 13 months, the valiant, romantic, quixotic streak in the Polish character—the tendency toward martyrdom—has been held in check. Why is it breaking out now? The answer, I think, is that the Poles are tired. Fear, frustration, and fatigue are setting in: the lines, the shortages, the anxieties about the coming winter. "It's terrible to live like this, the way *they* are making us live," my taxi-driver in Gdansk tells me. "They're starving us. They don't give us the freedom we need to save ourselves. Look what they're turning us into. Look at these lines. I'd rather fight them in battle than let them defeat us like this."

In May, people asked themselves whether they should expect a Russian invasion, and it was clear that the overwhelming majority of the Poles did not. In September, the question seems to have changed into whether one ought to *hope* for a Russian invasion, and a surprising number of Poles do.[14]

There is an early poem by the Greek modern poet C. P. Cavafy entitled "Waiting for the Barbarians." He describes an antique public square, the citizens huddled, the senate suspended, the emperor and his praetors decked out in their finest robes—everyone tense and expectant, waiting for the barbarians. Evening comes, and suddenly the crowd breaks up, overcome with sorrow and confusion: messengers have arrived from the farthest borders, and there is no sign at all of the barbarians. "And now what shall become of us without any barbarians?" the poet concludes. "Those people were a kind of solution."

Once again, the barbarian demurs. And suddenly the fever breaks. On September 22nd, with a few days to go before the opening of the second half of Solidarity's congress, the union's leaders and the government reach a tentative compromise on the crucial question of worker self-management. In a hastily called meeting of the union presidium—only four of the ten members are present—Walesa wins approval in a three-to-one vote. (Jan Rulewski, of Bydgoszcz, dissents.) The national parliament quickly passes the law, fighting back some attempts by Party hard-liners to gut its compromise provisions. If nothing else, the sense of imminent doom loses some imminence. Nevertheless, there are serious questions about the compromise, in which the Party basically preserves the right to appoint managers in certain strategic industries, and both the union and the Party will nominate managers in other industries, each side reserving a veto power, with deadlocks to be decided by an overseeing court. (The system will not go into effect until January 1st.) Many regional leaders in Solidarity think that the union cut much too soft a deal, and cut it too quickly—that the leadership was stampeded into an inadequate response by the state's (and the Soviet Union's) brilliantly orchestrated crisis. According to an alternative reading, Solidarity has only itself to blame for the scale of the crisis that its Eastern European resolution provoked. At any rate, as the second phase of the congress opens, there is no immediate guarantee that the delegates will ratify the scheme. And, indeed, once the congress reconvenes, on September 26th, the focus quickly shifts from the content of the compromise to the way it was achieved. What happened to democratic process? What about the congress's ultimatum to the parliament, with its call for a national referendum? What right does a small group of "experts" negotiating with a small group of government and Party representatives have to subvert the will of the entire congress? Why couldn't the leadership have waited at least until the congress reconvened, so that the compromise could have been discussed in full and in the open? And what kind of presidium meeting was that, anyway, with only four members present?

Once again, the weight of the moment falls on Walesa. Almost through the sheer force of his personality, he subdues the congress. He tells the delegates not to blame him for the fact that only four people showed up at that meeting. He was sick, he says, but *he* managed to make it—ask the others where they were. In the end, the congress votes a mild reprimand of its leadership for flouting the democratic process and, on the same day, fêtes Walesa on the occasion of his thirty-eighth birthday.

But again the cost is high. A few days later, when the congress holds its election for union chairman, Walesa wins on the first ballot, outpolling all three opponents. Still, he garners only 55% of the delegate vote, for a position that half a year ago he would most likely have won by acclamation. Walesa and his authority—the authority with which his constituents have endowed him—remain one of Solidarity's principal defenses against complete disaster. Most people count on it. But each time he gets taken to the wall—by the government, the Party, the Russians, or the union itself—he leaves part of that authority behind at the wall, like a smudge. At some point, there may not be enough to stave off a final confrontation. "This would be a fascinating experiment," the filmmaker Andrzej Chodakowski tells me outside the hall, "if we weren't its subjects."

On the question of worker self-management, the congress itself agrees to a compromise: the delegates, while not rejecting the parliament's law outright, still call on their leadership to hold referenda in the factories on certain sections of the law. Just what, exactly, will be done as a result of these referenda remains unclear. In a way, it doesn't matter—these issues are far from settled in any case. As the economic crisis persists, the question of management will continue to fester.

"A partnership being born in terrible pain" is how Tadeusz Mazowiecki once described the relationship between Solidarity and the ruling powers. Karol Modzelewski has put it another way: "We advance across a series of compromises, each of which is unsatisfactory: but the alternative would be disaster."[15]

My last few days in Poland, I took to asking people what they thought might happen over the next several months. Many were of course worried about the coming winter ("This may be the snowflake that breaks the giant's back"), about the possibilities of food riots or transportation breakdowns or old people freezing to death in their homes.

One health worker speculated that the time of greatest danger would come in early spring. "People will survive the winter, but early spring is when people will be at their weakest. It will become warm and wet and muddy, and our supply of soap may have given out completely by then, so people won't be washing—in other words, a perfect breeding ground for bacteria and the outbreak of epidemics. And let me tell you, the health-service system is overstrained already. We will not be able to handle such an outbreak."

Several people speculated about the Polish Army—whether it would obey orders to shoot at Polish workers.

"No. Look at them, they're just young kids serving their two years. They're just like us; they *are* us."

"Yes. You have to have served in the Army to know how they work you and work you on senseless, stupid tasks until you're so tired and disoriented and scared that you'll do anything they say."

"Well, the fact of the matter is that some will and some won't."

One morning, Nina Darnton told me, "On my most pessimistic days— well, not my *most* pessimistic days, which is when I'm trying to imagine an invasion, but on my dark days—I fear that *nothing* will happen, that the situation is completely stalemated, and that Poland will just become an open, festering sore, something like Northern Ireland, forever."

And yet, as Andrzej Chodakowski told me at our last lunch together, "It ought to be possible to imagine a happy resolution for Poland. We have such potential riches—mineral resources, fine agricultural land, a highly developed industrial base, an exceptionally well-educated population—perhaps especially that, the untapped creativity of our people! Poles are by nature hard workers—we're not like people who've grown up in the sun and would rather be out relaxing on the beach: we're eager to get back to work. It's a question of how to combine all of these elements into an integrated economy, which is really a political question. People will be willing to sacrifice if they believe in the integrity and competence of those who are asking them to sacrifice.

"There's so much slack in Poland right now. America or Japan or Germany would have to put in a tremendous effort to increase productivity by three percent. If Poland could ever resolve its political crisis, I bet we could increase our productivity by 30 percent!"

Perhaps Chodakowski is right, but during the first weeks following the conclusion of Solidarity's congress—I have in the meantime returned to the United States—Poland seems no closer than before to a resolution of its political quandary. Although tensions have subsided from their most recent peak—just before the second session—the atmosphere can hardly be described as calm. The government seems to be testing the unity and resolve of the union through a series of price hikes and provocative detentions. Individuals distributing Solidarity fliers, as they have been doing for months, are suddenly being arrested; such arrests occur principally in the middle of the busiest public squares, in the middle of the busiest times of day, as if the authorities were *trying* to spark public confrontations. Wildcat strikes are erupting throughout the country (involving over 300,000 workers by mid-October). The Communist Party, under intense pressure from the Soviet Union, ousts Chairman Stanislaw Kania, the nondescript bureaucrat who supplanted Edward Gierek after August 1980, and replaces him with General Wojciech Jaruzelski, already the Prime Minister and Defense Minister. (Jaruzelski, generally considered a moderate, derives virtually all of his paradoxical authority from the fact that as Defense Minister during the seventies he refused to order "Polish soldiers to fire on Polish workers"; were he ever to do so, that authority would immediately evaporate. Hence, in a certain sense, he can only retain what limited strength he has by refusing to exercise it.) Walesa, meanwhile, has been trying to deal with his own national commission, a body that was elected at the convention whose members generally espouse positions considerably more hard-line than his own.

As the month of October progresses, observers are reminded over and over again just how various the possibilities are for maneuvering when for all the world it looks like confrontation is already at hand. The two sides seem already to have collided; but when you fix your attention on the locus of collision, it turns out an infinitesimal gap still remains, and on either side of this thin sliver of avoidance, the two sides, tensed and flexing, are busy refining and redefining their positions. The moderate leaders on both sides seem to be simultaneously addressing both their opponents and the more hard-line elements among their own constituency. Thus, for example, Prime Minister Jaruzelski calls out the troops, in part, surely, to confront Solidarity with a show of force: but he does it in such a way (small units dispatched to thousands of rural outposts) that you end up thinking it's more a gesture to placate his Soviet overlords and their local clients in the Polish Communist Party. Conversely, Walesa calls an hour-long national strike, in part, surely, to confront the government with the continuing fact of the union's cohesion and determination, but in larger part because he's trying to stem the growing tide of wildcat actions being undertaken by the more radical elements within his own union. Jaruzelski responds by getting Parliament to pass a resolution (one that, admittedly, for the moment lacks any teeth) calling for an end to strikes. Walesa in turn responds by denouncing the resolution and proclaiming that Solidarity will never give up its hard-won right to strike; but within a few sentences, he is pleading with all the wildcat strikers to abandon their actions and return to work. As the month of October comes to an end, Walesa's authority is once again on the line: he is touring the country speaking at one strike-bound plant after another, trying to reassert the union's solidarity and get the workers back to work. It is becoming clear that in the months ahead we will be witnessing a race between the growing frustration of the union's membership and the waning authority of its leadership.

It is raining this evening here in New York. I am remembering the lines in Warsaw, the queues of sad black umbrellas, what rain does when it hits a row of unbrellas, how it drips from one onto the next and then the next, finally streaming into the last person's face and clothes, while his umbrella splatters his neighbor. I am remembering those children in the lines, the water splattering down onto them.

"It's easy for you to come through here with your notepads," my translator scolded me one afternoon after a particularly numbing series of interviews at the Solidarity congress, as we gazed on one such line, "to ask these people your clever questions, to point out their troubling contradictions, to take down your various impressions. In the end you'll pack up and leave, you'll go back to your comfortable office in New York, and type out your report—*but we'll still be here*, trying to see our way through this horrible, horrible winter, and what will your sentences do for us?"

That's fair. That's true.

Another friend told me, the day I was leaving, at the airport: "Oh, Poland, you know, the winter. You American reporters are always coming up with your impossible scenarios. Before it was the Russians, they were going to invade any minute; now it's the winter, no way we'll be able to survive it. You'll see: we'll survive. Winter will come and go, and Poland, miserable Poland, will still be here. Somehow, Poland always persists."

It is raining here in New York, and I am trying to put this manuscript to bed. It does not want to go to bed. Over the radio, I hear reports of a summit meeting between Walesa, General Jaruzelski, and Cardinal Glemp. It occurs to me that not one of these three people—the leaders of the three major institutions in Polish society today—held his position only 14 months ago. Who knows where they will be four months from now? Who knows where Poland will be?

On my last day in Warsaw, I happened to speak with Neal Ascherson, a fine British reporter who had just been proofing the galleys for his own book, which covers the Polish events up through the Communist Party congress in July. We were talking about how difficult it is to write anything about Poland today that will still be true when it's published a few months from now.

"Yes," he said, smiling, "but I guess this is what history feels like before it settles, isn't it? It's all wet and squishy and muddy and it gets in your shoes. . . ."

I feel like I've been writing on quicksand.

December 14, 1981: outside the former Warsaw regional headquarters of Solidarity. Where openness and hope had reigned just a few days earlier, there now stretched only the long dark shadow of a military regime—authority without legitimacy. *(UPI)*

THE COUP

— + · + —

December 1981

The old is dying and yet the new cannot be born. In this
interregnum, a variety of morbid symptoms appear.
ANTONIO GRAMSCI—*The Prison Notebooks* (1930)

DURING THE WEEKEND of December 11–13, as Solidarity's National Commission met once again in Gdansk, tensions were once again running high. Ten days earlier, General Jaruzelski had succeeded in quashing an occupation strike at a Warsaw firefighters' academy. The cadets had been demanding, among other things, that their training take place outside the military/police context into which firefighters are ordinarily subsumed in communist Poland. Following a standoff of several days, Jaruzelski ordered a helicopter raid on the academy, and Warsaw police followed their orders flawlessly, with no apparent compunction, forcibly removing the 300 cadets. During this operation, Solidarity's telex and telephone communications throughout the Warsaw area were temporarily severed. It was a scary, efficient performance, and one which undoubtedly should

85

have been taken as a warning. Activists in Solidarity, however, responded by becoming more, not less, radical. On December 6th, Warsaw regional Solidarity called on the entire national organization to join them in a day of protest, setting it for December 17th. On December 7th, official Warsaw radio claimed that secretly obtained tape recordings of a closed Solidarity leadership meeting in Radom earlier in the week included passages in which Walesa and others were predicting an imminent confrontation and advocating the overthrow of the government. (Walesa confirmed he'd made such remarks but claimed they'd been taken completely out of context.) On December 10th, the Soviet leadership fired off yet another anxious and anxiety-provoking note to the Polish party's central committee. Walesa, meanwhile, under heavy pressure from members of his own national commission, commented, "We do not want confrontation, but we cannot retreat anymore. We cannot be passive anymore as this would be detrimental to the union."

On Friday, December 11th, in Warsaw, the Polish foreign ministry asked French Prime Minister Maurois to postpone a three-day visit that had been scheduled to begin on December 16th. Meanwhile, in Gdansk, the more than one hundred members of Solidarity's National Commission convened their meeting and started out by serving notice that they would call a 24-hour nationwide strike if the government passed any laws giving itself emergency powers (such as that of banning strikes). Jan Rulewski of Bydgoszcz called for speedy elections to all representative institutions, and Marian Jurczyk of Szczecin called for free elections to Paliament no later than March 31, 1982. A Solidarity leader from Legnica raised objections to the presence of Soviet troops and their huge base in his home district. The next day, Saturday, December 12th, the National Commission voted to endorse its Warsaw chapter's call for a nationwide day of protest on December 17th. In addition, as Walesa looked on in frustrated silence, the commission took its most radical—and some feel, most provocative—action yet, voting to hold a February referendum in which the entire country would be canvassed for its opinion on four questions:

1. Are you in favor of a vote of confidence in General Jaruzelski?
2. Are you for establishing a temporary government and free elections?
3. Are you for providing military guarantees to the Soviet Union in Poland?
4. Can the Polish Communist Party be the instrument of such guarantees in the name of the whole society?

Many of those who voted for the referendum did so because they expected to be able to prove that the Polish people, guided by Solidarity, would answer the questions responsibly and sensibly—that is, for instance, voting "yes" on points three and four—thereby easing the anxieties of both the Polish Communist Party and its Soviet counterpart. In practice, however, the very suggestion of an electoral poll of this type in an Eastern bloc country was bound to be incendiary. When, a few hours later, the assembled delegates received successive bulletins that huge troop movements were under way throughout the country and that all communications to the Gdansk region were being cut, Walesa was heard to sigh, rebuking his fellow leaders: "Well, now you have the confrontation you were looking for."

During the early morning hours of Sunday, December 13th, police rounded up most of Solidarity's leaders, conveniently gathered as they all were in Gdansk for the National Commission meeting.[16] Meanwhile troops were taking up positions all over Poland, sealing off city after city. All internal telephone and telegraph lines were cut. All Solidarity offices throughout the country were seized along with most local leaders. Some sources put the figure of those interned in this first sweep as high as 40,000.[17] Jaruzelski's coup, in short, was one of the most effectively executed maneuvers in recent history: it will no doubt be studied by military tacticians and practitioners, both East and West, for decades to come.

Poles awakening to a dazzling clear morning, the first after two weeks of cold, gray skies, now learned of the imposition of martial law as, dressing for Sunday Mass, they turned on radios that were endlessly replaying General Jaruzelski's 6 A.M. address to the nation. In response to the country's dire situation, the general explained, he was invoking emergency constitutional powers, declaring "a state of war," and placing the government under the direction of a 21-man Army Council of National Salvation (WRON). Army generals and commissars would be taking over at all government ministries and at most large enterprises, and further directives would soon be forthcoming. The general insisted that these emergency measures would only be temporary. He concluded by quoting the country's national anthem, "Poland is not yet lost as long as we yet live."

Stern directives were indeed quickly forthcoming. After insisting that there would be "no turning back from socialism," the military council issued 20 separate martial law degrees—among other things sealing the country's frontiers; suspending basic civil rights such as freedom of press, speech, assembly, and access to communication; banning all public gatherings; instituting a strict 10 P.M. to 6 A.M. curfew; banning the distribution of printed material or even the use of any printing equipment, including office copying machines, without prior government approval; sanctioning mail and telephone censorship and eavesdropping (which would apply once either mail or phone service was resumed, since for the time being, everything was down); restricting all TV and radio broadcasts to one Warsaw-based channel; closing all educational institutions, with the exception of nursery schools, for an indefinite period (the regime was even wary of six-year-olds!); and authorizing the armed forces to use "coercion to restore calm, law and order," and the judicial system to engage in summary proceedings in the case of any violations of martial law (with penalties ranging from heavy fines to execution).

Notwithstanding which, the next morning, Monday, December 14th (the eleventh anniversary of the beginning of the troubles on the Baltic Coast in 1970), spontaneous occupation strikes broke out all over the country, at all the big history-laden enterprises: the Gdansk, Gdynia, and Szczecin shipyards; the Ursus tractor plant; the Radom munitions factory; the Nowa Huta steel mills outside Krakow; the Poznan machinery works; and the Silesian coal mines. The regime, however, was gradually able to break the backs of these occupation strikes one by one, and even to do so in a relatively bloodless manner. (The worst massacre apparently occurred in Silesia, at the Wujek mine, where nine miners were killed on December 16th, the anniversary of the worst violence in 1970, and the first anniversary of the dedication of the Gdansk monument to the martyrs of 1970.) By December 17th, the date Solidarity had initially set as a day of protest in response to the helicopter break-up of the sit-in by the firefighter cadets, most of the country had in fact been subdued.

I am recording these notes just two weeks following the coup and my comments are provisional. Precisely because of the success of Jaruzelski's news blackout, reliable, verifiable facts are hard to come by. It will probably be years before a comprehensive history of this sorry month can be attempted. Still, I would like to record a few impressions:

There is something profoundly disingenuous in much of the editorializing that has been coming out of the West since the coup. Western commentators continually speak as if Jaruzelski's imposition of martial law accomplished some utterly arbitrary emasculation of a healthy, thriving body politic. And yet, I can't imagine a more truthful portrayal of the actual situation in Poland that morning than Jaruzelski's own summation at the outset of his martial law address: "Our country is on the edge of the abyss. Achievements of many generations, raised from the ashes, are collapsing into ruin. State structures are no longer functioning. New blows are struck each day to our flickering economy. Living conditions are burdening people more and more . . ."

The fact is, Poland was probably not going to make it through the winter. Facing imminent famine and a collapse of its health-support systems, the country was lapsing into a state of near anarchy. It's not at all clear that Solidarity had either programmatic solutions or, any longer, the institutional cohesion necessary to develop those solutions.

Where Jaruzelski is being hypocritical, however, is in his steadfast refusal to accept his own complicity (and that of his "moderate" colleagues in the Polish Communist Party) in allowing the situation to have deteriorated to this point. There was a time (even as late as May) when the energies of Solidarity could have been mobilized on behalf of the nation's economic renewal. True, the privileged middle-level bureaucrats, the Red Bourgeoisie, would have had to give up some of their class prerogatives—but since the alternative was national ruin, perhaps that was not asking so much. Solidarity was willing to negotiate and to compromise—the moderate leaders in Solidarity still commanded enormous prestige and authority, and they would have been able to lead most of their members along such a path. Instead, they were confronted with endless provocations in the field and boundless bad faith at the negotiating table. "The ruling group is, in a sense, the owner of the means of production without having all the responsibilities of an owner," wrote Jadwiga Staniszkis, a brilliant Warsaw sociologist, shortly before the coup. "It participates only in the economic gains, and not in the losses. Since it is also quite prepared to issue dud checks, nearly all Solidarity's victories have had a superficial character." The fact that the best Jaruzelski could offer Walesa, as late as this past November, was one seat for Solidarity on an otherwise Communist-controlled seven-member Front of National Accord suggests that the so-called Communist moderates never really had any intention of hazarding a plausible middle solution. Is it any wonder that Solidarity's moderates never had any time to develop programmatic alternatives? In the face of such transparent bad faith on the part of their negotiating partners, they were continually scrambling just to maintain the union's cohesiveness. By the end, they were even failing at that.

Of course, the question of accountability for the Polish debacle becomes something like one of those wooden Russian dolls—blame mitigated by still larger blame. Jaruzelski and the other moderates in the Communist Party hierarchy most likely could never have negotiated in good faith because of the pressures they were under from their colleagues in the Soviet Politburo. Before we cast the Soviet leaders as the archvillains of the piece, however, it is important to remember that, completely independent of the false issues of Marxist dogma, the hatred between Russians and Poles is centuries old. The Soviet Union lost more than 20 million people fighting the last war on its western frontier. Can any other nation make a comparable claim? Is the Russian reluctance to see a fiercely romantic, potentially violent, and decidedly anti-Russian movement developing at its very border that hard to comprehend? Would the United States allow a similar manifestation in Mexico? It doesn't even allow one in El Salvador.

No, in Poland the very land seems cursed. "Geography," my Polish friend told me, "geography dooms us." And it dooms everyone who tries to master its lean imperatives. Jaruzelski's two speeches—December 13th and Christmas Eve—were true masterpieces. From reading them one comes away with the suspicion that this man really felt he had to act the way he did in order to save the nation. And perhaps he did. "But history," as Daniel Singer recently commented, paraphrasing Lenin, "doesn't judge by intentions; it judges by results. And it will judge Jaruzelski a butcher." Jaruzelski slaughtered a country's hope and condemned its people to desolation. Many of the country's best citizens were cast to the mercy of brutal prison guards and yet more brutal temperatures. (Jaruzelski may claim that there is still room to negotiate the existence of an independent trade union in Poland, but with whom does he intend to negotiate when the slightest signs of independent thinking have proven grounds for imprisonment?) He is in the process, apparently, of handing the country back to its worst elements, which is to say the Communist Party or rather that part of the party which has survived the past 16 months of desertions. (There are indications coming out of Poland that Communist Party resignations rose even more dramatically in the wake of the martial law decrees.) What remains of the Polish Communist Party as it enters 1982, for the most part, are its least attractive elements: the complacent, the incompetent, the corrupt, and a small but powerful minority of the truly evil—the fascist wing of the party, the perpetrators of the anti-Semitic purges of 1968, Moczar and his crowd. (Recall that as late as March 1981, Stefan Olszowski, one of Jaruzelski's principal heirs apparent in the Communist Party hierarchy and the darling of the Soviet Politburo, was praising the anti-Semitic harangues of the fanatic Grunwald Association.)

So it becomes hard to sustain one's objectivity in considering the deeds of Jaruzelski and his colleagues—especially for someone in my position. Many of the people I met in Poland—probably more than half of those I quoted in my reports—are today shivering in primitive detention centers. No one knows what will become of them. Granted, I end up feeling, Jaruzelski and his colleagues faced an unenviable set of options; granted, they may have thought they were acting to save the country; granted, if they hadn't acted someone else would have; granted all of that—still, it is *they* who did act and they who are responsible for the desolation in Poland today.

What's left to consider is how, in this country with its union of 10,000,000 SOLID, Jaruzelski's lightning coup could have been so remarkably effective at the outset, and then what the prospects for Poland's new regime may be in the long run.

As for the first question, three factors stand out. The first involves the nature of the army in Polish society. As late as June 1981, when a poll ranked Solidarity the second most respected institution in Polish society, just after the Church, the army came in third, just after Solidarity (the party ranked fourteenth). For Poles, the army up till now has been a bastion of nationalist feeling, so much so that a general could legitimately expect to get away with concluding his declaration of martial law by invoking the country's national anthem. The issue's even more subtle than that, although it was staring us all in the face the whole time. "No," my Polish friend had insisted when I asked him whether Polish soldiers would fire on Polish workers. "Look at them, they're just like us. *They are us.*" They are us. And while so many commentators predicted that Polish soldiers would never fight their brothers and fathers and sisters and lovers in the Polish workforce, few acknowledged that, by the same reasoning, Polish workers would never fight them. In any case, as things developed, Jaruzelski was able to keep the issue fairly moot: the army generally was held in abeyance, deployed in noncritical functions—used, for example, to encircle occupied factories but seldom to invade them. That was a task reserved for the highly loyal (and—remarkably—still intact) 25–30,000-member Internal Security Forces, the zomos: they did most of the dirty work, one factory at a time.

So, the question becomes, why didn't the Poles fight the zomos? Presumably there was no love lost between the workers and these minions of the Communist Party. I think the answer is that they would have, back in May. But by December something had happened, something intangible but pervasive. People were so busy speculating on how Poles would behave in the event of an actual civil war that they had failed to notice that one had already started deep within each individual, particular Polish soul. In most Poles, it seems, there is a part which is burning, heroically, defiantly hopeful and idealistic—but it exists side by side with an aspect which is fathomlessly desolate. Poles *know* that Poland always loses. It is precisely out of the darkness of that knowledge that the flame of their hope still somehow occasionally gleams. Gleams . . . and then gutters out again. By December, the desolation was coming back to the fore, was beginning to drown out the hope. Jaruzelski waited to strike until most Poles already secretly sensed their cause was lost.

Or, phrased another way—and this brings us to our third point—Jaruzelski struck at the very moment when it was most important that individual Poles not be abandoned to their solitary fantasies—and he struck in such a way as to leave them with nothing but those fantasies. Robbed of Solidarity, they were relegated to solitude. "The key to Jaruzelski's strategy," the London *Sunday Times* reported, "was to isolate and thereby neutralize every group, and to deprive them of *any* information, save his own decrees. This was achieved with ruthless ingenuity. Poles could not telephone each other, nor could they write letters, because the post had stopped. They could drive until their fuel ran out—all petrol stations were closed—but not very far, because of the roadblocks. Newspapers, other than government ones, were banned. Sports events were cancelled and small gatherings prohibited. In Gdansk police even broke up a queue outside a food shop. In other words, almost every possible forum for ordinary people was banned or obliterated" (Dec. 20, 1981).

Solidarity was a movement that lived by breathing the openness it exhaled. Jaruzelski's brilliant insight was that the way to extinguish the movement was not so much by attacking it directly as by smothering the openness it lived on. For months, everyone had known everything. Now, suddenly, no one seemed to know anything: Were strikes going on? Had there been many deaths? Who and how many had been arrested? Where was Walesa? What was the Pope doing? Nobody knew. Might your neighbor be an informer? Why had your husband failed to come home before curfew? How could you get word to your wife that you'd failed to leave early enough to avoid the curfew and had hence decided to spend the night at the office? People became so consumed by their private anxieties and misgivings that they had little time for anything else.

It comes down to something as clichéd as this: Information is light. It was precisely the sudden lack of information that rendered everything so stark. We experienced it here in the West: Without substantive information, the kind we'd become used to, we tended to abandon ourselves to our darkest, most desolate fantasies. *Any information* would have been better than this. Imagine how it must have been for the Poles. No wonder that for the most part, after a few days of resistance, they seemed to crater.

As I write, these last few days in December, two weeks into the new regime, it would seem that Jaruzelski has succeeded in imposing his martial law, for now. The last remaining holdouts, for the time being anyway, are a couple of thousand miners in Silesia. (Think about those miners, by the way, for a moment. Can you imagine what their lot has been for the past two weeks, cooped up in those dark, low, primitive shafts, the very walls bleeding a clammy, black, winter dampness—no information, no ventilation, no light, no contact with loved ones, only an abstract terrible sense of the impending future? Poland has an uncanny capacity for secreting such concrete images of its own situation: The country is its own best poet, it is always singing itself.)

But what can Jaruzelski have hoped to accomplish in the long run? Clearly, he hoped that, following the initial shock, he would be able to get the country back to work, that a touch of military discipline might help pull the country away from the brink of bankruptcy. Indeed, during the first days of the new regime, several Western bankers seemed to share that expectation. "Many U.S. bankers," reported the *Wall Street Journal*, "see Soviet-style authoritarianism as their best hope for recovering the $1.3 billion that Poland owes them." The *Journal* story went on to quote an unnamed bank executive to the effect that "Most bankers think authoritarian governments are good because they impose discipline. Every time there's a coup d'état in Latin America there's much rejoicing and knocking at the door offering credit" (Dec. 21, 1981).

Of course, such expectations quickly proved ludicrously far off the mark. Although Jaruzelski's shock forces were able to break the occupation strike of the mammoth Ursus tractor plant just outside Warsaw within its first few days, for example, reports out of Poland this week suggest that during the initial ten days of martial law, the several thousand workers at the plant have produced precisely *one tractor*.

The problem never was getting people to show up for work; it was getting them to work enthusiastically, to boost their productivity. There doesn't seem to be any way that Jaruzelski's regime will be able to accomplish that. According to a report out of Gdansk, workers on one side of a ship were busy all right: they were busy unloading all the freight the workers on the other side of the ship were busy loading. Meanwhile, elsewhere, assembly line workers are said to be busily turning out parts that don't match. The entire country is quickly becoming a Polish joke. The stalemate I saw back in September has merely been carried to a higher level. I sometimes imagine that if Poland were a chess match, the two masters would have abandoned it a long time ago, declared a draw, shoved the pieces off the board, and started again from scratch. What does one do in a chess match which has achieved stalemate when one's not allowed to quit the game?

Perhaps all one does is wait. The latest graffiti on Warsaw walls reads, "The winter is yours, but the spring will be ours!" Perhaps, perhaps.

For the time being, however, the Poles have been relegated once again to their longing. It is a longing centuries old—one which seems to have insinuated itself into the souls of anyone who has tried to live on that low, flat plain. The Chassidic Jews, whose movement was also born there two centuries ago, told wonderful stories about that longing. Elie Wiesel, the survivor of Auschwitz, recalled one of those stories in his 1970 book, *One Generation After*:

> Having concluded that human suffering was beyond endurance, a certain Rebbe went up to heaven and knocked at the Messiah's gate.
>
> "Why are you taking so long?" he asked him. "Don't you know mankind is expecting you?"
>
> "It's not me they are expecting," answered the Messiah. "Some are waiting for good health and riches. Others for serenity and knowledge. Or peace in the home and happiness. No, it's not me they are awaiting."
>
> At this point, they say, the Rebbe lost patience and cried: "So be it! If you have but one face, may it remain in shadow! If you cannot help men, all men, resolve their problems, all their problems, even the most insignificant, then stay where you are, as you are. If you still have not guessed that you are bread for the hungry, a voice for the old man without heirs, sleep for those who dread night, if

you have not understood all this and more: that every wait is a wait for you, then you are telling the truth: indeed, it is not you that mankind is waiting for."

The Rebbe came back to earth, gathered his disciples and forbade them to despair:

"And now the true waiting begins."

Or, as Antonio Gramsci, the great Italian communist political theorist, insisted to his followers from the bowels of the prison to which Mussolini had remanded him: This has become a season for "pessimism of the mind, and optimism of the will."

—*December 27, 1981*
New York City

Spring 1982. Solidarity and KOR leaders under detention at Bialoleka prison.
Top (l. to r.): Rulewski, Kuron, Onyszkiewicz.
Center (l. to r.): Modzelewski, Wujec, Gwiazda, Michnik.
At right: Kuron (shirtless) and Rulewski.
(*Photographer unknown*)

A STATE OF
WAR

——————+ +——————

October—December 1982

PART ONE

A VISITOR WHO CAME, as I did, to witness martial law in Warsaw in the fall
of 1982 with memories of how things had seemed the previous fall (the
endless lines in front of near-empty stores, the increasingly frantic political deterioration in the face of an oncoming winter) and with precon-
ceptions drawn from martial law in places like Chile (grim soldiers at
roadblocks, stadiums crammed with prisoners, the full power of the state
projected in overt repressive terror)—such a visitor in Warsaw could be
quickly brought up short. For one thing, the lines had pretty much disappeared; stores were by no means lavishly stocked, but there did seem
to be some basic foodstuffs on the shelves and a generally calmer aspect
to the market. On the surface, it seemed clear, things had improved.
Meanwhile, although one did occasionally see a group of three or four
soldiers walking (not really marching) by, they hardly seemed threatening. If anything, they presented a Buñuelesque aspect: you might be
sitting in a park watching children play in a sandbox, and a small squad-

ron of soldiers would shuffle past, incongruously, heading nowhere in particular, with no one really seeming to mind.

To be sure, these were Army soldiers and most Poles this autumn were still managing to conceive of their Army (if not its leadership) as an authentic nationalist institution. The ZOMOS, the gray-uniformed élite trouble-shooters who answer directly to the Party, and who still carried out most of the regime's dirty work—they were another story. But you hardly ever saw them. Unless trouble was occurring somewhere, they were judiciously confined to barracks. In Warsaw, the centrally situated Hotel Warszawa had been converted into lodgings for the ZOMOS, and Warsavites jokingly referred to it as the Zomotel. For that matter, Warsavites did a lot of joking about the ZOMOS. ("Why do the ZOMOS always have all those scratches on their faces on Friday night? Because that's the night they try to teach them to eat with forks and knives.") One editor told me with great delight how the people at his workplace had called the police to report a suspicious-looking meeting taking place in a room down the hall: the ZOMOS arrived within minutes, tore down the door, and broke up a meeting of the publishing house's Communist Party cell.

During the 16 months of Solidarity's officially permitted existence—between the Gdansk strike of August 1980, and General Wojciech Jaruzelski's coup on December 13, 1981—people often referred to the Polish renewal as "the self-limiting revolution." Everyone seemed to recognize that things could go only so far—that toppling the Communist Party, for instance, or giving way to violence would likely provoke a Soviet invasion. Meanwhile, the country's internal situation continued to deteriorate. The coup on December 13th, although shockingly sudden, seemed in retrospect shockingly obvious. On that cold Sunday morning, as one mordant joke had it, a gang of thugs had gone and attacked an insane asylum. For the first several months thereafter, most accounts agree, the mood of Poland was one of stunned, bleak shock. Spring brought with it feeble signs of life—demonstrations in early May, an increasingly visible underground presence, and an increasingly irreverent and sometimes daring public attitude toward the regime. During the months of martial law, however, Jaruzelski and his colleagues were engaged in a sort of self-limiting counter-revolution. If they didn't launch a full-scale overt repression (thousands of Chileans were killed in the first months of the Pinochet coup, and people in Santiago certainly weren't going around in public places telling jokes about soldiers), this was partly because they couldn't: they didn't have the forces at their disposal.[18] The ZOMOS were spread thin, and the regular Army, although it could be deployed to surround striking factories or to patrol city streets in small squadrons, could not be relied upon to enforce Chilean-style discipline. "The Army's a slate hammer," a friend of mine in Warsaw commented over lunch in an open-air café. "And the regime knows it. If Jaruzelski ever has to bear down hard with it, it may well crumble in his hands." Jaruzelski probably conceives of himself as a patriot; he probably believes that by his actions he saved Poland from an onrushing civil war and a Soviet occupation. But he must know that full-scale frontal repression might easily provoke the Poles into precisely the civil war he imagines he has prevented—and then the Soviets would certainly come. So he himself limits the counter-revolution—or, rather, he limits it to more subliminal levels.

The result is that life in Warsaw this autumn could sometimes seem disconcertingly open. One evening, I went to a production of *Antigone* at a Warsaw theater. In Sophocles' play, Antigone and her uncle Creon confront each other over her right to give a decent, worthy burial to her brother. (In the steel town of Nowa Huta the very afternoon of that performance, a similar issue had been tested as thousands of mourners defied the authorities by attending the funeral of a young man killed in street violence a few days earlier, so the topic could hardly have been more relevant.) In the original play, Antigone is a model of honorable civil disobedience, but Creon is no simple tyrant—his speeches are laced with "on the one hand"s and "on the other"s. This Warsaw production played Sophocles more or less straight except that the Creon character had been completely stripped of his balancing circumspection and came off as a power-mad megalomaniac. The production had apparently been passed by the censors: it was being presented at a regular theater, regularly advertised. (Andrzej Wajda, the film director, was also preparing a production of *Antigone* for presentation on the Krakow stage later in the winter.) A few nights after that, I saw a lively rendition of Eugeniusz Szwarc's *Smok* ("The Dragon"), an anti-Stalinist allegory in which noble Lancelot comes to town to slay a virgin-eating dragon and is told by the town's officials that everybody *likes* the dragon.

Many excellent actors were available for such productions this autumn in Warsaw, because virtually all of Poland's actors were engaging in a boycott of the country's state-run television—once one of the finest cultural institutions in Eastern Europe—and have been doing so since the coup. In view of the fact that most Polish actors ordinarily derive the major part of their income from television, it was a truly heroic commitment. Despite continual pleading by the Ministry of Culture and Art, they refused to be seen on television or heard over the radio; every evening Poles could tune in to witness the results of their continued defiance and the regime's hapless attempts to cope with it. At one point, Deputy Prime Minister Mieczyslaw Rakowski was quoted as saying, "If no major actor wishes to accept a part on television, we will show mediocrities." And Polish television has indeed become an endless round of panel discussions, old reruns, and Soviet imports. The scriptwriters for one popular radio soap opera (in continuous production since the late fifties) had to work feverishly to try to account for the sudden disappearance of almost all the show's principal characters (one brother was said to have gone off to work in East Germany, the father was in a sanatorium); finally the situation became untenable, and the show was cancelled.

Occasionally, a performer would ignore the boycott, as did the pianist Halina Czerny-Stefanska; when she subsequently gave a public concert, the audience applauded her appearance on the stage and continued to applaud through all of her attempts to play. When, once in a while, a writer appeared on television supporting the authorities, he'd be likely to open his front door the next morning and find piles of his books, returned by neighbors, blocking the exit. Meanwhile, many of the better art galleries in Warsaw (Poland has a distinguished avant-garde and modernist tradition) were closed, with little signs on their doors saying "*Remont*" ("Under repair"). "Poland's artists are on spiritual strike," a dealer told me. "They are producing, but for the future, not for today."

One afternoon, at the tourist art gallery occupying one side of the lobby of the Victoria, the city's plushest hotel, I was casually looking over the sappy landscapes and second-rate portraits when I was stunned by a powerful image of a young woman: her face was creased with suffering and a large crow was perched in her hair, its beak squarely embedded in her forehead, drawing blood. The regime's Military Council of National Salvation, WRON, is known unofficially by a variant of its acronym, *wrona*, which is the Polish word for crow. I stared at the image for some time and then turned away to find a bellhop looking at me: he simply nodded and smiled.

A few weeks earlier, I was told, a reviewer in *Polityka*, one of the major political journals in Poland, had published a long article on *The Polish August*, the fine book about Solidarity by the London *Observer*'s Eastern Europe correspondent Neal Ascherson; the *Polityka* critic had started out by lambasting the book as profoundly antisocialist and then, as if to prove his point, had quoted at great length from many of the book's most "objectionable" sections.

The Polish official press agency has several vitrines around town in which it displays inspirational photographs; one day I came upon a crowd of young people laughing in front of one of them. Behind the glass the display's designer had contrived a fetching contrast of, on one side, General Jaruzelski and, on the other, Poland's newly canonized saint— Father Maksymilian Kolbe, the martyr-hero of Auschwitz. Kolbe's eyes were fierce and yet serene; you couldn't see Jaruzelski's eyes behind his dark glasses.

For all its censorship and propaganda, the Polish aboveground press is still the most open in Eastern Europe, by a mile. Last fall, for instance, even though Lech Walesa was still under internment, the Warsaw newspapers were reporting that he was being considered as a candidate for the Nobel Prize. Some of the best reporters were dismissed from their jobs (the militantly pro-Solidarity journalists' association was dissolved during the first months of martial law), but many of them have surfaced in small, out-of-the-way venues. Stefan Bratkowski, the former head of the association, now writes regularly for the women's magazine *Moda i Zycie* ("Fashion and Everyday Life") and for *Niewidomy Spoldzielca* ("Blind Cooperativist"), the magazine of clubs for the blind, which has become perhaps the best-written and most widely prized journal in Poland today, even though much of it is in Braille.

One no longer comes upon the remarkably evocative Solidarity posters along the streets, but many of Solidarity's graphic artists have gone back to designing covers for books, and a visit to a bookstore can be a bracing experience. (Ironically, according to an editor friend of mine, the early months of martial law, with most of the newspapers suspended and their presses hence available for other uses, were a boom time for Poland's previously parched book-publishing industry.) Several new books have covers that, given the political situation, seem downright subversive. One features a prisoner, bound, gagged, and scrunched in a corner (this for a novel about the Warsaw ghetto uprising); another shows a pair of hands tied brutally behind a prisoner's back (a book about partisans in the Second World War); and a third simply offers a brooding black crow (a children's book). The recent spate of state-published books includes new editions of Poland's émigré Nobel laureate, Czeslaw Milosz.

Graffiti are everywhere: "WRON WON ZA DON" ("Crow, go back across the Don River"). "COME BACK EDDIE, ALL IS FORGIVEN"—a reference to Edward Gierek. "WLADYSLAW, WELCOME TO THE UNDERGROUND!"—a reference to Wladyslaw Gomulka, Gierek's predecessor as party secretary, who died and was buried in September 1982. At the studios of Film Polski, someone had hung a small cardboard notice on the door of the room that used to serve as the unit's Solidarity office: "Back in a moment." One morning, in the center of a mass-housing project on the outskirts of Warsaw, I came upon a single word scrawled large in bold, black spray paint: "RASTAFARI!"[19]

In an attempt to lure young people off the streets, the regime has been pouring money into dance clubs—a policy that has led to an upsurge of Punk groups. Many of them belt out lyrics that are not exactly what the regime had in mind. "I can take the crisis," goes one refrain, "just spare me the crap." The city's top band, Perfekt, used to electrify its audiences with a song that went, first loud, "YOU DON'T HAVE TO BE AFRAID," then soft, a whisper, "of Jaruzelski"—over and over again. Jaruzelski recently had this group dissolved.

For a while after the imposition of martial law, people went around wearing V-sign pins. Jaruzelski has been greatly annoyed by this profusion of V signs. "There's *no such letter* in the Polish alphabet," he pointed out, correctly, in an early speech, and the pins were banned. People subsequently took to wearing rabbit-ear buttons, till they, too, were banned. Then people started wearing tiny resistors taken from transistor radios (the Polish word for resistor, *opornik*, has the same connotation as the English), until these, too, of course, were banned. Recently, they've started wearing black enamel jewelry. It took a while for the regime to figure out what that was all about, but it turned out that during the 1863 rebellion against czarist Russia, women who sold their gold and silver to support the cause of Polish liberation were reduced to wearing black enamel. The regime couldn't very well ban black enamel jewelry. Occasionally, after talking with someone for hours, I'd notice that the dandruff-sized speck on their lapel was in fact a tiny plastic pin bearing, in micro-miniscript, the traditional *Solidarnosc* logo, with the red letters and the flag coming out of the *N*. One day, I encountered a man walking down the street boldly wearing what seemed to be a traditional, full-sized *Solidarnosc* pin. Only, when he got close up I realized that the letters on the pin didn't spell out "*Solidarnosc*" but, rather, the phrase "What are you looking at, stupid?"

Everyone in Warsaw seemed to have a little box of "war paraphernalia" hidden somewhere in a cupboard. (From the start, for legal reasons, Jaruzelski himself had been referring to martial law as "a state of war.") I was shown a finely tooled wooden jigsaw puzzle: four pigs combined to form the face of Jaruzelski. I was shown some postcards, famous illustrations from a traditional Polish story for children: one showed a noble young prince languishing sadly in prison—the cards had been taken off the market. I was shown new, fresh ten-zloty banknotes, dated 1982, with the words "*Wrona Skona*" ("The crow will die") clearly bled into the watermark. And several times I was shown two commemorative stamps. On December 16, 1981, three days after the coup, philately shops throughout Warsaw began selling postage stamps commemorating the dedication, a year earlier, of two monuments, at Gdynia and Gdansk, to the martyrs of the 1970 massacres. During the first few days after the coup, the commissars were apparently so busy attending to other things that they failed to notice the stamps, which featured beautiful, inspired renditions of the two monuments. By the time they got around to stopping the sales, everybody seemed to have copies. No one, though, was trying to use them to mail letters.

One of the first things a visitor in Warsaw notices these days is that Victory Square is boarded up. Until 1918, this large, empty plaza in front of the Victoria Hotel was the site of a huge and hugely hated Russian Orthodox church, the symbol of czarist domination of this Catholic country. It was torn down following Polish independence, in 1918, and the vast square remained empty, a site for official public ceremonies. In 1979, in the presence of more than a million rapt Polish Catholics, Pope John Paul II and Cardinal Stefan Wyszynski jointly celebrated Mass in the square. After Wyszynski's death, in May 1981, the spot became a sort of shrine, and Warsavites regularly brought flowers, which they strewed along the ground in the shape of a long cross. After the imposition of

Graffiti from the state of war: victory through passivity; Solidarity behind barbed wire (with intimations of Auschwitz); the word "Solidarity" being demolished by an advancing tank (and yet, below the bloody massacre, the letters are already re-forming, only larger).

Two official Polish postage stamps commemorating the first anniversary of the dedication of monuments in Gdynia and Gdansk to the martyrs of December 1970—"mistakenly" released December 16, 1981, three days *after* the coup.

martial law, the cross seemed to sprout an "M" under one arm, an anchored "P" under the other, and a sweeping "V" at its base. The "M" was for "Mary," and the anchored "P," or "PW," recalled the Polish Home Army's "*Polska Walczaca*" ("Poland is still fighting"). Every few days, the police would come and blow the shrine away with their water cannons, but the next day Poles would simply start to rebuild it from scratch. Finally, the regime decided to board up the whole plaza for repairs, and they were undertaken with a vengeance. Behind the wooden fence you could hear tractors rumbling. "Some functionary downtown," a taxi-driver outside the nearby Europejski Hotel told me, "has been pushing for repairs of the plaza for years. There was never enough money to do it. Now, suddenly, it turns out the guy was a genius, he's been given a promotion and put in charge of the emergency."

The flower cross soon sprang up again, a few blocks away, in an alcove near the entrance to the Old City outside St. Anne's Church. This time, flowers and boughs were piled even higher—sometimes as high as two and a half feet—with fresh flowers at the top covering what was quickly becoming a compost heap. Among the wreaths were scattered photographs of Lech Walesa, Cardinal Wyszynski, and Pope John Paul II; Solidarity banners; and personal messages inscribed in red on white ribbons. The cross is constantly surrounded by a crowd of people; old, black-garbed women lead them in patriotic and religious hymns (in Poland, there's no distinction). One evening by the cross, as I was watching the devotional candles flicker and listening to the singing, I was quietly asked by my neighbor if I'd heard the rumor about Victory Square. The government, he said, had decided to erect a fountain at the old site of the cross, so as to prevent its reappearance. "A fountain," he repeated, his eyes glistening. "Don't you see? A spring . . . a miracle!"

In the midst of martial law, the regime seemed to be bending over backward to observe the form of whichever laws it hadn't simply decided to cancel. This, too, created some incongruities. One woman I spoke with had taken maternity leave on December 1, 1981—two weeks before the coup. Everyone else in her section had been fired in the wake of martial law, but she, who had been, if anything, the leader of the activists in the section, was continuing to receive monthly checks; since she was "on leave," the government couldn't touch her. Even more surprisingly, for ten months after the imposition of martial law the union's 40,000 full-time staff members continued to be paid their full salaries by a regime-administered trust fund, since the union, though suspended, was technically still in existence. Hence, by some monumental quirk in the law the regime was paying the salaries of 40,000 of its most active opponents, even those it had imprisoned—in effect, directly subsidizing the work of the underground.

One day, I happened to meet a Polish scholar who had received a visa for America and was getting set to leave the next day. He'd had to report to a special government office to have every single sheet of paper he planned to take out of the country catalogued, approved, and stamped. I commented that the practice seemed appallingly oppressive. He smiled, and said, "Oh, no. You just take it there and they approve it—they don't even look. Most of the lower clerks were themselves Solidarity members, and they hate the regime as much as we do. You have to remember, this is martial law Polish style." And he was right. At first, martial law Polish style can seem surprisingly breezy. You find yourself thinking, What's the fuss? But when you've stayed on a few days, first impressions give way to second looks, and you come to realize that beneath its breezy surface martial law Polish style can be very grim.

The reason for the virtual disappearance of the endless lines at the shops, for example, is simple and, as I learned, has nothing to do with an upturn in the economy. Quite the contrary. As one friend of mine in Warsaw put it, "I don't stand in line anymore, because I can no longer afford to buy what's at the head of the line. Neither can anyone else, so there are no more lines." Through martial law, Jaruzelski has at least been able to accomplish one thing that several regimes before him had failed to do: to increase food prices without a proportional increase in wages. Thus, for example, in one year the official price of a quarter kilogram of butter has gone from 27 to 60 zlotys; a single egg has gone from 5 to 18 zlotys (that's if you can find it at regular stores; on the black market, prices range from 20 to 25 zlotys per egg); coffee is up 130% to 1400 zlotys a kilo; apples, sometimes as much as 200%. On July 26, the government's Main Statistical Office issued a report that celebrated the fact that during the first six months of 1982, wages in the socialized sector of the economy were up 40%; the report also noted, however, that the cost of living for families in the same sector had risen 104% (for pensioners it was up 115%). Thus, real employee family income had dropped 25% in one year!

The average salary for an industrialized worker in Poland today is 10,800 zlotys per month; teachers, clerks, nurses, and small firm employees usually earn less (a nurse makes between 7,000 and 8,000 zlotys); a pensioner receives under 5,000 (which incidentally is up from under 3,000—one of the major lasting achievements of the Solidarity era). One kilogram of good quality meat today costs between 550 and 700 zlotys; a kilo of poor quality meat (mainly bone, fat, and gristle) costs between 110 and 180 zlotys. (Since October, 1.5 of the 2.5 kilos allowed on each individual's ration card must be redeemed in "poor quality" meat.) Pork costs 600 zlotys a kilo; sausage about 350.

When I was in Warsaw in September 1981, a popular joke concerned a man who finally reaches the head of the line at a meat market and asks the two butchers behind the counter if they have any beef. No, of course not, he's told, all out. How about some veal? Nope. Do you have any pork? No. Sausage? No. Lamb? No. Chicken? No. Finally the man leaves, dejected and empty-handed. "That man must be crazy," the first butcher says to his colleague. "Yes," replies the second, "but *what a memory!*"

This fall, you'd see such supplies occasionally, but they were unafford-able, and the jokers were instead asking if you knew how to make a Polish sandwich: "It's simple," they explain. "Take a ham ration card and place it between two bread ration cards." Church officials, who have been moni-toring the food situation even more closely than the government, report that 30% of the Poles can no longer afford to buy all the food allotted them on their meagre ration cards. This is probably just as well since during every month in 1981, according to a recent Radio Warsaw report, 1,500,000 more ration cards were issued for meat, 2,000,000 more for sugar, and 1,750,000 more for butter than should have been, given the available monthly supply.

There is another reason you don't see as many lines as you used to. In many cases, there is simply *nothing* in the stores. This is particularly true of clothing, where shortages have become severe—and calamitously true in the case of children's shoes. In a country where almost ten percent of the population is under the age of four—that is, a country where almost ten percent of the population has definitely grown a shoe size or two in the past year—it is virtually impossible to procure new shoes for children, and, facing the winter, parents are tense and desperate. Even the black market seems to be giving out. In addition, it has now become impossible to get over-the-counter drugs and vitamins without a doctor's prescription. "You can't even get a simple aspirin," one friend of mine in Warsaw complained. "Everybody in this city is walking around with a headache."

There are countless ways of calibrating the devastation of the Polish economy. During the first seven months of 1982, according to the official Polish news agency, Poles consumed 13% less food and purchased 30% fewer manufactured goods than they did during the same period a year earlier, and 1981, of course, was no banner year. The government continues to cast the current shortfalls as a hangover from the chaos of 1981.

Although the strikes of 1981 can surely be blamed for only a small number of the country's economic problems (in many cases, workers struck at assembly lines that were already idle), the apportionment of blame is at this point fairly moot. When the generals seized power in December, they claimed they were acting to save the nation—to save the nation's economy, that is—and the relevant question is whether in any sense they can be said to have accomplished this.[20] Although they did succeed in raising prices, that has tended only to exacerbate the suffering of most Poles, and the economy in general seems none the better. Jacek Kuron, one of the leading theorists of the Solidarity movement, wrote from his prison cell late last winter, "The state of the economy stands in no need of description. If one is to believe the authors of the military coup when they claim that they acted in order to save the economy, one may say that the operation was successful but the patient died."

Jaruzelski, for all his brilliance as a military tactician, has utterly failed to solve the central dilemma of modern Polish history—that of legitimacy. Gierek tried to buy it, and failed. Jaruzelski has been trying to command it, and is failing as well "You can bully people into obedience," Daniel Singer recently noted. "But you cannot achieve with bayonets what Solidarity would have found it difficult to accomplish when the workers had the feeling of gaining mastery over their own fate."

A bit of graffiti I came upon frequently in Warsaw consisted of the image of a snail; protruding from the shell, in place of its head, was a hand with fingers extended in a V sign. "Victory through passivity," a friend of mine explained. "It's a variation on a symbol of resistance during Nazi times: then it was a turtle, but the strategy is the same." A few weeks after the imposition of martial law, the Warsaw underground organization issued a tract called "Basic Principles of Resistance." Principle No. 6 read, "Work slowly; complain about the mess and incompetence of your superiors. Shove all decisions, even the most minor ones, into the laps of commissars and informers. Flood them with questions and doubts. Don't do their thinking for them. Pretend you are a moron."

To be sure, the intensity with which Poles threw themselves into creative nonactivity during the first months of martial law has given way to something more tired and mundane. Workers show up, and then work with sullen deliberation. But if the passivity of Polish workers is no longer paralyzing the economy it is still preventing the recovery. Jaruzelski can make the workers show up at the factories, he can even make them work, but he cannot make them work enthusiastically, and at this stage nothing short of enthusiasm will suffice to save the economy.

Of course, on top of the attitude of the workers Jaruzelski is confronted with the rampant dilapidation of Poland's physical plant. According to the French journal *L'Alternative*, 40% of Warsaw's buses are now out of circulation for lack of batteries. Of 620,000 tractors in Poland, all of which are desperately needed for agricultural production, 100,000 have broken down and will not be repaired until Poland generates enough hard currency to buy the necessary spare parts. One evening, I had a chance to speak with one of the thousand workers who service Warsaw's central-heating system. "The quality of the pipe we are now laying is so bad that it lasts only four years," he said. "We tear up the road, lay the pipe, and repave the road knowing that in four years we are going to have to come back and tear up the road again. The main pipes are all right—they're from before—but the feeder pipes are new and rotten. They come from the Huta Warszawa steelworks, and the poor guys over there simply don't have the specialized steel and the necessary equipment. They sent a shipment to the Soviet Union for the Siberian pipe-line and it was rejected. We have to lay about 20 kilometers a year if we're to keep on schedule and get back where we started within four years."

I asked him how much they'd laid in the ten months since December. He broke into a toothy smile, shrugged, and said, "Two kilometers."

Does that mean that Warsaw will be without heat in three years?

"Ah, no," he replied. "Not necessarily. It works like this: Today, we have a thousand people laying pipe; in two and a half years, some bu-reaucrat will discover the emergency and launch an offensive and we'll have five thousand people laying pipe. *But it will be the same pipe.*"

The low morale of the workers and the dilapidated condition of the physical plant are often aggravated these days by the stupidity of the authorities. "I'll give you an example," a Warsaw writer who spends time in the country told me. "This happened in the village where I go. The authorities spent months trying to coerce the local farmers into selling their grain to the government cooperative. They invoked patriotism and humanitarian concern, and so forth, and about half of the farmers gave in and sold their crop. Then, finally, just this week, in an effort to get the rest, the authorities raised the price they were willing to pay—and the other half, the recalcitrant half, happily brought their grain to mar-ket. So the first guys have learned a lesson for next year: they got stung; they should have held out, too."

Besides all these difficulties, Jaruzelski has been having to deal with Western trade sanctions and banking pressures. The impact of the sanc-tions has been relatively mild; it's not as though the Poles would have had any hard currency with which to buy anything if the sanctions had not been imposed. (Such impact as has been felt has been confined largely to agriculture: farmers have been slaughtering their herds for lack of American feed.) Western bankers, for their part, have generally been turning over the loans; that is, lending Jaruzelski money to pay the interest on his debt, so that they can avoid declaring Poland in default—a prospect that no one relishes. But even when Jaruzelski is able to pro-cure a little hard currency beyond this debt servicing, he has to pour it into consumer items—food, clothes, etc.—and has virtually nothing left to invest in spare parts or raw materials or capital improvements. So it's not surprising that, according to Daniel Singer, domestic output, which had been down seven percent in 1979–80 and thirteen percent in 1981, fell another eight percent in 1982.

Faced with such statistics, it's easy to start wondering how the Poles are getting by at all. From what I could gather, many of them aren't. People aren't starving yet, but the government's own figures list 30% of all Polish workers as now living below the poverty line, along with 50% of Poland's pensioners. Virtually everyone is spending more than he is earning. For some, this means the last year or so has seen the gradual liquidation of their life savings. (A common joke has it that the average Pole earns 5,000 zlotys a month, spends 7,000, and saves the rest.) How will these people make it through 1983? Many people are getting by thanks to private foreign aid: either parcels distributed through the churches or—more often, perhaps—small gifts of hard currency from friends and relatives in America or Western Europe. In Poland, people of every class and region seem to have relatives abroad, and the monthly gift of, say, five or ten dollars can make all the difference—especially given the telescoping effect of black-market currency exchanges. For all the talk about the relative effectiveness of boycotts at the governmental level, I have no doubt that what is keeping the Polish economy from complete collapse these days is the unceasing influx of hard currency in small denominations like this; without that steady assistance the country might well have exploded months ago.

Many people get by precisely by playing the black market in currency or entering the entrepreneurial subterranean economy. The official exchange rate for dollars has doubled from an arbitrary 32 zlotys in 1981 to an equally arbitrary 86 in 1983. Nevertheless, the street rate (the actual rate) remains between 350 and 400, and profits are to be made in the interstices.[21] The need of average people for hard currency in Poland today is perhaps more extreme than ever. One of the few burgeoning areas of the economy is the PEWEX shops. "They're opening up all over," a friend of mine tells me. "And everyday, it seems there are more and more things which can only be bought at the PEWEX shops. A very distressing development is the recent creation of PEWEX shops for meat. Soon, the only way we'll be able to get good meat is for dollars."

The government therefore turns a blind eye to the black market in currency (it needs the hard currency in the country, and people need it in their pockets), just as it tends to turn a blind eye to many other aspects of the subterranean economy. One architect in Warsaw told me, "This country runs *because* of corruption, not in spite of it. Any time something works, I assume that money is passing under the table somewhere—and I assume as often as not that I may be the one having to pass it." Thus, to be allowed to fill your car's gas tank, it usually takes 500 zlotys to the station manager before he even turns on the pump meter. To get a new suit can take 1500 zlotys for the shop assistant over and above the cost of the suit. One shop assistant told me that he took tips "so I can afford to pay other tips down the line—and also so I can afford to feed my family."

Shortly after the imposition of martial law, Jaruzelski made a great show of evenhandedness, claiming that he was going to pursue official corruption with the same zeal with which he attacked antisocialist tendencies. However, as time passed, the anti-corruption campaign lapsed. "It turns out he's the creature of apparatchiks," a friend told me. "Or maybe they just all have to hang together. To the extent that high-level corruption is uncovered in the bureaucracy, it usually results in lateral transfers rather than demotions or dismissals." (One exception proved to be the circus trial of Gierek's media czar Szczepanski, which was still continuing through increasingly bizarre, prurient, and entertaining permutations as late as this fall. One began to pity the poor lizard.)

In the midst of the economic debacle, there is a thriving expansion of the entrepreneurial spirit. The regime encourages this spirit partly by not cracking down on illegal enterprises and partly by completely absenting itself from various sectors of the market. Three ex-journalists, for example, are making a small fortune repairing and refilling pocket cigarette lighters—people come to them because they have nowhere else to go. (Government shops are incapable of performing the task, and have no new lighters to sell.) I met a onetime engineer who now runs a small toy-manufacturing shop. He employs several former factory workers. Although he pays the workers twice what they would be earning on the factory line and must regularly bribe various government clerks and contrive complicated transactions to obtain the necessary parts, he still manages to make a tremendous profit. "But," he cautions, "keep in mind that the profit is in zlotys, so to some extent it's worthless, because there's nothing to buy."

Everywhere you looked in Warsaw last autumn, it seemed, people were huddled in corners engaging in some sort of anxious transaction: bills for bills, bills for objects, objects for objects—an awkward ballet of bulging trenchcoats, dangling cigarettes, and furtive glances. Michael Dobbs, of the Washington *Post*, has noted that "the economic chaos creates a climate for social ills such as alcoholism, prostitution, and drug addiction that Marxist ideologists often portray as the hallmark of life under capitalism." One Pole in Warsaw told me in disgust, "This isn't communism. It isn't even capitalism. It's pre-capitalism—everyone for himself." Another person said, "The Communist Party in this country seems willing to sacrifice everything, including any pretense of communism, simply to retain its hold on power."

Nothing in Warsaw last autumn could disguise the despair of people thinking about the country's and their own economic future: the one chance, as they saw it, to salvage both had now been scotched. In addition to everything else, that's what December 13th had been about: not only would they no longer be permitted to save their economy but its management was reverting to the very bureaucrats who had masterminded the fiasco in the first place. "Year by year now," one Warsavite told me sadly, "we will fall further behind." At the university one afternoon, a young woman student commented, "What can I expect for my future? There is no new housing, and now there won't be. I will have to live with my parents till I am 45, unless I marry, in which case I will live in the living room of my husband's parents."

"There is just no hope anymore," another young woman, a former Solidarity activist, told me. "No world of illusions within the realm of possibility, no viable fantasies of improving one's lot."

In Poland, you can usually anticipate the tides of unrest simply by consulting the calendar. In this intensely Catholic country, dates are everything. At the beginning of 1982, for instance, you didn't need to be clairvoyant to know that early May—with both May Day and, two days later, the anniversary of the promulgation of the 1791 Polish constitution—was going to be tense. Or that a crowd would no doubt gather in Poznan—if nowhere else—on June 28th, the anniversary of the 1956 massacre in that city. Or that midsummer would be troublesome, with its cavalcade of anniversaries: August 1st, the launching of the heroic, ill-fated Warsaw Uprising, in 1944; August 14th, the start of the Gdansk strike in 1980; August 15th, General Jozef Pilsudski's rout of the Red Army in 1920; August 26th, the arrival of the Black Madonna at Czestochowa, exactly 600 years before, in 1382; August 31st, the triumph of the Gdansk strike; and September 1st, the start of the Nazi blitzkrieg into Poland with the storming of Danzig (Gdansk)—the attack that precipitated the Second World War, in 1939.

No matter how hard the regime bore down on the underground, the people would be restive. Poles don't have to be mobilized around some arbitrary date: they know which days to take to the streets, and they'll always be there—in spirit, if not in body. So you also knew that something was going to happen on November 10th (the second anniversary of Solidarity's registration as a legal union) and in December, with its wrenching series of anniversaries: December 14th through 18th, the 1970 massacres in Gdansk, Gdynia, and Szczecin; and, of course, December 13th, the first anniversary of the imposition of martial law. To anyone looking ahead, one of the few calm periods seemed likely to be mid-October: no particularly memorable dates for a few weeks in either direction. Apparently, Jaruzelski and his colleagues, looking at the same calendar, decided that that would be a nice, innocuous period during which to ban Solidarity. (The union had technically only been "under suspension" the previous ten months.) Polish history is a bit like the game Battleship: successive regimes seek out empty spaces on the calendar to spring their repressions, thereby creating new horrors for subsequent memorialization. Thus, slowly the calendar blots up, new dates emerging where there were few before. Therefore, under Jaruzelski's direction the Sejm, Poland's parliament, banned Solidarity on Friday, October 8th. The following Monday, the Lenin Shipyard in Gdansk was back on strike—an astonishing spectacle, and one that for a few moments seemed likely to spread. Workers sat straddling the wall staring out at the tanks.

On the great white letters "L-E-N-I-N" above the entry gate they'd super-imposed, in red paint, "s-o-l-i-d-a-r-n-o-s-c." After the second day, how-ever, with the militarization of the yard, the strike faltered and collapsed.

Sitting in my hotel one afternoon in October, about a week after the collapse of the Gdansk strike, I was rereading some of the documents I'd brought along—texts from the high good time of Solidarity—when I was struck by a phrase in an essay by Halina Bortnowska. Bortnowska was one of the most deeply respected activists during those 16 months— a Catholic intellectual who enjoyed unusually good relations with the steelworkers in her home town, Nowa Huta, outside Krakow. In Janu-ary 1981, in *Tygodnik Powszechny* ("Universal Weekly"), the distin-guished Krakow Catholic journal, she characterized Solidarity as "a concrete, historical social movement which is now one of the most im-portant expressions of what I call the 'subjectivity' of Polish society, its capacity for acting as a subject rather than the object of history."[22]

Polish society had briefly recaptured its subjectivity through the recov-ery and projection of its solidarity—the sense that ten million people, united, moving together, could transform themselves from history's ob-jects into its subjects. Bortnowska's phrase seemed particularly striking to me because it helped clarify the struggle currently taking place in Poland between society and the regime: Jaruzelski and his colleagues are intent on transforming Poles from subjects back into objects. The key element in this process is the obliteration of their sense of solidarity— both their capacity for unity and their capacity for action. This helped account, in part, for the surprising openness I'd witnessed during my first few days in Warsaw. In all sorts of ways *that don't finally matter*, Jaruzelski was willing to let the Poles vent steam. The regime could handle individual street demonstrations, semi-subversive plays, splashes of graffiti, even job actions at individual, isolated factories; the one thing to be avoided at any cost was having all the workers go out on strike at all the factories at the same time. As long as that didn't happen, the sense of complete subjectivity would not be revived.

In the meantime, there were all kinds of ways in which the regime could slowly begin to reimpose a sense of objecthood—through the econ-omy itself, for one. Of course, the regime's planners might have preferred an early fiscal upturn and a renewed prosperity, but as long as that wasn't happening the dire economic shortfalls could be put to repressive uses. People who were spending most of their time scrambling for food and clothing for their families had less time to devote to subversive aspira-tions or subjective nostalgias. Furthermore, with the economy in such bad shape, the threat of dismissal or arrest became all the more effec-tive: workers might think twice, three times, five times before deciding to participate—or, more often, not to participate—in a strike or a demonstration. Those who did participate knew they were risking the very livelihood of their families. This, by the way, is not a strategy that is unique to the ruling parties in Poland: we in the West frequently hear statements to the effect that one "side benefit" of the current recession and the high rates of unemployment is that they help to "discipline" the work force—to undermine unions, to make them temper contract demands or accept contract concessions, and so forth. In Poland, however, the mechanisms are much more severe. "What you have here is a bureaucratized terror regime," Roman Laba, an American Fulbright scholar in Warsaw, insisted to me one day. "It doesn't have to project force on the street all the time: the terror is built into the system by virtue of the fact that the state is the sole legitimate employer. It simply means an awful lot more for a worker to be dismissed or for him to contract an arrest record here than it would in the West." Fired workers often find that the regime has issued a "wolf ticket" on them—a form edict that effectively blackballs them from employment at any other state-run enterprise. At best, such a worker will know that he will only be entitled by law to the lowest possible pay at his next job, with no promotions for at least a year. (Any director who tries to pay him more is subject to a fine of between 20,000 and 50,000 zlotys.)

During the early phases of martial law, a particularly demeaning tactic employed by the authorities was to require loyalty oaths and reaccreditation hearings. Workers who weeks earlier had been embracing the cause of Solidarity were now required one by one to sign an oath in effect renouncing that prior allegiance. A loyalty oath is a piece of paper in which one surrenders one's subjectivity; a reaccreditation hearing is a place where one can grovel, desperately pleading with the authorities to be allowed to be reduced once again to the status of an object. Either that—forswear, grovel—or risk losing one's job in a harrowing economy.

Marek Nowakowski, one of Poland's finest short-story writers, has written a series of brilliantly observed vignettes about martial law, called *War Stories*, which he has been courageously publishing under his own name. He was the first cultural figure to renounce the use of a pseudonym; within weeks of the coup, these remarkable miniatures began appearing—at first in typescript (each person who got a copy would take it home and make a new set of carbons, passing them along in a sort of chain-witness) and then in underground journals. In one story, "Rat," a factory director who was previously fairly sympathetic to Solidarity calls in an underling, a former union activist, and, following a long, edgy prologue—the meeting is clearly demeaning to *both* parties—nervously asks the activist to sign a loyalty oath. (The underling's is the narrative voice):

I raised my head and stared. "Where is this paper, then?" His entire face lit up. He beamed. Breathed relief. He quickly slid his hand into a drawer. How deft those fat fingers had become! He plucked out a small piece of paper from a pile of others. Delicately, with two fingers, he placed it on the desk. He began to slide it toward me. All the while smiling ingratiatingly. His eyes disappeared within folds of wrinkles. Shining eyes. He was still saying something in a friendly voice, but I no longer heard what it was. He had begun to change in my eyes. A backwards metamorphosis. It was repulsive. But it was happening. He was shedding his human skin, assuming animal form. Those hairy paws. Pudgy, yet agile. The pointy nose . . . all he lacked was a slippery tail. I recoiled. My eyes swam. I jumped up. I could no longer see anything human in him at all. I have high blood pressure, nerves, sometimes things go to my head. I banged my fist on the desk. "This paper—you couldn't even wipe your ass with it! It's too filthy!" I rose and stood over him. He retreated into his chair, shielded his face. "I won't hit you," I said. "It's not worth my hands." I put on my cap and went to the door. [trans. Agnieszka Kolakowska]

The activist soon finds himself transferred from his former position to a pig farm that the enterprise runs as a side operation; he feeds the pigs and hunts for rats, trapping them occasionally, spiking them, and summoning up images of his boss.

In another Nowakowski story, called "Reaccreditation," a panel of five examiners convenes at a publishing house (representatives from the culture ministry, the Army, the Party, the publishing house, and, "at the end of the table, one person of unknown allegiance") and calls in, one after another, three employees for individual review. Each, however, arrives more drunk than the one before—it's clear they've all been up the whole night dousing their anxiety. Finally, the Army representative, a colonel, reddens like an apoplectic, pounds his fist on the table, and exclaims "This is a farce!" and the hearing is adjourned to another day.

I heard countless stories about reaccreditation hearings, and met many people who had been fairly shattered by their moment of decision.[23] Shortly after martial law was declared, the regime offered to release many of those it had interned and arrested if they would merely sign declarations of loyalty, agreeing to refrain from engaging in activities "harmful to the state and the government of the Polish People's Republic."

Soon after, an internee at the Bialoleka prison, near Warsaw, who signed his name "Andrzej Zagozda" managed to smuggle out a tract entitled "Why You Are Not Signing." "Zagozda" was widely believed to be Adam Michnik, the passionate, highly regarded Solidarity theorist. He wrote:

A young woman, the wife of a Solidarity activist, was arrested and taken away from her sick baby—which, she had been told before-hand, they had decided to place in a children's home. She signed the declaration. My friend was torn away from his mother, on her own and dying of cancer, and told that "there will not even be a lame dog to make your mother tea." He signed the declaration. . . . It is difficult to condemn either choice here. Ostracism would achieve the government's aims: for it is precisely their aim to break social resistance and human solidarity by creating divisions and conflicts. However, if one takes a position of tolerance and understanding, one cannot thereby assume that the very act of signing the declaration of loyalty is in itself "morally indifferent." It is not. Every declaration of loyalty is an evil, and a declaration coerced from you is an evil into which you have been coerced. The only difference is that sometimes it is a lesser evil. The act of signing deserves understanding, always sympathy, but never praise.

For all the unpleasantness of the loyalty oaths and the reaccreditation hearings, I met few people in Poland who begrudged their fellows whatever choice they'd come to. The fifth of Warsaw Solidarity's "Basic Principles of Resistance" advises, "Do not denounce ordinary people. Your enemies are: the policeman, the eager conformist, the informer." And most people agreed. (They judged others leniently; themselves, sometimes, less so.)

In Krakow, the Solidarity underground contrived a strategy that had all the marks of Halina Bortnowska's thinking. In workplaces where resistance was not strong enough to organize mass refusals of loyalty oaths, the underground leadership urged signing en masse: "It is not important what papers we sign under duress but how we act. Loyalty oaths are a form of psychological pressure. We will not allow ourselves to be cut off from each other so that an individual must choose between fellow-workers and his conscience." At one point, Jozef Glemp, Primate of the Polish Catholic Church, issued a statement in which he observed that oaths elicited under coercion had no force: one could swear to anything under such circumstances and not be bothered by one's conscience, for the oath was not binding. In heavily Catholic Poland, such a statement from such a source provided many suffering people with considerable solace.

One day in Warsaw, a young man pulled aside his jacket lapel and showed me a metal pin affixed to his shirt: it was a superbly modelled hand, with two fingers thrust upward in the familiar V sign. Only, the insides of the two fingers were notched, like a zipper. "Two fingers together and you have the symbol of oath-taking, the sign of capitulation," he explained. "But all you need to do is unzip them and you have the sign of defiance." So many people signed and many didn't, and finally it didn't really matter: thousands of people were fired anyway as the authorities attempted to promote their quiet terror.

During the early stages of martial law, however, the authorities were confronted with an astonishing display of social solidarity—of recalcitrant subjectivity, Halina Bortnowska might say—when they attempted to use the weapon of mass dismissals. In late May, for example, when thousands of workers had been fired in the wake of demonstrations on the thirteenth of the month, the Warsaw underground leadership issued the following appeal:

> Now the time has come to *share* what little we have, not just to give away what we can spare. This is another test of our solidarity. . . . Nobody must be left without help! Nobody must be left alone! Nobody must remain in fear of tomorrow!

Such appeals quickly led to the formation of social-help committees in factories, institutions, and parishes, and these organizations proved remarkably effective. Furthermore, many fired workers found work in the burgeoning private sector—the small shops that were cropping up all over to attend to tasks and services the government could no longer provide. By summer, however, many of the entrepreneurs who had taken to employing fired workers were being visited by bureaucrats and pressed to dismiss them or else face charges for running illegal enterprises. Even so, the capillary network of social support seemed to be holding up. In early fall, therefore, the regime launched one of its most frightening offensives—the campaign against "social parasites."

To hear Polish television's newscasters tell it, the economy was being dragged down by hosts of drunkards, laggards, and black marketeers. There were nightly reports featuring individual case studies of the loathsome behavior of these vermin. In October, in response to the supposed resultant groundswell of public indignation, the regime proposed, and the parliament quickly passed, a social-parasite law. In essence, everyone was required to find new employment within three months of becoming unemployed. The state knew who the unemployed were, because it knew that *it* was no longer employing them. Anyone still unemployed after three months would have to account to a local administrative body for the means of his livelihood. If this body determined that the livelihood was inappropriate (for example, being supported by relatives or friends or foreign royalties) or was "dangerous and harmful to the rules of co-existence in the community" (pretty much anything the state chose to characterize as such), the applicant would be declared a social parasite and would be liable to up to two years' "limitation of freedom"—which could mean forced induction into a road gang in the hinterland. In addition, social parasites and their families could face eviction from their lodgings. In Poland, where it now takes up to 20 years to get an apartment, which is then zealously passed from grandparent to parent to child, such a threat is truly terrifying. Although the law was supposedly designed to attack, for example, black marketeers, everyone knew that those characters would easily be able to bribe their way out of prosecution, and that the law's true target was fired activists. (The law seemed perfectly timed to jam Solidarity's 40,000 union organizers who'd suddenly became officially "unemployed" as a result of the delegalization of the union, on October 8th.)

Another example of how the desperate situation of the economy is being used by the regime as a lever of repression—this time in a more active way—came with the government's announcement, after the delegalization of Solidarity, that the organization would be replaced by new unions. Most people's initial reaction to the establishment of these unions was one of utter revulsion. They had no intention of taking part in this obvious charade. The regime, however, soon began to float intimations that certain supplies would be available *only through* the new unions—things like children's shoes. And, one by one, Polish families found their subjective resistance giving way to objective abjection. This process was aggravated when a strict boycott of the new unions became official underground policy, for now each family had to face its difficult decision in solitude rather than in solidarity.

The subjective revival represented by Solidarity had allowed—indeed, required—an unprecedented openness in Polish public discourse. The regime's campaign of repression, for its part, has relied heavily on a renewed countervailing offensive by the state's propaganda apparatus. The Polish regime's propaganda, however, is of a somewhat different sort from that which one usually associates with totalitarian regimes. There is, for example, relatively little celebration of supposed economic triumphs. "If anything," one friend of mine in Warsaw observed, "Jaruzelski's is a propaganda of despair: 'You think things are bad now—just wait, they're going to get worse. You're lucky we don't just line you all up along a wall and shoot the whole lot of you.'" Although my friend was exaggerating, it is often astonishing to witness the blatant cynicism projected by government representatives, especially Jerzy Urban, the principal government spokesman. One day, for example, he was asked by a reporter whether he thought the Western sanctions would have an impact on the Polish economy. As Polish television cameras whirred in the background, transmitting his words throughout the country, Urban looked the reporter in the eye and replied coolly, "The authorities will always eat their fill." He almost seems to revel in taunting his fellow-citizens. The despair he provokes arises partly from what he says and partly from the way he says it—the way he seems to know that there is nothing anybody can do to touch him anymore. He is the country's nightly reminder of the apparatchiks' revenge.

In addition, there is incessant denigration and ridicule of the regime's opponents—Solidarity and its heirs in the underground. Solidarity was a good thing, the propagandists acknowledge condescendingly, *in the beginning*, but then it was coopted by intellectual radicals, and by the end it was leading the nation into civil war. Demonstrations are dismissed as the antisocial excesses of small bands of hooligans, and coverage usually focusses on damage to property: broken windows, punctured tires—"this at a time when the nation is desperately short of funds, and glass, and rubber." (In the words of a popular saying from the early days of martial law: "Three persons together are an illegal gathering. Nine persons together, an antisocialist demonstration. Ten million members of Solidarity, a handful of extremists.") According to government propaganda, these young hoodlums are usually provoked by outside agitation—foreign spies and Western radio transmissions.[24]

Jaruzelski's is not a propaganda that aims at convincing but, rather, one that seeks to confound and to demoralize. One afternoon, I was visiting a screenwriter friend who had his radio tuned to the Third Channel, Poland's youth-oriented station. During my 1981 visits to Warsaw, the radio had often featured disconcertingly apt Western rock songs: Gloria Gaynor's "I Will Survive," Bob Dylan's "When You Gonna Wake Up?," Simon and Garfunkel's "America" ("She said the man in the gabardine suit was a spy. I said, 'Be careful, his bow tie is really a camera' "). This trip, things were toned back to the seemingly irrelevant: the empty disco pulse of "That's the kind of love I have for you," or Billy Idol's "Hey little girl, what have you done?" At one point, the music gave way to a half hour of what was billed as free discussion. "Listen," my friend said. "We call this whipping up foam—lots of words but completely empty, nothing of substance." The earnest young panelists were saying things like "I think the situation should be improved. It needs improving. Life is not very easy in Poland, but I think we should take up responsibility for the country, we young people. What do you think, Comrade?" *"There!"* my friend interrupted. "They always do that, they're never able to pull it off completely. Ordinary people in Poland never call each other 'Comrade.' "

Does it work, though? Does the propaganda wear people down, confuse and demoralize them? "People have ceased to buy newspapers," according to an article in the underground journal *Tygodnik Wojenny*. Government newspapers fail to sell up to 80% of their printed copies—especially in Warsaw and in Krakow. "The circulation of *Trybuna Ludu* [the Communist Party daily] has already been reduced from 1.5 million to 750,000." (This picture contrasts sharply with the situation of *Tygodnik Solidarnosc*, which was merely suspended until October 8th, at which point it was formally banished. In a farewell communiqué issued shortly thereafter through the underground, the staff boasted that the paper had seen 37 issues, with a total of over 20 million copies in circulation, and that "we were a paper of which not one copy was ever returned.") As for the television news, most Poles during the 16 months of Solidarity assimilated one of the movement's main slogans, "Television lies," and few people are taken in outright. In the town of Swidnik last spring, people instituted the custom of an evening promenade, everybody in town out walking in the warm crepuscular light during the 7:30 evening news. The authorities soon forbade this practice, and people responded, throughout the town, by ritually cleaning their carpets, beating them at the windows, every evening at 7:30. There was nothing the authorities could do about that. Some people in Warsaw call the news "The Children's Hour" or "Fantasy on Parade."

And yet, of course, the propaganda does have an impact. In a different context, the English Marxist critic and novelist John Berger once wrote, "Propaganda preserves within people outdated structures of feeling and thinking whilst forcing new experiences upon them. It transforms them into puppets—whilst most of the strain brought about by the transformation remains politically harmless as inevitably incoherent frustration. The only purpose of such propaganda is to make people deny and then abandon the selves which otherwise their own experience would create."[25]

One afternoon, a former Solidarity activist, a highly intelligent young woman, told me, "To some extent, the propaganda is working. People develop a strange parallel mind-set. They hear the same thing over and over and over again, and after a while it does get through, and they find themselves thinking, 'Those Solidarity extremists really were bastards.' But the strange thing is that this in no way affects their hatred of the government, which remains constant—if anything, becomes more pronounced. My granny's a good example. She's sort of reverting to her second childhood, and she's in awe of the radio. I go to visit her and she'll say, 'What was Solidarity doing? It was leading us into civil war.' But in the next sentence she'll say, 'Just who does this Jaruzelski think he is, anyway?' People like me here in Warsaw are tied in to the sources of authentic information—especially the intelligentsia, with their foreign contacts and the widespread circulation of *several* underground bulletins. But in May I was in the mountains, cut off from my usual sources of information, and on May 13th I heard a radio report that there were bands of young people actually burning the Polish flag—and I didn't know what to think. *One doesn't know what to think.* A chasm opens up, and you wonder. I mean, you know the government people are bastards, but you wonder. Still, when the moment comes, when the strikes start, it won't have mattered: everyone will know what to think and everyone will join the strikes."

Perhaps. But there's another possibility. Although the regime may never be able to establish its own legitimacy, this incessant campaign of vilification, sustained over a period of years, may succeed in sapping the legitimacy of the opposition. If that happens, and there is a new uprising, and no one in the country is left with any authority, then where will Poland be?

The history of the Polish struggle, as we have seen, is often a struggle for Polish history; that is, it gets played out, generation after generation, in terms of models derived from the rebellions of earlier generations. Each attempt to oppress the Poles (by the czarist Russians, the Nazi Germans, or, more recently, the Soviet-sponsored Polish Communist Party) has had to concentrate on an attempt to suppress their sense of their own history. In turn, each upsurge of Polish resistance has been characterized by a sudden, dramatic upwelling of historical convictions and memories that turn out to have persisted, by way of rich subterranean traditions, throughout the long periods of occupation, partition, or repression. In August 1944, for example, the freedom fighters of the Warsaw Uprising went to their barricades amid crackly recordings of Chopin's "Revolutionary" Étude (composed in 1831 in commemoration of the previous year's Polish rebellion), and in 1968, the students at the University of Warsaw were catalyzed to rebellion when the government closed a theater production of Adam Mickiewicz's 1833 millennial paean to Polish national identity, *Dziady*. One afternoon, a young Polish woman, a former student from that 1968 generation, recalled for me a trip she'd taken to Bulgaria about five years ago. "We can't understand it," her Bulgarian hosts had chided her, "how you Poles can get so agitated about the cancellation of a play, going to the brink like that over a *mere* piece of theater." She'd blown up. "Of course, you wouldn't understand," she recalls shouting, "you who have replaced 600 years of Ottoman domination with another 30 by the Soviets and so have no literature of your own, no history, no way of imagining what a work of art could mean for a people!"

The convolutions of Polish history—its "repetition compulsion," as a friend of mine calls it—reached a new level of complexity and subtlety with Jaruzelski's seizure of power. It happens that the Polish constitution has no provisions for the declaration of a state of emergency. The only relevant clause outlines procedures for declaring "a state of war"—to be used whether the enemy is external or internal. Hence, on that December morning in 1981 General Jaruzelski literally found himself declaring war—"war on society," as Solidarity's pamphleteers quickly pointed out. And it wasn't only Solidarity's tabloids that harked back to the situation during Poland's last war, the Nazi occupation of 1939–44.

Indeed, the military regime had only itself to blame, in many ways, for the compounding confusion. That the organizers of the coup, with all their months of prior planning, could come up with nothing better than "WRON" as an acronym for the new executive body of commissars charged with administering martial law suggests an almost pathological need to confess. For all the cartoons and jokes about the crow at war with the Polish eagle have a history; in fact, the same jokes were being told between 1939 and 1944, when the subjugated Poles habitually referred to the Nazi eagle as *wrona*. As if to blur the distinction further, the regime itself, during the first months of martial law, flooded television with countless old Second World War movies. This attempt to pander to Polish patriotism (and, incidentally, to counteract the complete effectiveness of the actors' boycott) backfired. To begin with, these stories of Communist partisans at war against the occupying Nazi Army were utterly at variance with the "true" history that Poles had been reviving and celebrating during the previous 16 months—a history in which the patriotic Home Army had been seen to bear the brunt of the fighting against the Nazis, unassisted by the relatively inconsequential Soviet-supported People's Army. But even without this complex undercarriage of history, the regime's television celebration would have backfired, because what it kept showing was uniformed enemies—Nazis—being heroically challenged by plainclothes resistance fighters. The uniformed figures on the TV news were supposedly patriotic Poles, but during the endless succession of movies they were always Nazis. Little wonder that within days the crowds confronting the zomos in the street were pelting them with the epithet "Gestapo!" (One man I spoke with, a 60-year-old historian sympathetic to Solidarity, kept complaining about the inaccuracy of the chanting crowds. "*Not* Gestapo," he would moan. "The Gestapo were the *plainclothes* secret police. What they *mean* is SS!") Meanwhile, on walls throughout Warsaw that strange, powerfully evocative Home Army graffito was reappearing in lush profusion:

By January 1982, Poles were invariably discussing their situation in terms of such phrases as "before the war" and "since the war," meaning December 13th but summoning up images of the occupation. The regime was clearly becoming troubled by the rampant confusion—or, rather, equation—of the state of war with the situation during the Nazi occupation. One early gambit to deal with the problem was a series of parliamentary proposals, floated in May, to recast the Polish constitution so that there *would* be a "state of emergency" as well as a "state of war" and then to redub the current crisis an emergency. Nobody seemed much taken with, or even remotely fooled by, that tack, however, and the proposals languished for a while (they were in fact enacted the following year).

Still, as the months wore on, the propaganda machinery became increasingly sophisticated, and by the fall the regime was engaged in a full-fledged campaign of historical cooptation. The result was something like Vichy France—that is, a puppet regime, clearly under the thumb of a foreign power, trying to legitimize its claims to authority through appeals to an ersatz nationalism. Under Pétain's stewardship, the Vichy regime was continually waving the tricolor and exalting French national values and French historic victories. Under Jaruzelski, the post-December authorities in Warsaw went through all sorts of contortions in their attempts to wrap themselves in the symbols of Polish nationalism. There was talk in the parliament, for example, of returning the crown to the head of Poland's eagle. (It had graced the national symbol in the years before the 1795 partition and again during the brief interlude of independence between the wars but had disappeared in 1944, with the arrival of the Communists.) A special honor guard was formed by the military and garbed in the distinctive, long-suppressed uniform, with its diamond-shaped hat, of Poland's pre-1939 Army.

Odder yet was the growing insistence of the regime-sponsored Sikorski cult—a continuation of a curious campaign that had been launched even before the December coup. During the Second World War, General Wladyslaw Sikorski was the leader of the London-based government-in-exile, an idolized, unifying figure for all occupied Poland, and the ultimate commander of the Polish Home Army. As such, he became an enemy of Stalin, who had no use for the London-based regime in his conception of postwar Europe. After the Nazis declared war on the Soviet Union, in the summer of 1941, however, Churchill managed to patch together a wary modus vivendi between the two leaders, which lasted until April 1943, when Hitler's troops uncovered the mass graves of Polish officers and intelligentsia massacred by the Soviets at Katyn. Within days, relations between Stalin and the London-based regime were severed. (Stalin would presently begin sponsoring his own highly disciplined, though ludicrously undermanned, People's Army. Then, on July 4th, Sikorski was suddenly killed when his plane crashed, under mysterious circumstances, off Gibraltar. (Many Poles feel that the flight was sabotaged by Stalin's agents.)

Why would Jaruzelski have wanted to resurrect the memory of Sikorski in the first place? Partly, no doubt, as a preemptive alternative to the growing cult of Marshal Pilsudski, the heroic victor in the 1920 battle against the Soviet Red Army outside Warsaw. Sikorski, it could be argued, had at least been realistic enough to conclude a pact, even if only temporary, even if highly unstable, with the great fraternal neighbor to the east. One of the more ludicrous sideshows in Poland during the latter half of 1981, therefore, was a government-induced controversy about where Sikorski's ashes should be returned to from their current resting place in England. The contrived competition played off such contending sites as the capital, Sikorski's birthplace, and the Wawel Cathedral in Krakow, and ended only when Polish nationalists and conservative MP's in London managed to block the return of anything having to do with Sikorski to any place in Poland. This absurd dénouement nevertheless failed to still the Sikorski campaign, which rose to new heights following the imposition of martial law. Indeed, the largest single swath of funds available to the Polish national film industry is currently being poured into an extravaganza production (as extravaganzic, that is, as any production in Poland can be these days) entitled *Death in Gibraltar*, which is being directed by Bogdan Poreba, the highly despised *auteur* among whose previous credits can be found the chairmanship of the noxiously anti-Semitic, semi-official Grunwald Patriotic Union (active 1980–81).[26]

If the Sikorski cult seems doomed to farce, the regime's eerie celebration of the Warsaw Uprising, launched last summer, appears much more corrosive to public morale. Faced with a profusion of "PW" graffiti and the defiant, unifying emotions that such graffiti arouse, the regime simply decided to coopt the symbol and declare the entire rebellion its own. Suddenly, special official commemorative exhibits sprouted all over Warsaw, with large "PW" banners. Most of the generals who make up the Polish junta had in all likelihood spent August and September of 1944 on the other side of the Vistula, with the Soviet Red Army, while Warsaw was razed and much of its population killed, wounded, or driven from the city. Only after that inferno had most of these onetime junior officers deigned to liberate Warsaw. Yet today, as generals, they embrace the idealism of that rebellion, through some weird, Vichyesque logic, as their own.

The most galling exhibit of this kind was housed in a former factory near Warsaw's central train station: it included elaborate reconstructions of barricades, bombed-out rooms, and even the escape routes through the sewers in which the Home Army survivors had fought their last, hopeless battles. On my visit to the factory, I was accompanied by a Polish journalist friend, and we toured the exhibit sadly. The regime has been very clever in the ways it has manipulated this minicult of the Uprising. The fighters are portrayed as valiant, heroic idealists, misled by foreign (London-based) agitators and agents. The central point, hammered home again and again, is that they were wiped out, they were destroyed, they suffered excruciating deaths, *and nobody came to their rescue*. Rebellion (drones the continual subliminal message), resistance, is utterly futile. Outside again, my journalist friend was shaken and angry. "It's as though they took our flag and trampled it into the ground," she said. "Over and over and over again. The bastards."

The Poles, ever resourceful, had nevertheless already managed to hijack the legacy of the Uprising back from the regime. Less and less was one seeing the simple "PW" graffiti on Warsaw walls. It had undergone a not so subtle metamorphosis into a new, unmistakable sign:

Still, the "PW" and other Vichyesque campaigns were taking their toll. Here, as everywhere, the cynicism and duplicity of public life were once again threatening to drain language of meaning. Halina Bortnowska, in her 1981 article, had identified Solidarity with "a general and passionate protest against the hypocrisy poisoning all communications in life," adding, "Falsity acts like carbon monoxide in the blood: saturation leads to a cessation of life functions." It wasn't so much that the "PW" campaign or any of the regime's other propaganda barrages (such as the "Celebration of Polish Motherhood," another juggernaut of the summer) were convincing anyone; rather, they were exhausting everyone. You spent so much energy fighting the regime's lies that you had little left to fight the regime. Perhaps that was the whole idea.

The "PW" campaign did have at least one humorous aspect, however. One evening, Polish television's nightly news featured a report on General Jaruzelski's visit to the exhibit at the abandoned factory. Stiffly, behind the perennial dark glasses, the General toured the various displays. At one point, the news montage found him emerging from a section of the exhibit that documents the battle of the sewers, the *Kanal*; Jaruzelski was suddenly just standing there beneath a huge, downpointing sign: "KANAL." I sat looking at the TV in my hotel, dumbfounded, imagining that millions of Poles at that very moment must have been having the same thought. Afterward, I tried to imagine how footage of Jaruzelski emerging, rat-like, from the sewers could possibly have made it onto the evening news. I envisioned the cameraman, a secret whimsical saboteur, "just happening" to frame that particular angle; his field director, a craven opportunist, only recently promoted to the job (as the replacement for a predecessor who'd refused to sign a loyalty oath), too dumb to notice; back at the studio, an editing assistant, noticing but just following the orders of his ideologue-literalist boss to splice in that scene, that particular take ("Eagerly carry out even the most idiotic orders," No. 8 of the underground's "Basic Principles" had read. "Do not solve problems on your own. Ridiculous rules are your allies"); a bit higher up, the show's assistant director (a middle-level commissar, perhaps), noticing but wary of being the first to notice, of being thought seditious for noticing, and hence letting it pass; his boss, the news director, too preoccupied with the tortuous convolutions of the ever so subtle innuendo in the program's text to bother with its imagery; the newscaster, his eyes pinned to the text he is reading for fear of getting a single word wrong (and these words are by no means easy; they are not the sort of words that might suggest themselves), the image on the screen behind him, unfurling—Jaruzelski, the sewer, the "KANAL" sign pointing squarely at him—into living rooms throughout Poland.

To repress: to press people, like good little objects, back into their boxes, and the boxes back into the wall.

The forces of repression in Poland haven't stopped at economic constrictions, loyalty oaths, reaccreditation hearings, and propaganda. In the cases of citizens who still refuse to knuckle under, the regime relies on such traditional means as military force, interrogation, arrest, and incarceration.

Over the months since martial law was imposed, several fatalities and considerably more injuries have occurred during battles between the regime's forces and its opponents. It is difficult to get accurate figures. We know, for instance, that nine miners were killed in Wujek in December 1981, and that at least three civilians died in Lubin on August 31st, and we know the particulars of several other confrontations as well. We do not know how many soldiers and zomos have died in the various clashes. The government does not release these figures, but rumor has it that they are high, and it doesn't take much imagination to realize that the fate of a lone zomo, caught behind the lines of a surging crowd or cornered in a blind alley, would not be an enviable one. ("Do you know what to do," goes another common joke, "if you come upon a critically wounded zomo in the street?" "No." "Good.")

Nor are the government's figures on civilian casualties reliable, and not just because of the regime's obvious interest in playing down such figures. In many cases, people try to avoid letting their injured friends or relatives fall into the hands of the authorities, for fear of the consequences: casualties are taken home or to church sanctuaries to be cared for—sometimes even buried—in private, without government knowledge or interference. Still, even given the hazy state of documentation, the relative absence of massacres has been one of Polish martial law's most striking features; there have, for example, been no individual episodes as violent as those in Poznan in 1956 or in Gdansk in 1970 (or, for that matter, in Watts in 1965 or Detroit in 1967), and the regime has tried to limit overt displays of state power.

When such displays do occur, the zomos have borne the brunt of the action. These 25 to 30,000 crack troops are the subject of considerable speculation among average citizens, who cannot imagine what enticements would transform an otherwise normal Pole into such a symbol of betrayal. It is known that a ZOMO private receives a salary many times higher than his Army counterpart, with bonuses for individual street actions; that the best available food supplies are lavished on ZOMO billets in towns; and that in the countryside ZOMOS live with their families in relative luxury and isolation. It is thought that many ZOMOS are of peasant stock and come from remote areas, and it is rumored that others are violent criminals who have been offered ZOMO service as an alternative to prison terms. It is also rumored, perhaps less reliably, that ZOMOS are regularly souped up with drugs in anticipation of street confrontations.

The ZOMOS are backed by an army made up largely of conscripts. Throughout the Solidarity period, the regime attempted to sequester those draftees who had been called up before August 1980, and hence had no firsthand knowledge of Solidarity, from those who came in afterward. These soldiers were fed a steady diet of propaganda and misinformation during the 16 months of Solidarity, and their contacts with family and friends were severely limited. Furthermore, the members of the classes of autumn 1979, and spring 1980 (Polish boys born in 1961–62), found their normal two-year service extended into a third year, so that the government was able to rely on a largely "uncontaminated" army well into 1983. It is interesting to realize that for decades to come a thin wedge of a generation will be moving through Polish history, like a small bulge through a boa constrictor: men who alone in their society did not experience the surge of Solidarity.

Even with its Army thus isolated, however, the regime consistently tried to avoid situations where it would have to rely solely on these troops, since it was never sure of their loyalties. These young men are only now being released from service, and are subject to immediate recall if the situation should demand it. Solidarity's pamphleteers are going to considerable lengths to dissuade people from turning their backs on them. One piece explains, "The soldiers who blocked with tanks the gates of factories on strike and who stopped and searched us on the streets are now coming home, back to society. We must not turn away from them. This is our great opportunity. . . . Should the conscripts of 1980 return to barracks, the *Wrona* must not find in them docile executors of orders." Meanwhile, the underground is having increasing success in smuggling pamphlets to the soldiers still in their barracks. One such piece included a poem by Ryszard Krynicki:

DON'T SHOOT

Soldiers, don't shoot at us!
Don't shoot at your brothers.
We are defenseless, and you
Will have to come back to us.

> *Those who drafted you*
> *And are ordering you now*
> *To shoot*
> *Will one day deny giving the orders.*

The arrests, internments, and interrogations were probably most frequent during the first months of martial law, when the regime suspended civil liberties and instilled fear and insecurity into the entire society. Throughout the 16 months of Solidarity, the regime's security apparatus —the thousands of police, plainclothes agents, and informers—had been held in check by the authorities and ridiculed by the population as a whole. "Let him listen," my friend at the Hotel Forum bar had insisted, back in May 1981, after pointing out a police spy. "Maybe he'll learn something. There's nothing they can do to us—we're ten million strong." Well, they did listen; they took their notes, compiled their files, nursed their bile. And after December 13th, with Solidarity stunned and reeling, they acted.

It's difficult to get precise figures on the internments and arrests. The regime admits to over 10,000 internments, of varying lengths; that is, cases in which individuals were preemptively detained without charges at one of the 78 internment centers that quickly sprang up all across Poland. In addition, there were thousands of arrests for violations of martial law—engaging in strikes, participating in street demonstrations, distributing leaflets, operating underground presses or radio stations, hiding materials, and so forth. Many of these cases were tried in summary military courts, and sentences were often quite severe. In New York City, the Committee in Support of Solidarity, which has for some time been monitoring the official and underground presses, occasionally releases lists of hundreds of names and sentences. Each name may represent the ruin of an entire family. The lists make unhappy reading:

Andrzej Adamczyk, Gdansk, worker at the Gdansk Repair and Installation Works. Sentence: 4½ years. Charge: Unknown.

Jan Andrzejewski, Lubliniec, worker at Production and Energy Installation Enterprise. Sentence: 3 years. Charge: Participating in a strike in December 1981; he suffers from asthma.

Andrzej Bachorz, Bytom, employee at Trade Cooperative. Sentence: 5 years. Charge: Participating in publication of the newspaper *Biuletyn.*

Kazimierz Jasernik, Bielsko-Biala province. Sentence: 3 years. Charge: Painting Solidarity slogans.

Krzysztof Legowski, Torun, student at Kopernik University. Sentence: 3 years. Charge: Distributing leaflets.

Edward Matia, Legnica province, baker. Sentence: 1½ years.

Charge: Participating in street demonstrations on August 31 or September 13, 1982.

Stanislaw Trybus, Libiaz, miner at the Janina coal mine. Sentence: 3 years. Charge: Trying to escape from Poland; desertion from his workplace after its militarization.

While I was in Warsaw, I spoke with many people who had spent time in prison or under internment. Most of them were members of the intelligentsia, and, as one of them said, "women, the ill, the elderly, and intellectuals—we all got off better than the others. We were generally better treated, because the regime wanted to be able occasionally to trot us out to auction before the Western press." A veteran of Bialoleka prison, which houses many of the most prominent internees, told me stories of long, rambling games of Monopoly, and of internees passing the time teaching each other foreign languages—especially English. A priest who was busy compiling arrest records for his district so he could supervise distribution of aid packages to the various prisons put the matter simply: "If you're an intellectual from Warsaw or Krakow, you'll have it relatively easy. If you're a worker from the provinces, it can get very hard." Even among the intelligentsia, there was an unusually high rate of tuberculosis and other diseases; the wife of Jacek Kuron, for example, died of pneumonia following several months of detention. I was unable to speak with Halina Bortnowska on this trip because, although she was out of prison, she was in the hospital, suffering from "brain inflammation"—most likely a form of meningitis, and a distressingly common illness.

Among the prisoners who were not intellectuals, however, there were frequent reports of beatings. The *Uncensored Poland News Bulletin*, a London-based biweekly digest of official and underground sources, has become one of the best surveys of information on these and other matters: the editors regularly provide thorough documentation of cases of prisoner maltreatment. In one issue, for example, they outlined the story of Jerzy Mnich, a worker in the Manifest Lipcowy coal mine, who was accused of having organized a strike there in the early days of martial law. During the strike, Mnich suffered a heart attack and was hospitalized. On January 13, 1982, he was in the hospital, on an I.V., when police barged in, pulled him off the I.V., and transferred him to Katowice police headquarters, where he was severely beaten during interrogation: "He was forced to kneel on a stool with his hands pinned by handcuffs high above his head to a grating. He was then beaten on the soles of his feet and heels. He was then treated with a dose of tear gas—straight into the eyes." Subsequent medical diagnoses revealed severe burning of his retina and increasing blindness. He was released from custody in March but remained in the hospital until August. Following his release from the hospital, he was dismissed from his job at the coal mine, on the pretext of "inability to fulfill the conditions of his employment." Owing to his partial blindness, Mnich must now live off a meagre "invalidity pension, third class." There have been countless such cases, scores of them reported in the *Bulletin*. True, Poland has perhaps been no more strict in its repression in this regard than other dictatorships, East and West (if anything, maybe even less so, in terms of the ratio of prisoners to population), but there is at the same time a particular horror in being delivered into the hands of a security apparatus whose very existence you had been helping to jeopardize just a few months earlier, and whose members you had for a time truly frightened.

The arrests and internments, an old-timer explained to me, have reverted to the Stalinist pattern; that is, they have become unnervingly random. Several people will be engaged in the same activity; two will be taken into custody by the police; one of the two will be released, the other given a heavy sentence, and no one can figure out why. The practice does succeed in sowing insecurity and suspicion throughout the society.

Of course, many more people are taken in for occasional interrogations than are given prolonged sentences. Again, the idea is to spread as much insecurity and provoke as many crises of conscience as possible. "You're hauled in," one woman told me. "You don't know what's going to happen. You are kept up all night. They change shifts, but you stay there and they keep asking you questions. Hundreds of questions. Then they throw you into an overcrowded cell for a few hours—mine had fourteen women in a room designed for two—and then they start all over. My mother, who went through the Stalinist prisons, used to advise me, 'Keep your answers short and remember everything you've said, so they can't trip you up.' It's good advice, only, you get so tired. They threaten you, they demand that you sign a piece of paper. They turn friendly— you know, that fake friendliness—and the next minute they are threatening to haul in your family. And then, for no apparent reason—you haven't signed the paper or anything—they release you. They warn you to be careful, they'll be watching and they may come pick you up again at any time."

In "Why You Are Not Signing," the article that was smuggled out of Bialoleka prison, "Andrzej Zagozda" argues that the moment of interrogation is the fulcrum of all relations in the state of repression. At that moment, everything comes down to the relationship between the interrogator and his prisoner. Of the interrogators "Zagozda" writes:

> It goes against common sense to make agreements of any kind with these people who interpret the very concept of an agreement very loosely indeed, and who violate common agreements—with people for whom the lie is their daily bread. You have surely never met anyone who had anything to do with the secret police and did

not feel cheated by them. For those people, whose gaze is dead, yet restless; whose mind is blunted, yet skilled in the art of harassment; whose soul is defiled, yet greedy for social acceptance—for those people, you are nothing but stuff to work over. They have their own particular anthropology: they believe that anyone can be convinced—that is, bribed or frightened. For them, there is only the problem of the price paid and the pain inflicted. Although they work mechanically, every slip you make, every fall, gives meaning to their life. Your capitulation is not only their professional success, but their raison d'être.

"Zagozda" continues:

You are therefore arguing with them about the meaning of your own life, about how there is no meaning to theirs, about endowing every human life with meaning. You are continuing the argument of Giordano Bruno with the Inquisitor, of the Decembrist with the Czarist police superintendent, of Lukasinski with the Czarist exterminating angel, of Ossietzky with the blond man in the Gestapo uniform, of Mandelstam with a Bolshevik Party member in a uniform with the blue N.K.V.D. lapel. You are taking part in an argument that will never end—the argument of which Elzenberg says that the value of your involvement is measured not by the victory of your idea but by the value of the idea itself. In other words, you win not when you gain power but when you remain true to yourself.

"Zagozda" appears to be invoking Kant's Categorical Imperative as a strategy for revolutionary practice: You should always act as if through your action you were legislating for all mankind. Although the regime, as I have already noted, borrowing from Bortnowska, is trying to transform Polish society from a subject back into an object, "Zagozda" seems to say that if the prisoner, alone in his confrontation with the interrogator, can retain his own subjectivity, he is in a certain sense retaining it for all society. "Zagozda" concludes:

It is over this that the battle is being waged: functionaries want to squeeze out of us a declaration that we have abandoned hope. . . . Those declarations are supposed to transform us into servile, base creatures. . . . But by refusing to engage in conversation with the functionary, by refusing to cooperate, by rejecting the status of a collaborator and informer, by choosing the human condition of a political prisoner, you are preserving hope. You throw this, your declaration of hope, like a sealed bottle into the sea—from your prison into the world, among people. If you tell at least one person, you have won.

You know how keen is the feeling of desolation. You think that you are helpless in the face of this policy—a military machine that was set in motion on a December night. But you know, as you stand alone . . . you know, thanks to your favorite poet, that "the avalanche changes its course according to the stone over which it flows." And you want to be that stone that will change the course of events.

But in Poland today it's almost easier to be in prison. "Zagozda" in his essay says as much: "Bialoleka is a moral luxury and an oasis of freedom. . . . Indeed, I think it is easier to bear than the morally and politically complicated situation on the other side of the barbed wire." Alone, you can imagine that you alone are everything. Outside, with the others, where subjectivity was all along conceived in terms of solidarity, it's much more difficult to keep it alive by yourself. And often prisoners released from detention are thrown back upon themselves. I heard many sad stories of people who had behaved heroically in prison but were being shunned by their friends in the underground once they were out— they were too obviously under surveillance, too dangerous to be relied upon for sensitive missions. For all the solidarity that I heard celebrated in Poland during my visit (the people taking care of each other, sharing their meagre livelihoods with those less fortunate), I also saw something very disturbing: Polish society is now riddled with suspicion and intrigue. One morning, a man told me he suspected that the man I was going to visit next was a collaborator—a suspicion soon repeated by this next man regarding the first. Perhaps they both were, perhaps neither. At the neighborhood level, low-life opportunists of all sorts were busy spreading rumors, accusing rivals of being underground activists or of being police agents—depending on whether they were trying to impress the police or the neighbors in their attempts at personal aggrandizement. The regime nurtures this atmosphere, plays groups off against each other, fosters the disintegration of the society's prior solidarity. Meanwhile, the general social consensus of August 1980—a vague but confident sense of knowing what needed to be done to save the economy and renew the nation—has itself fragmented. Most people haven't a clue what to do. They certainly don't know how to get rid of the regime, but, increasingly, they seem to be losing faith that they would know what to do if they ever could get rid of it.

A crucial development in the history leading up to the formation of Solidarity was KOR's gradual forging of links between intellectuals and workers between 1976 and 1980. If Polish society did recapture its subjectivity during the 16 months of Solidarity, it was surely in part because these two classes discovered each other's common aspirations, and both joined up with Poland's other principal group, the peasants. Conversely, since the onset of martial law the regime has been trying its best to sever those tentative connections.

If the regime has had some success at this, it is partly because toward the end of the Solidarity period these ties were already starting to unravel. By the second session of the Solidarity congress, in September 1981, many angry workers were frustrated by the constant calls for moderation coming from the intelligentsia, and were beginning to ignore them. Some intellectual advisers did not get enough votes to make it onto the union's national commission at the end of the congress—notably Walesa's key adviser, the medieval historian Bronislaw Geremek. Furthermore, although there had been a great deal of interaction among workers, peasants, and intellectuals at the level of committees and problem-solving groups, there was apparently little purely social interaction—the creation, that is, of new networks of friends. Perhaps there wasn't enough time, or perhaps the inherent rifts between the groups were simply too great.

One intellectual activist, who had seemed to be in the very center of things in 1981, told me a year later, "During Solidarity, we'd seen this quick mixing of the three groups, but this is largely gone now. On the morning of December 13th, I looked through my address book and realized that I didn't have *any* street addresses of workers. My office books, of course, had phones and addresses, but I could no longer get to them. I had a few phone numbers, but the phones were down. I'd met these people countless times at committee meetings and parties, and I knew them by their first names, but they hadn't really entered my social group. Today, I've reestablished contact with a few of the workers, but these are the activists, and it's hard to get a real reading on what's going on in the factories from people who have invested so heavily in their own plans and hopes. It's hard to believe that I could be saying this one year after the way things were in 1981, but now I really haven't the slightest idea how workers in the factories feel on any given day about any given issue." Another intellectual activist said, "The government is doing its best to cut off contacts between intellectuals and workers. When such contacts occur, it's usually the worker who suffers, not the intellectual, who may have his own contacts, and hence protection, in the West. You hesitate to put these people at risk, and solidarity therefore withers." The principal contact across these class barriers now consists of the underground newspapers—this is one reason they are considered crucially important. There has also been a resurrection of the Flying Universities (classes for workers held in a rotating series of apartments), which characterized the months leading up to August 1980.

In its attempt to further erode relations between workers and the intelligentsia, the regime has launched a process that may culminate in show trials of prominent KOR leaders. On September 3rd, following a wave of street demonstrations on August 31st, the second anniversary of the Gdansk agreements, the Chief Military Prosecutor accused KOR of being responsible for fomenting and masterminding this and other terrorist violence, and issued arrest warrants for Adam Michnik, Jan Litynski, Jacek Kuron, Henryk Wujec, Jan-Jozef Lipski, and Miroslaw Chojecki. KOR itself, which had never consisted of more than 40 full-fledged members, had by then been disbanded for almost a year. At the time of its disbandment, its members had noted that whereas they had formed the group, in 1976, to protect workers, it was now the workers, through Solidarity, who were protecting all of society; hence their organization had become superfluous. Of the six persons cited in the arrest warrants, one (Chojecki) had been stranded outside Poland at the time of the coup and had not returned; another (Lipski) had spent most of his time since the coup in Polish internment camps, although he was at the moment in London undergoing emergency treatment for a very serious heart condition. The four others had been confined at Bialoleka since December 13th. It was at first blush a little difficult to imagine how any of them could be held responsible for events that had taken place outside the prison walls since that date.

Adam Michnik noted in a letter he smuggled out of prison a few days later, "The audacious statement that the street demonstrations of August 31st were organized by interned members of KOR (which ceased to exist a year ago) is—and I say this in spite of my indubitable sympathy for KOR—a somewhat exaggerated tribute by the prosecutor's office to the capacities of the members of KOR." (In the case of Michnik, the charge of terrorism struck me as especially outrageous. I had vivid memories of the events at Otwock, a town near Warsaw, on May 8, 1981, at the height of Solidarity time. On that day, a crowd of townspeople, furious over police mistreatment of two local youths, had converged on the police station, surrounded it, and were on the brink of setting it afire. Several Solidarity leaders rushed to the scene, but Michnik was the only one who proved effective. Despite the fact that he ordinarily talks with a severe stutter, he managed to deliver a dramatic and eloquent speech—single-handedly calming the crowd, defusing the situation, and saving the police.)

In the course of the fall, it became evident what the regime was up to with these prosecutions. KOR was being relentlessly attacked in part because it had symbolized the unity of workers and intelligentsia. There was also the ongoing attempt to create the fiction of a Good Solidarity and a Bad Solidarity: an initial good core of workers and worker aspirations which had been subverted by a secret cabal of opportunistic intellectuals with their own demonic agenda; hence the need to dissolve the old organization and start from scratch with new unions. There was, in addition, a subliminal whiff of anti-Semitism. Two of the six indicted KOR members, Michnik and Litynski, were Jewish, and a third, Lipski, although he was of pure Polish stock, had recently composed a famous essay on Polish ethnocentrism, which provided, among other things, perhaps the most lucid, balanced, and thoughtful account of native anti-Semitism ever advanced by a Pole. (Even in the early months of 1982, the regime's propagandists had been slandering Lipski for the unseemly, un-Polish "secularism" of his views—a truly astonishing charge from a supposedly atheistic Communist Party apparatus.)

A few words about anti-Semitism in Poland today—a subject that has become even more convoluted than usual during the past year. It is clear that the regime, or elements in the regime, tried to use anti-Semitic devices during the first days of the coup. On the morning of December 13th, downtown Warsaw blossomed with a profusion of abhorrent posters. I was shown the tattered remnants of one such poster by a man who had torn it off a wall near Solidarity's Warsaw headquarters that morning. Once we'd reassembled the jigsaw puzzle of pieces, the image showed a photo-collage of a bearded rabbi swathed in ceremonial garb speaking into a phone, with the phone wire coursing down the side and along the bottom of the poster and back up the other side into a receiver being held by Bronislaw Geremek, the noted Solidarity adviser. The headline read, "THE DOMESTICATION OF THE POLES IS ONLY BEGINNING!" The text, in a telexlike typeface, read:

> "Hello, Baruch!"
> "This is Bronislaw."
> "No need for that. To them you're Bronislaw, to us you're Baruch. Listen, Begin congratulates you for what you're doing, but he has two new instructions: (1) Rein in Walesa on a shorter leash, and (2) Fire that bastard Jurczyk or he'll blow the whistle on all of us."

A month or so before, Marian Jurczyk, a Solidarity leader from Szczecin, had made an anti-Semitic slur, to the effect that many Communist Party leaders weren't even truly Polish, and he had been immediately reprimanded by Solidarity's National Committee. The Solidarity organization had had an excellent record throughout its history of educating Poles about the way previous oppressors had used the anti-Semitic canard as a device for diverting attention from real issues and fragmenting opposition. Partly because of the effectiveness of that educational campaign, partly because of the immediate firestorm of world opinion, partly because of the sheer implausibility of the slander in a country whose Jews had nearly all perished in the Holocaust or emigrated since, the regime's anti-Semitic insinuations were quickly muted. "It's interesting," Roman Laba observed to me in Warsaw. "This regime is utterly without any ideological focus beyond its own survival, and is hence exactly the sort of regime that often has recourse to anti-Semitic campaigns. But except for those early slurs and now this hazy stuff surrounding the KOR trials, it has pointedly avoided anti-Semitism."

The situation is a complicated one. Several leading dissidents are Jewish, but so are several of the regime's leading apologists—notably, the government spokesman Jerzy Urban. (Some people suspect that, as a Jew, Urban has specifically been put in a role where he will be drawing popular hatred, only to be summarily jettisoned later on. Urban himself, meanwhile, is not above anti-Semitic intimations. He recently lambasted the Catholic Krakow weekly *Tygodnik Powszechny*, perhaps the most widely read independent Polish journal published today, for being "idolatorily philo-Semitic.") One young Jewish professional whom I had met on my previous trips commented this time that the low-level, vestigial anti-Semitism that persists among many Poles is compounded of "complete ignorance and immense curiosity," but that he himself has never felt it as personal antipathy. He also spoke of the paradoxical fact that Poles who are vaguely anti-Semitic are nevertheless rabidly pro-Israeli. "It's almost as if they didn't connect the two—didn't realize that Israelis are Jewish. They just see Israelis as brilliant fighters against the Soviet Union's allies in that part of the world. I had people coming up to me and saying that they applauded the Beirut massacre because the dead were all Communists anyway."[27] (Similarly, I heard tales of how during the early phases of the Falkland crisis the Poles hadn't known whom to support—both Prime Minister Thatcher and President Galtieri seemed resolutely anti-Soviet—but once the Soviet Union came out in favor of Argentina they all started rooting for Britain, and even showered the British Embassy with flowers the day after the sinking of HMS *Sheffield*).

One joke I heard while I was in Warsaw had the feel of a story that had been kicking around Eastern Europe for generations: A long line of people is waiting outside a bakery when the commissar steps out and asks if there are any Jews in line. A few step forward and he says, "Not enough bread for you—go home." A few hours later the line hasn't moved and he steps out once again and asks if there are any people in line who aren't members of the Communist Party. About half of the line steps forward and he says that there won't be enough for them either and tells them to leave. A few more hours pass, the line still doesn't budge, and finally the commissar comes out and says there will be no bread at all today and tells everyone to go home. One of the remaining people says to his friend, "Did you see that? *Did you see that!* The Jews *always* get preferred treatment."

Oddly, the regime's barrage of anti-KOR propaganda, anti-Semitic or otherwise, seemed to be giving the group a sort of second virginity. The workers had grown to resent KOR for having been too moderate, and here was the regime painting it as too radical. If anything, the campaign was backfiring. Still, throughout the autumn the prosecution continued to gather evidence—35 volumes' worth, according to Urban—and prepare for what may become a harrowing spectacle. The maximum possible penalty, given the charges these men face, is death. (In the fifties, similar trials in Poland, Czechoslovakia, Hungary, and other countries of Eastern Europe did result in capital sentences.) It is easy to imagine the regime wanting these men dead—some of them have been causing problems for a quarter of a century. Therefore, world vigilance will be crucial. Michnik, in his September letter, urged people outside Poland "to do all within your power to insure that we have an open trial in the presence of observers and lawyers from democratic countries." Then, in a bitterly sarcastic aside, he singled out two of the regime's less active opponents in the West: "I should like to remind the Chancellors of Austria and West Germany, who find in their hearts so much understanding for our generals, that even the Communist Dimitrov [the man accused of setting the Reichstag fire in 1933] was tried by a Nazi court in the presence of international observers."

When and if the trial begins, there will be at least five defendants. On September 15th, less than two weeks after his indictment, and despite his perilous physical condition, Jan-Jozef Lipski voluntarily boarded a plane in London to return to Warsaw. (During the week immediately before the departure he had just completed his history of KOR, an extraordinary volume scheduled for English-language publication in 1984 by the University of California Press.) In a statement composed during his last night in London, he wrote, "KOR was both an institution and an idea, and part of the idea was that we shall pursue our aims without attempting to use force. It might be said that this is not particularly meritorious when you have no force to use anyway. But it is not quite like that. Even a small group of people can use terror, let alone such a widespread movement as that inspired by KOR. It is precisely because we have been against terror that we shall be accused of being terrorists: it is a convenient way to muddle up the image of KOR." A few paragraphs later, he recorded his belief that, despite government propaganda, "the majority of Poles will watch for news from the courtroom keeping their fingers crossed, for our sake and that of our families. God bless them, but let them not hope for better sentences, for these are already determined, or will be before the prosecutor reads the charges. You need to keep your fingers crossed that in crucial moments we should not lack courage, that nerves should not paralyze the intellect, and that we should be able to remember and associate facts correctly. The Crow will do a lot to insure that we are not heard. But we shall be heard."

Shortly before he left for Poland, when incredulous reporters asked Lipski why a man in his condition would even consider returning to face certain imprisonment and possible death, he replied, "I do not intend to become an émigré. I do not want to give the government propaganda machine the possibility of telling the workers that an intellectual will always get away, while the workers have to face the consequences of their actions alone. It is a question of solidarity."

Poland 1982: a church altar where a new corpse has been added to the long sad massacre which is the national historical memory. From behind the window, the Black Madonna looks on. (*Photographer unknown*)

October—December 1982

PART TWO

IN THE UNITED STATES, when someone wants to dismiss or defuse a problem he'll say, "That's history," meaning that it doesn't matter anymore. During visits I made to Poland in the 16 months of Solidarity's life span, as I reported earlier, I was often confronted by Poles relating long-past events and insisting that nothing could matter more. This is why I was especially taken aback one evening in Warsaw last fall when a heavily besotted young woman at a sombre drinking party took me aside and began recalling the events of the previous year. "Solidarity is history," she said morosely. "It's over, and we have to start thinking of it as history, as part of Polish history. We Poles don't spend enough time thinking about our history."

As a legal, aboveground entity, Solidarity began to become history with the imposition of martial law. But the intense and blatantly open discussion of political issues that characterized Poland before martial law has in no way subsided. Its tone, of course, has changed, and sometimes (grudgingly) its volume, and often its tense. Now, in addition to arguing about what the underground should be doing, one can argue about what Solidarity should have done. Was the coup inevitable? At what point had the regime locked into its military strategy? Did Solidarity go too far or not far enough? Was there a point when, by acting differently, Solidarity might have won?

On December 13, 1981, Solidarity was one day short of 16 months old. That's if you consider its birth to have occurred on August 14, 1980, the day the workers in the Baltic port of Gdansk launched their 17-day occupation-strike of the Lenin Shipyard. And current second-guessing starts right there, with the conduct of those negotiations. "Solidarity made a crucial mistake at the very beginning," Jadwiga Staniszkis, a prominent young Polish sociologist, told me in Warsaw during my October visit. Staniszkis has written a long, detailed sociological interpretation of Solidarity's history, *Poland's Self-Limiting Revolution* (which has already been published in France and will be available in the United States in 1984 by way of Princeton University Press). In many ways, her provocative, often quirky analysis makes her the first revisionist historian of Solidarity. She seems to delight in upending received versions of the history of the movement. "It was a mistake urged on by the experts, the intelligentsia who had come to advise the workers during the August negotiations and who ended up by muddying an otherwise pure situation," she said. "I am referring to the inclusion in the Gdansk agreements of language recognizing 'the leading role of the Communist Party.' If the workers had had their way, they would never have agreed to that compromise. It was urged on them by the intellectuals, and it warped everything that followed."

"If it hadn't been for that compromise," a friend of Staniszkis' who'd been listening to our conversation interrupted, "nothing would have followed. There would have been a deadlock, and probably a bloodbath." This is certainly the more traditional view.

"The real turning point, however," Staniszkis persisted, ignoring her friend's comment, "came six months later, with the Bydgoszcz crisis." In this opinion Staniszkis is not alone. By March 1981, a pattern of confrontation and avoidance was emerging: The authorities would agree to certain concessions, stall in every way possible in carrying them out, be confronted by the threat of further strikes, agree to speed up the implementation, and, once the strike threat was lifted, revert to stalling tactics. People were getting angry and increasingly frustrated, putting pressure on Lech Walesa and the union leadership to project a firmer line. The Polish Communist Party, meanwhile, was in growing disarray. Fully one-third of its members had themselves joined Solidarity and were calling for more active democracy within the Party. On March 19th, in the north-central town of Bydgoszcz, which lies halfway between Warsaw and Gdansk, a phalanx of policemen swinging billy clubs stormed a sit-in of Solidarity representatives who had gathered at a local council chamber to demand action on behalf of the area's farmers and peasants. By far the most violent incident up to that point, it was clearly a provocation by recalcitrant, hard-line elements in the regime. Three Solidarity activists had to be hospitalized, including the charismatic leader Jan Rulewski. Posters featuring photographs of his face, horrifyingly battered, went up all over Poland. Solidarity's leadership declared a nationwide strike alert, set March 31st as the date for starting an unlimited general strike, and demanded that those responsible for the attack be disciplined.

The next ten days were the most suspenseful in the union's history. As Warsaw Pact troops undertook their highly publicized Soyuz '81 maneuvers in and around Poland, Walesa and Deputy Prime Minister Mieczyslaw Rakowski entered into desperate negotiations. On March 27th, Solidarity held a four-hour warning strike as a show of strength (it was adhered to by virtually everyone), and people continued to mobilize for the March 31st deadline. Moscow stepped up its demands that the Warsaw regime hold firm. Walesa, for his part, was under tremendous pressure to call the strike, ostensibly around the issue of Bydgoszcz but really as a protest against the regime's entire attitude. A collision seemed inevitable, and Soviet intervention highly probable. At the last moment, Rakowski and Walesa reached agreement—a document of Byzantine complexity which finally said nothing at all. Walesa jammed the settlement through his executive committee, and the strike was called off. The next day, several of Solidarity's top officials—most notably, Karol Modzelewski, the union's brilliant press spokesman— resigned in protest over the collapse of Solidarity's internal democratic process during the negotiations.

"March was the moment when a general strike might have worked," Staniszkis told me. "The entire nation was united and resolute. The Party, by contrast, was paralyzed in its polarization and self-doubt. I guess I'm the sort of radical who likes her situations pure, and Bydgoszcz was as pure as they come; that is, until the intelligentsia—Walesa's expert advisers—got in the way and contrived their stupid compromise. That agreement pulled the plug. It left everyone deflated and demoralized. The transparency of the union was gone forever. The hierarchy of semantic competence now reappeared: decisions were no longer being framed in clear language that all workers could understand. Instead, we reverted to the tortuous double-entendres and ambiguities which had characterized discourse between the intelligentsia and the regime all along. You had to be an intellectual to understand them, and if you weren't you lost interest, and hope. If you're not sure you're going to be willing to carry out your general strike, you shouldn't threaten it. Afterward, it was too late. Those who opposed the general strike in March wanted one by November, but by then it was hopeless. The nation's unity would never be recaptured."

"We should have gone out on strike after Bydgoszcz," a Warsaw psychologist agreed the next day, when I told him what Staniszkis had said. "We didn't strike then when we were strong and they were weak, and after that it was just a series of defeats for the union leadership."

How had he felt at the time?

"Oh, I was tremendously relieved. We all were. This is definitely backseat hindsight driving. It's very common now to hear how we should have struck on March 31st, but don't let anybody fool you: on March 30th, we were scared to death. It seemed like certain disaster. And, for all the criticism of the lack of democratic process which followed, few of us questioned the basic decision not to strike. All my reservations then I still hold, by the way—it's just that now I see the alternative, and it's worse."[28]

When I mentioned the consensus about March 31, 1981, as the turning point to a Western diplomat, he disagreed. "Clearly, Bydgoszcz was important," he said. "But, in retrospect, I think the turning point came a bit later, in early summer. As long as the Communist Party was continuing to reform itself—and you must remember, those were very heady days, all that internal debate and self-criticism, all those open elections at the local level pointing toward the July Party Congress—everything was still possible. A renewed Party might have been able to reach an honorable accord with society. In June, though, the Polish Party's Central Committee received a very stern warning from its Soviet counterpart, in which it was told in no uncertain terms that this groundswell reformation was to stop. And from one day to the next it did. It took a few days for people to notice, but the Party Congress that finally did convene in July was completely controllable, and no great changes occurred. After that, the situation deteriorated at a progressively faster rate."

The subsequent rigidity of the Party, particularly in the face of the collapsing economic situation, led to an increasing radicalization on the part of Solidarity. The authorities, in launching their coup, as we have seen, blamed Solidarity's extreme behavior during the first half of December for the imposition of martial law in the middle of the month. And yet some Poles, speaking in retrospect, insisted to me that the final decision to stage a coup had already been made by late September. They referred me to a speech by the Politburo hard-liner Albin Siwak on September 30th, in which he told a meeting of Communist Party leaders gathered in Krosno that a six-man Military Council of National Salvation (WRON) had been formed, with Generals Jaruzelski and Czeslaw Kiszczak (the eventual Interior Minister) at its head, that militia and Army forces were being prepared for action, and that the council would wait two months before using these forces—that is, until popular support for Solidarity had dwindled further. As reported at the time in the No. 44 issue of the Solidarity press agency's *A. S. Bulletin*, Siwak also indicated that "a decision to rescind the registration of the independent free trade union Solidarity is to be expected."

Siwak's speech helps one to understand the significance of some of the other dates that Warsavites now cite as decisive. For instance, many point to October 18th: On that day, Kania was dismissed, and was replaced by Jaruzelski, who now concentrated the authority of Prime Minister, Defense Minister, and First Party Secretary in his person—an arrangement virtually unprecedented in world Communist practice since Stalin, and one that would prove essential in the imposition of martial law. Others point to October 23rd, the day Jaruzelski sent small groups of troops into the countryside. (Even though they were withdrawn on November 19th, the maneuver now appears to have been either a dry run or a preparatory incursion, or—probably—both.) Still others consider November 9th, following the summit between Jaruzelski, Walesa, and Archbishop Jozef Glemp, when the best that the authorities could or would offer Solidarity by way of compromise was one seat on a seven-member "front of national accord," with the Party and its puppets retaining all the other seats—a cynically preposterous offer—as the point of no return. And others refer to December 2nd and the raid on the Firefighters' Academy.

Although Poles seem to enjoy this point-of-no-return game, trying to pinpoint the date when the regime had locked itself into its coup strategy, few in Warsaw this autumn seemed to think there was much Solidarity could have done to prevent it. Hardly anyone takes the regime seriously when it claims that it acted only because during those last few weeks, and especially those last few days, Solidarity had finally gone too far. If ordinary Warsavites do begrudge Solidarity's stewardship in those final days—and many of them do—it's rather because they feel that the leadership should have seen the coup coming. People are a bit ashamed at how much of a surprise Jaruzelski's coup proved to be. "For all the talk about general strikes, and all the tension preceding December 13th," a taxi-driver told me, "when it came down to it, they weren't prepared with anything—*any* response."

"I still can't stop thinking about those miners in Silesia that Christmas morning," another Warsavite told me. "How they were still holding out there deep underground in those cold, wet tunnels—convinced, *absolutely convinced*, that all of Poland was on strike with them, and that the line the authorities kept feeding them, that the country had by then been largely subdued, was an obvious, shallow trick. They wouldn't even believe the testimony of their own wives. And, of course, they were right. We should have been on strike. *The union should have prepared us to be.*"

"Solidarity was trapped—still is trapped to some extent—by a number of myths that it refused ever to reconsider," Aleksander Smolar, a Polish émigré scholar, recently told me in Paris. "One of them was the myth of national unity. In all its rhetoric, Solidarity insisted that the nation was united against a tiny ruling clique, whose members, in turn (although this tended to go unsaid), were merely the lieutenants on the scene of a foreign overlord. That was simply not the case. When it came to the test, there were tens of thousands, probably hundreds of thousands, of middle-level Polish bureaucrats who felt terribly threatened by the 16-month experiment and sided with those who undertook the coup, and it would not have been possible without their support.

"Another myth that impeded clear thinking on the part of Solidarity was that of the Army. Poles cherish their Army as an institutional expression of ongoing Polish nationalism. This is a carry-over from the 1930s and before, and 28 years of membership in the Warsaw Pact has not affected it. Solidarity's leaders could not bring themselves to believe that the Army would allow itself to be used against them. The fact is, however, that on December 13th many of the senior and middle-level officers acted as they did precisely because they felt they were saving Poland. The Army turned out to be a perfectly useful tool for suppressing the movement."

"One of the main problems with Solidarity was its inability to get people to change their way of thinking, from social to political categories," another political theorist, this one in Warsaw, told me a few days later. "Hannah Arendt's was the preeminent critique of Solidarity *avant la lettre*. Her great theme was how to make a spontaneous revolution into a political movement. And Solidarity was a textbook case of failure in that regard. There were all these word games—we represent society and hence are merely 'social,' the Party is 'political,' we have no interest in 'politics'—and they had a certain strategic value, but they were also revealing: they were accurate. I'm not saying that it would have changed things—probably what happened would have happened anyway—but at least Solidarity could have done better, been truer. There were three main political questions: Poland versus the Soviet Union; Solidarity versus the Party; and the attitude of governments in the West (what kind of interest did they or should they have in Poland?). But, for all the talk during the 16 months, those questions were hardly ever framed in political terms. Instead, they were addressed either through magic—the cult of symbols and symbolic dates—or through conspicuous exclusion. I understand it, but it's unfortunate that no one had the courage . . . Look, every political idea about compromise, even in the long-range future, is a bit nasty, is morally ambiguous, especially in our economic circumstances. And Solidarity was loath to embark on that kind of journey. Instead, there was the endless discussion of the Soviet massacre of Polish officers at Katyn in 1940. Someone should have said, 'Forget Katyn! Let's leave Katyn out of this—it was 40 years ago! What we have to worry about is these particular working conditions at this particular factory.' But the fact of the matter is that a lot of people *were* more interested in a proper memorial to Katyn than in rebuilding —or scrapping—their factory."

"That love of symbols makes Poland very strong in defeat but frightfully shaky—almost unmanageable—in victory," someone else remarked.

However, my psychologist friend disagreed when I recalled for him the political theorist's comments. "Of course we weren't political," he said. "We were *pre*political. We were fighting to create a space where politics could take place. We just never made it. And ours is not a political problem today, either, the same way the German occupation was not a political problem." Saying that Solidarity was "not political enough" presupposes that the regime would have been willing to engage in a political discussion with the mass movement—that the regime would have been interested in a national political compromise—and there is precious little evidence to support that assumption. ("The myth of a 'national compromise' is another one of those elusive fallacies to which the Poles are subject," Aleksander Smolar told me in Paris, referring to the periods both before and after the imposition of martial law.)

"Solidarity had no clear, certain aims and no concept of coexistence," the Solidarity leader Adam Michnik wrote in an article entitled "The Polish War," which was smuggled out of Bialoleka prison last spring. He continued:

> Naturally, it was easily provoked and diverted into participation in unimportant side issues. It was preoccupied with ad-hoc problems, it was messy, incompetent, unable to predict the moves that its opponent was likely to make. Solidarity knew how to strike but was unprepared to wait. It could attack directly but it could not withdraw. It had a general-outline program but no gradual means to implement it. It was powerful in the factories among workers but weak at the negotiating table. It had to face an opponent who could not speak the truth, could not administer, could not maintain promises, but who could manage one thing—the crushing of social solidarity. Solidarity was a giant with steel legs but hands of putty. . . . The Communist regime was a giant with putty legs but hands of steel.

"December 13th was inevitable and unavoidable," an activist friend told me. "And yet in an open organization, where all decisions were public and most were subject to vote, there was no way to prepare for it."

"As early as the spring of 1981," a Warsaw historian recalled, "I felt that the only way Solidarity could survive was through dictatorial discipline. The tragedy, of course, was that its main impulse was democratic. People wanted that internal democracy more than anything else—that was what could make them feel they were something. Naturally, the young workers knew very little of what democracy was all about—one of the main things it's about is knowing when to stop the debate—but where, how could they have learned?"

Ultimately, all discussions of the purported inevitability of the coup become discussions of geopolitics, questions about "that very large country," in the words of the satirist Slawomir Mrozek, in a recent short story, "which is also fraternal and which, although quite independent of our country, is so close to us that one doesn't have to leave their country to be in ours, and one doesn't have to leave our country to be in theirs." Edward Gierek, during his ten years as Party Secretary, used to taunt his critics with the phrase "This isn't Australia!"—by which he meant that Poland was no island, let alone one conveniently bobbing somewhere in the South Pacific. The boss of an editor friend of mine—my friend is the former Solidarity representative of her unit, her boss is a liberal Communist Party member—to this day pleads with her in exasperation, "What would you have us do? What specifically? And don't say 'Take the entire country to the moon.' " It's basically the same point. And yet the journalist Daniel Singer told me one afternoon in Paris, "I don't think everything is decided by the Russians. That whitewashes the role of Jaruzelski and his colleagues. There was always room for maneuver—wider before, narrower now—and I think that most of the time the odds were *against* the Russians' intervening. It's important to make that distinction."

Of course, not all discussion of Solidarity is critical—second-guessing and second thoughts. Long after the coup, many of Solidarity's achievements persist and are cherished. "What we have left," another friend told me, contradicting those who deprecated symbolic politics, "are the great gestures: the 1970 memorial in Gdansk; the film *Man of Iron*; the Eastern European Resolution. That is why I don't condemn those actions. They are the lamps that will sustain us through this next dark time." In addition, there are the concrete gains (those that have not yet been taken back by the regime): the *Walesowki*, as they are called in fond tribute to the union's leader—"Walesa's dividends." Free Saturdays, still, for most workers (except coal miners)—a major breakthrough. Increases in pensions and wages, especially large for the lowest-paid workers. A substantial increase in salaries for working mothers, along with maternity leave. "Western reporters misunderstood Solidarity's line on women's issues," a young woman journalist told me one evening in Warsaw. "You were misled by our call for 'a return to the traditional role for women' into imagining that Solidarity was somehow hopelessly sexist. Rather, by our insisting on family values Solidarity was trying to correct the outrageous exploitation of women in this society, where they are expected both to hold factory or menial jobs (for which they are terribly underpaid) and to take care of their families—stand in line, cook meals, mend clothes, clean house. In Lodz, the textile center, we found in one study that the average woman works at those various tasks 19 hours a day! An entire city's work force living near the edge of physical and nervous collapse. So Solidarity's success in attaining some child-care centers and, especially, maternity leave and higher wages for these women was and remains terribly important. Those 16 months made a terrific impact on family life in Poland."

Later in our conversation, this journalist helped me to understand another aspect of Solidarity's achievement: "I was one of those who felt from the beginning that it wasn't going to last, that this was an eruption of truth which would of necessity eventually be crushed, but that it would prove victorious in the end, because this truth would permeate society *for generations*, and people would not forget this time of freedom, and would know that what was around them was abnormal. I mean, during the first several months after the coup I was numb—I didn't talk to anyone, I didn't read or try to write. But recently I had a chance to take a look at a few back issues of the journal I worked on during the 16 months before the coup, and I was shocked. Working there day to day, I hadn't fully realized what a flow of truth-telling was taking place—all words impossible to say before or after. And I now realize that I will have to go back and reread the entire production."

"The changes in consciousness went extremely deep," another Pole told me. "Workers would come home after eight hours on the line and would then spend an hour or two *reading*. When people ask me why Solidarity wasn't prepared for 'the war,' all I can say is that you can ask that only if you didn't know the situation. In an open, democratic organization, there was no way to organize an underground in anticipation of something like December 13th. The only thing its leaders could do was to change consciousness, and they did that—that was their accomplishment and is their legacy."

A middle-aged art dealer said, "I used to live in an internal emigration. I tried not to pay attention to what was going on. That changed in 1980. It has changed for good."

Although daily life and conversation in Poland this autumn were suffused with analogies between Jaruzelski's state of war and Hitler's occupation, many of them were forced; in most ways, Poland under martial law had little in common with Poland in 1943. A failure to see clearly the distinction between the two periods—a tendency to emphasize the similarities—has had deleterious effects on the group that calls itself, harking back to the forties, "the underground." Rhetoric flies ahead of lived reality, and the activists in hiding are often disappointed at the lack of seemingly appropriate social response. And yet the fact is that the kind of response that would have been appropriate in 1943 just is not today.

"A mass underground movement can develop only where police have difficulty in infiltrating the community," Jan Nowak wrote in *Courier from Warsaw*, his recent memoir of the resistance to the German occupation of Poland. "The Nazis had created such a gulf between the occupation forces and the population that they had virtually no access to Poles. . . . The Germans tried to force the hostile population to submit through the use of total terror, disregarding all political methods. Terror exercised on the principle of collective responsibility of both the active and the passive segments of the community increased social cohesion and the feeling of mutual solidarity by its very nature. . . . The invaders proved to be rotten psychologists. Because of the constant escalation of repression, terror lost its power to terrorize. People simply stopped being afraid, because they had nothing much to lose."

Jaruzelski's regime may be deemed rotten at many things, but its leaders are by no means rotten psychologists. Over a year of martial law has left Polish society riddled—not solid, as it was, say, in 1943, or in early in 1981. Almost everyone has fond feelings for Solidarity, but these feelings are laced with others, and seldom these days is everyone feeling the same absolute, unalloyed defiance of the regime at the same time. Alex Smolar, observing Poland from his base in Paris, told me, "The regime will be able to achieve 'normalization' if it can manipulate public morale in one of three ways. First, if it can make the people come to blame and hate Solidarity as the *cause* of their problems. Well, this just isn't going to happen. Second, if it can make the people come to hate certain leaders or elements of Solidarity for having led them astray. This is clearly one of the regime's strategies, but it also seems fairly unlikely to work. But there's a third possibility, and that's if the regime can get people to come to see Solidarity as a glorious but hopelessly impossible dream—a wonderful moment of vitality that just never had a chance of translation into prolonged success, this, after all, being tragic Poland. People would then presumably sink into an exhausted stupor. This is a much more realistic possibility, at least in the short run." And it is precisely this possibility that the underground in 1943—as opposed to today—never had to face. To paraphrase Nowak, people may stop being defiant because they have nothing left to gain.

This fall, the staff members of the Solidarity weekly *Tygodnik Solidarnosc* (a paper that had been under suspension but was now being formally dissolved) issued a final leaflet. They recalled the words that the weekly's currently interned editor, Tadeusz Mazowiecki, had used in the paper's very first issue: "As a society and as a union we have embarked upon a road never travelled before. No plans, models, maps fit our situation. We have to create them for ourselves. We have to be faithful to that hope that has been born among us." They then went on to note, "These hopes and dreams have now been pushed into the underground."

But this was not the sort of time that could be expected to allow for an efficient, secure, confidently structured, and disciplined underground. "You can't just take a ten-million-member organization underground," a friend observed. "Nor can you really have leadership without an organization—a leadership floating free, issuing directives with no real chain of command for effecting them. Such a command structure existed in the early forties, but it doesn't today. And it can't be replaced by vague good feelings of the population as a whole—it just doesn't work. No wonder these guys are having such a hard time."

Although Solidarity managed to set up fairly effective clandestine organizations in some large factories and in some towns—notably Wroclaw, where the Solidarity leadership during the last weeks before the coup had the foresight to withdraw all of its chapter's funds (over 80 million zlotys) from the local banks, and hence entered martial law amazingly solvent—these organizations have failed to coalesce around a unified strategy. Where Solidarity has proved effective in the months since the coup is in establishing networks of support and communication. In some factories, there are even systems of dues collection for the purpose. The Catholic Church at the parish level is intensely involved in this activity, and also in documenting arrests and acts of violence. This sort of loose network may someday prove important in mass mobilization. In any case, in the short run it attempts to minimize the damage to the social fabric—to social solidarity.

More visible—indeed, tremendously impressive—evidence of underground activity can be found in the extent of clandestine printing. This is an area where the Second World War analogy stands up. One reason the underground printers are so effective today is that they can draw on lessons in technique and concealment derived from prior generations of underground printers. (A proliferating feature of the Polish landscape, however, is phony disinformation leaflets, allegedly printed by Solidarity cadres but in fact the work of government propagandists. Here it is the regime that has learned from the Polish Second World War underground's strategy of producing phony Nazi literature designed to demoralize the German occupying army.[29])

As of August 1982, the Warsaw-region underground's weekly *Tygodnik Mazowsze* reported on its own inventory of 250 ongoing underground journals nationwide (56 in the Warsaw region, 14 in Silesia-Dabrowa, 10 in Gdansk, and so forth), with press runs ranging from several hundred to 30,000. Many of the issues I saw seemed better printed than the ones I'd seen in 1981. This was true of newspapers, and even more so of books, although the writer Marek Nowakowski commented, "People don't really care about the quality of printing; in fact, the worse something is printed, the more carefully it seems to be read."

One evening at a party in a Warsaw suburb—over 60 people crammed into two tiny rooms, drinking vodka, listening to Western rock music on a cassette, and then giving way to loud communal singing of patriotic hymns, some of which dated back to the 1863 rebellion—I happened to run into a friend from my previous visits. These days, he confided amid the noise and the singing, he's co-editing *Wezwanie*, a thick quarterly that is one of the most important underground journals—its title contains a pun, signifying both "an appeal" (a call to action) and "a subpoena" (a call to witness or interrogation). He told me—and other Poles subsequently confirmed—that the magazine is read by both workers and intelligentsia.

"One of the most valuable things about the Solidarity period was the way it forced many of us in the intelligentsia to reexamine how we use language," he said. "During the years before 1980, we had developed terrible habits of thinking and speaking—ours was an Aesopian language, filled with convoluted jargon. When we began writing articles for the workers, they brought us up short. They'd come back to us and say, 'What do you mean here? This is too hard. You have to work too hard to understand it. Can't you just say what you mean?' We were forced to see how the density of our language—which we had developed as a kind of adaptation to repression—itself *served* repression, since it kept us separate from our natural allies among the workers. So one of the great labors since 1980 has been the invention of language that is clear and yet flexible and intelligent. We try to write in a kind of spoken Polish. And we're getting better, I think."

Four issues of *Wezwanie* have come out so far, each of several hundred pages, and the circulation is now 3,000. My friend continued, "Our recent issue includes analyses of the state of war and how we should respond; historical analogies; a section called 'Dreams of the State of War,' which is just that; another on the war through the eyes of children;[30] an attempt to construct a composite portrait of police interrogators—how they behave, who they are, what they ask. We have a group of psychologists working out psychological profiles of the regime leaders."

I asked him whether printing and distribution presented problems. "Not really," he said. "It's very well organized. This is one field in which Solidarity was prepared for the coup. For 16 months, for example, printing equipment was being hidden away, and although plants are regularly seized, we still have plenty of machines in storage and more being smuggled in. The underground printing operations from the seventies never really surfaced during the 16 months, precisely because of the fear that there might be renewed repression—so they are still intact. Smaller pieces—leaflets, things under three pages—can be printed overnight or in off-hours at regular, aboveground plants. Larger journals and tabloids are printed in the secret plants. The printing of the big Warsaw-region weekly is scattered among five plants around the city—all of them working simultaneously on the same copy, in case anything should happen to any one. We figure the life expectancy of a clandestine plant to be four months. In a well-run police state, once a plant starts up it shouldn't take more than two months to expose it, but the authorities here are still a bit slow. During Nazi times, I'm told, the life expectancy was six months, so they're better than that. If we're lucky, when a plant falls our people have time to escape and all that's lost is the machinery. Then within a few days the same people can start up again somewhere else. But we're not always lucky, and the minimum sentence is three years."

How, I asked, does the system actually work in practice?

"Money changes hands at each step—that's the key. Thus, when writers turn in their stories I pay them immediately, so that I don't have to see them again. They are paid according to their material needs. Then, when we editors have put the entire finished copy together, we take it to the printer, who, in turn, pays us a lump sum. For a run of 3,000 copies, we are paid the equivalent of the cover price of 1,200— this ends up meaning, after we reimburse ourselves for the writers' fees, that we editors each make between 7,000 and 10,000 zlotys a month." This is a bit under the salary of a factory worker. "In theory, we never see the copy again. The printer arranges printing and distribution. The cover price of the current issue is 400 zlotys. When a distributor comes to pick up, say, a hundred copies, he pays the printer 40,000 zlotys up front, and recoups this as he passes the copies along, in groups of ten perhaps, to the subdistributors—usually workers on the factory floor, or other people in various enterprises—who, in turn, of course, recoup their money with each individual sale."

He picked up a copy of a book on a nearby table—a new, illustrated biography of Walesa—and said, "See?" He was pointing at the price— 300 zlotys—and, beneath that, the legend *"Nie Spekuluj"* ("Do not speculate"). "There is endless opportunity for speculation, especially since many of these editions are limited way below demand, but we try to keep it down and are to a certain extent successful. Besides, people are expected to pass copies along to their neighbors."

I asked him whether the printers were in it for the politics or the money.

"Nobody in Poland is in anything for the money," he said, laughing. "Not, at any rate, when the money in question is zlotys, which are all but worthless. I think idealistic motives prevail. The printers are well paid, but that is because they are taking the biggest risks, and they want at least to set something aside for their families in case they are caught. They also have to deal with obtaining ink and paper, which is the single most difficult part of the operation and requires considerable bribes."

He paused, and then continued, "That's how it's supposed to work. Actually, there are a hundred and ten thousand errors in the conspiracy. We have a distressing accumulation of functions—we even have people working for several papers at once. Everybody talks too much, including me." He smiled as he cast a glance around the room. "And then, if you're an editor, it's hard not to have direct contact with the printers again and again—you don't just let something go, you go back and check it and make corrections up to the last minute."

I had been taking notes during the conversation, and as I was putting my note pad away he asked if he could have my pen.

I said of course, but why?

"Fine-point ball-point," he replied. "Tremendously useful in doing corrections on stencils—you can hardly do without them. That's why the authorities have pulled them off the market. If you know anyone coming into Poland, tell him to bring fine-point pens."

Throughout 1982, the widespread distribution of underground litera-ture made it possible for all Poles to listen in on, and in many cases contribute to, the fundamental strategic discussions taking place among the members of the underground leadership. Indeed, even those interned or in prison were frequent contributors. They would read position papers in newspapers smuggled into the camps and then smuggle their own comments out to the same newspapers. Prison walls proved re-markably porous membranes.

A basic premise underlying virtually all these discussions of strategy was a continuing insistence on nonviolence, or, at any rate, a refusal to sanction terrorist tactics. This insistence became increasingly urgent as the leadership tried to fend off the appeal of such tactics to a populace reeling under bureaucratic state terror. "Violence breeds violence," Jacek Kuron, the longtime dissident activist and a co-founder of KOR, warned at the outset. "The not-so-patient, the not-so-thoughtful will tend toward terror, the double-edged weapon. Terror breeds terror, and the spiral of terror cannot be broken by terror."

The underground committee in Krakow, heavily influenced by the city's Catholic intelligentsia, took a very strong stand. On January 4, 1982, it issued a statement in which it branded terrorism a nineteenth-century invention of the czarist secret police, designed at once to isolate the resistance and to allow for a hardening of police power. The com-mittee urged fellow-Poles not to succumb to provocations: "We condemn terrorism as incompatible with our Christian heritage and contrary to the program and practice of our Solidarity union. It is a tactic as ineffective as it is pernicious. . . . We refuse to resort to violence in the face of violence. We are determined to fight lies and direct attack, but only by standing in the truth and without the use of force."

The consensus against the use of terror disguised wide-ranging under-lying differences among Solidarity's strategists. Or, to be more exact, Solidarity's leaders displayed profound differences when they tried to articulate a basic strategy that might lessen the appeal of random terror. Jacek Kuron launched the debate from prison in February 1982, with his essay "A Way Out of the Impasse." Noting that the government's inability to repair the economy and its simultaneous refusal to negotiate in good faith with society were forcing things toward an eventual chaotic debacle ("an explosion"), he argued that it was up to the opposition to present the authorities with a plausible ultimatum, one that would compel them to either compromise or risk being swept away.

"For this reason," Kuron wrote, "we must organize ourselves—differently from before August 1980—organize ourselves around a main center, and display absolute discipline before it." That center would begin to prepare for a major, coordinated, "simultaneous offensive against the centers of power and information throughout the country." Elsewhere, he noted that "the ultimate means of exerting such pressure and currently the last chance for a compromise would be a general strike," but he was somewhat ambiguous on whether he was prepared to defend such a strike through centrally coordinated (as opposed to individual terrorist) violence: "Throughout the many years of my opposition activity, I propagated the principle of avoiding all forms of violence. I therefore feel obliged to speak out, to say that at present preparing ourselves for overthrowing the occupation in a collective action seems to me the least of all evils." It was also unclear whether he was advocating these preparations because he seriously proposed undertaking such an offensive or because he imagined such preparations to be the only way to force the regime into serious negotiations: "People from the government camp must know that the time left for them to initiate a compromise is strictly limited."

Kuron's essay quickly spawned a remarkable controversy, with contributions from both inside and outside prison finding their way into the clandestine press. Zbigniew Bujak, the leader of Warsaw's underground organization, wrote from his hideout, "I find that the main point of Jacek Kuron's article is contained in the assertion 'If you don't want war, prepare yourself for it.'" He went on to contradict Kuron, arguing that in the short term, at least, Poles were mature enough to avoid giving way to a social explosion they knew they could not win. Hence, there was no need for the underground to be organizing toward centralization and a head-on confrontation with the regime. Besides, under current conditions such organizing would be impossible. Instead, Bujak advocated a strong *decentralized* movement, with a variety of techniques of action. "Only such a movement—multifarious and undefined—will be elusive and difficult to overcome." At one point, referring to this strategy as "trench warfare" or "positional battle," he acknowledged that "this road is not one of rapid and effective success, but one of long, hard work, demanding activity from a significant part of society."

Wiktor Kulerski, a colleague of Bujak's in the Warsaw underground, agreed, arguing for an "informal" movement, composed of independent, though loosely linked, groups. "Such a movement," he wrote, "ought to lead to a situation where the government will be in control of empty shops but not the market; employment but not the means of livelihood; the state press but not information; printing houses but not the publishing movement; telephones and post but not communication; schooling but not education." Such a program, pursued over the long term, Kulerski argued, would lead to a rotting of the regime and to its eventual recognition of the necessity for compromise and negotiation.

In a letter smuggled out of Bialoleka prison and subsequently published in the underground, Kuron's longtime associates and current prisonmates Adam Michnik and Janusz Onyszkiewicz tended to side with Bujak and Kulerski: "The view is heard that a general explosion here is inevitable, and the problem is to organize it properly. But in politics, we feel, nothing is inevitable. . . . It seems to us that Solidarity must avoid total confrontation. Common sense demands that one avoid battle on a field on which the enemy is stronger." Michnik and Onyszkiewicz went on to advocate taking a long view, and forming an underground society with flexible tactics: "A short strike of definite time limit, yes. A strike till victory, no." They concluded, "In other words, we support the strategy of 'positional battle,' or even 'guerrilla warfare,' and not that of a general, all-out confrontation. To give it more color: Only by such a strategy could the Shah have been overthrown, the Vietnamese have gained victory, and Spain have achieved democracy." (This last passage, incidentally, offers a remarkable series of antecedents to be embraced by a group that many in the West persist in seeing as antisocialist, and even proto-capitalist.)

In a polemical reply to his critics, published in the spring, Kuron noted that he didn't need to be lectured on the merits of an underground society—he had been one of the inventors of the concept back in 1976, with the creation of KOR. "But now we are talking about methods of action; and methods depend first of all on the existing conditions— which today are totally different from the conditions before August 1980." Reiterating his position, Kuron became less ambiguous on the question of violence. "No program can be built on the hope that the generals and the secretaries will voluntarily agree to a compromise," he wrote. "It has to be assumed that violence retreats only before violence, and it has to be announced unequivocally that the movement will not hesitate before the use of violence." He sketched out in greater detail his proposal for a general strike, which would be "accompanied by attacks on selected power and information centers, with the knowledge that a minority in the Army and the militia would choose to take our side." He added, "Another possibility is to announce that such an attack will take place if the striking workers are attacked first." So as to be absolutely unequivocal, he then repeated himself: "I am urging you to announce

that if the authorities do not . . . come to an agreement with society—
then the movement will be forced to resort to violence."

Kuron concluded, "Please forgive my playing the philosopher. I know
how hard you are working and how considerable your achievements
have been. Still, we find ourselves at an impasse, and although we probably do not yet measure up to the situation, we have to rise to it. It is we
who have to show a way out of the situation that we perceive as a situation with no solution. You have not chosen for yourselves a burden so
great, but unfortunately you cannot now discard it. You have the
Golden Horn."[31]

As the spring of 1982 gave way to summer, the debate on strategy
became a matter of assessing the temper of the times: Should the crisis,
and hence Solidarity's response, be seen as short-term or long-term?
Specifically, should the underground leadership be moving toward a
general strike? (The question of whether such a strike should be de-
fended by violent means was held in abeyance for the moment.) Wladyslaw Frasyniuk, the underground leader in Wroclaw, for instance, issued
a statement on June 1st in which he argued against haphazard, one-shot
street demonstrations but in favor of building up organizations within
the factories "capable of protecting social interests by using as [their]
ultimate weapon the general strike. The situation in our country is
such that this ultimate weapon may soon prove to be necessary. Thus,
all our actions are and must be subordinated to preparing for such a
strike."

A late-summer issue of the Warsaw underground's *Tygodnik Mazowsze*,
however, included a wide range of dissenting opinions. Solidarity members of the Polish Academy of Sciences, for instance, warned that the
defeat of a general strike would mean the end of Solidarity: "That is
why it can be declared only when there is a realistic chance of success,
or when the end of Solidarity is anyway inevitable. A general strike can
only be declared once—it must not be postponed or called off once
declared." Another contributor wrote, "It is necessary to have a sense of
reality. A belief that a general strike would immediately force the authorities to make concessions or would lead in two or three days to a change
of government has nothing to do with reality. . . . A bloody confrontation will certainly lower resistance: cowards will break down, the best
will die or land in prison, the rest will give up or resort to terrorism.
. . . We have to tell the people the truth: no spontaneous or organized
strike will bring about independent free unions."

Another contributor, dubbed "Geopolitician" by the editors, wondered
what the political landscape might look like one week into a general
strike, and offered four scenarios: (1) "Like Napoleon, let us begin
the battle and later see what comes of it." (2) The military government
dissolved, martial law lifted, negotiations in progress between a new
government team, Solidarity, and the Church. (3) The strike crushed by

the secret police and the Army, "with innumerable casualties and 100,000 people in prison camps." (4) An intervention by the Warsaw Pact. "Geopolitician" concluded by evaluating the four possibilities: "I will not comment on the third and fourth scenarios. No. 2 unfortunately does not stand a chance. As for No. 1, let me just say: Napoleon had *guns.*"

Through the end of September 1982, the battle between the underground and the regime had "played itself out something like a game of chess," as Neal Ascherson, the Eastern Europe correspondent for the *Observer*, told me in London. "The government would make some move, and Solidarity would sit there and look at it—hmm—and then might call out the workers on a two-hour demonstration, as on August 31st. The regime would look at that and then fan out its ZOMOS to the principal centers and cut off all the phone lines, perhaps impose a few curfews, because that's the required next move in *its* playbook. Depending on the effectiveness of that tack, Solidarity would plan its next move." For all the tension, it was a fairly stylized progression. "We're still at the stage of police-baiting," one Pole told me in Warsaw in October. "The crowds gather and they're angry, but not yet with the sort of what-the-hell anger that boils over into revolution." The underground leaders, for their part, had not yet arrived at a consistent long-term strategy.

During October, something happened to the chess match: it became a rout. Having survived the dangerous spring and summer, the regime now moved quickly to consolidate its position against the backdrop of the oncoming winter, the prospect of which was once again dulling public response. Intent on lifting martial law by the first anniversary of the coup, December 13th, if possible, the regime was determined to institutionalize most of its principal features into civil law before that date. This would prove particularly tricky, because of the high level of public frustration and anger and the general paralysis of the economy, but the government leadership rose to the challenge, keeping the opposition and the people off balance through a brilliant series of psychological ploys. The underground leadership, at least in the short term, sank before the onslaught.

In retrospect, it is clear that the end game began in the immediate aftermath of Solidarity's triumph on August 31, 1982, the second anniversary of the Gdansk agreements. Although the union had been able to mount demonstrations in 66 cities, 25 of them "serious," according to the government spokesman who provided the figures (presumably a reference to the degree of violence used by the authorities)—had been able, that is, in the face of strenuous warnings from both the government and the Church, to project hundreds of thousands of supporters onto the streets throughout Poland—the government still contrived to claim a victory of sorts: not every Solidarity member had been there, and certainly not all ten million; in fact, more hadn't than had. (One particularly cynical bit of propaganda on August 31st consisted of a TV tour of the factories where, lo and behold, everyone was working. Of course they were: Solidarity had not called for a strike, only for demonstrations after work.) Furthermore, during the next few days the regime was able to use the August 31st disturbances as an excuse for launching its KOR prosecutions, putting the blame for the immediate troubles on people who had been interned the entire time.

As October began, it was clear that the regime was planning to settle the question of Solidarity's ongoing existence once and for all. With tensions rising, Archbishop Glemp cancelled a trip he had been planning to take to the United States. (Notwithstanding which, the local Communist Party newspaper in Lodz ran an exclusive story on "some regrettable attacks against the head of the Catholic Church in Poland during his recent visit in the United States," reporting, "The instigators of these brawls—and this a term used by the American press—were . . . Poles. At least, that is what they call themselves." Apparently, someone forgot to get word to the editor that the trip had been called off.) On Tuesday, October 5th, with the union's delegalization by the parliament looming, the regime scored a decisive coup: the arrest, in Wroclaw, of Wladyslaw Frasyniuk, perhaps the most popular of the five members of Solidarity's underground Temporary Coordinating Commission (the TKK), and the leader of a local underground organization that up to then had been thriving. Whether Frasyniuk's capture at that particular moment was a lucky accident for the regime or a planned preemptive strike, it could not have come at a better time. It meant people would already be demoralized on Friday, the eighth, when the delegalization bill sailed through parliament. On the ninth, when the members of the TKK met to frame their response (Frasyniuk's place having been taken by his lieutenant Piotr Bednarz), their tone, and to a certain extent even their authority, seemed shaky.

The statement issued that weekend by the TKK outlined a twofold response: a total boycott of the new, replacement unions ("To break ranks with such a boycott amounts to a betrayal of the ideals of the independent trade-union movement"); and a day of protest, on November 10th, the second anniversary of Solidarity's registration, that would include a four-hour warning strike ("The outcome of this strike will determine the future strategy of our union"). Both calls were controversial. Many felt the boycott to be worse than an exercise in futility. Since desperately scarce supplies would in all likelihood be funnelled through the new unions (children's shoes, for example), individuals would be abandoned to the solitude of their own doubts and self-loathing as, one by one, they had to cave in and join. Far from fostering solidarity, the boycott would spread hopelessness. Within less than a year, the government would be able to claim that one or two million people had joined the new unions, with more joining every day, and this would be construed as a government victory precisely to the extent that Solidarity had chosen to make an issue of it.

Some critics argued that instead of boycotting the new unions, Solidarity members should have swarmed to join them, overwhelming the structure and hijacking the incipient organizations for their own purposes. Although this tactic would probably not have worked (the law had been very cleverly drafted in such a way as to leave final authority for approving any new union to the regime), it still would have been possible, according to other critics, to let the issue ride virtually without comment. Solidarity should simply have ignored the new unions, they argued. One Warsaw writer pointed out to me a few weeks later, "The TKK could have just said, 'Fine. People can join the new unions or not—it's a matter of complete indifference to us. The only thing that matters is that Solidarity still exists, and here we simply decline to recognize your order of delegalization. Solidarity could be dissolved only by a vote of the ten million members who voted, by joining, to create it. This hasn't occurred, and the union survives.' "

The choice of the November 10th date was also dubious. Although those who chose it did so because they felt that such a vast action would require considerable planning, to many it seemed too far off. The anger was at its peak now—why wait? "The regime was very smart," a friend told me in Warsaw, "acting as it did at the beginning of October and counting on the TKK to wait for one of their anniversaries to make their response, knowing the nearest one was over a month away."

As it happened, many of the workers refused to wait. Breaking ranks (or attempting to lead a vanguard, depending on your point of view), the shipyard workers in Gdansk launched a strike at the first possible moment—on Monday, October 11th. They chose a strategy of eight-hour, first-shift strikes on successive days, to be pursued indefinitely. The government's swift response—cutting off communication to the Baltic region and militarizing the yards (in effect, summarily drafting all the workers into the Army and subjecting them to military discipline)—confronted the workers with a tragic dilemma, particularly when the strike did not spread immediately to other centers. Many of the young workers in Gdansk, according to subsequent accounts, seemed willing to risk courts-martial. But older workers with families and responsibilities toward young children soon buckled, and the strike collapsed at the end of its second day. "What can you do when they're holding a gun to your head?" one returning older worker asked a Western correspondent.[32] Early the following day, Wednesday, the Warsaw-region underground leaderships found itself calling for sympathy strikes to support workers in Gdansk who by that time had already returned to work—a fact that becme embarrassingly clear by midafternoon. At the same time, demonstrations did occur that afternoon in Nowa Huta, a steel town outside Krakow, and here the rampaging police and militiamen claimed one victim—Bogdan Wlosik, a 20-year-old worker, who died of gunshot wounds.

Having both contained these strikes and highlighted the disarray of the union's underground leadership, the government now began a concerted propaganda campaign to undermine support for the November 10th strike. Part of this campaign was based on fear. One began to hear reports of dissidents—notably the Gdansk activist Anna Walentynowicz —being sent to mental hospitals (a commonplace in the Soviet Union but hitherto unheard of in Poland), and rumors that future prisoners might face deportation, to Siberia, presumably (a truly harrowing prospect).[33]

On October 20th, government television covered the funeral, in Nowa Huta, of Bogdan Wlosik. The footage failed to show the crowd of 20,000 with their banners reading "We Will Never Forget," "One Dies for What One Lives for," "It Is Better to Die Standing Than to Live on Our Knees," and the quasi-Messianic "Bogdan Died for Us." Instead, the monitor showed a grim sequence of the casket being lowered into its grave as the anchorman intoned, "The unnecessary death of a young man was and will remain a warning. The dramatic conclusion of the Nowa Huta excesses has demonstrated yet again how unpredictable is the switch from a stormy demonstration to stones, crowbars, petrol bottles, and on to percussion grenades and provoked shots." It was a grim little speech at once baldly obscene and disarmingly effective. Meanwhile, the evening news continued its drumbeat of sensationalist stories about "social parasites" (leading up to the October 26th passage by the parliament of the social-parasite law) coupling these with repeated warnings that anyone participating in the November 10th strike stood a good chance of being fired, and hence, implicitly, of becoming the sort of social parasite who now could legally be shipped off to a work camp.

In the face of this campaign, the TKK met again, on October 20th, and, instead of pulling back from its November 10th strike call (as many I spoke with that week in Warsaw wished it would), raised the stakes. Noting that "because the regime has proved deaf to the nation's voice . . . Solidarity is entering a new phase of the fight," the TKK extended the duration of the November 10th strike from four hours to eight, tacked on a second day of protests for November 11th (the anniversary of Poland's independence in 1918), and projected actions for the December 13th anniversary of martial law, framing all this as preparatory to a general strike in the spring. Ironically, with the general strike's principal advocate on the TKK, Frasyniuk, under arrest, the group, led by the moderate Zbigniew Bujak, was now taking what looked very much like Kuron's radical position—even to the point of echoing his language.

"The methods adopted so far," their statement read, "have not managed to turn the authorities back from their path to catastrophe, so we must reach for the ultimate means—the general strike."

Having fomented an atmosphere of increasing fear and doubt, and having induced Solidarity's leadership itself to raise the stakes, Jaruzelski's regime moved quickly to close the trap: the last few days before November 10th were brilliantly orchestrated to obliterate any chance of a successful strike. On November 8th, to the horror of many Poles, Archbishop Glemp apparently made his long-delayed deal with Jaruzelski. In exchange for the government's agreement to allow a visit by Pope John Paul II in June of 1983, the Archbishop joined the General in a statement expressing "common concern for maintaining and consolidating calm, social harmony, and work." In other words, "Don't strike." Furthermore, Glemp called all the bishops into a two-day conclave at Czestochowa, to begin November 10th; they would thus not be in the field, with their parishioners, at the time of the strike. (Many of the bishops had previously shown themselves to be considerably more radical than their Primate.) The announcement had a devastating impact on Solidarity's momentum. By declaring, in effect, that "normalization" had already occurred, Glemp's statement served as a self-fulfilling prophecy. The Church had cut its best possible deal and in so doing had cut Solidarity out. The government's concession on the visit of John Paul II was likewise a brilliant move. By saying that the Pope would be able to visit in June, the regime was both expressing bold confidence that conditions would indeed have normalized by then and, somewhat more subtly, warning Poles that only their failure to behave themselves —for example, on November 10th—could jeopardize that visit.

Moreover, on the very day that Glemp and Jaruzelski issued their statement, the regime announced another blow to the underground: the arrest, in Wroclaw, not only of Frasyniuk's replacement on the TKK, his lieutenant Piotr Bednarz, but also of 11 other high local-organization officials. This left the impression that an organization that had until just recently been Solidarity's most highly developed was now completely devastated—and also, incidentally, the impression that the regime was beginning to play with Solidarity the way a cat plays with a mouse. The handling of the arrest on the TV news was particularly demoralizing. Bednarz was shown handcuffed and being led by police as a microphone was thrust in his face.

"Is your name Piotr Bednarz?"

Silence.

"You are refusing to talk, are you not?"

"That's right."

Then the commentator broke in: "Piotr Bednarz did not want to talk to journalists. Let us remind you, then, what he said in the program broadcast by the so-called Radio Solidarity, which has since been liquidated." And then one could hear, in a pathetically crackling recording, Bednarz saying, "The TKK urges all members of the union and all working people to go on an eight-hour strike on the tenth of November during the first shift." The regime was so self-confident at this point that it was actually broadcasting the appeal.

On Wednesday, November 10th, when virtually nobody struck and only a few thousand people showed up for demonstrations, hardly anyone was surprised. "The closest thing to a demonstration," John Kifner reported from Warsaw in the *New York Times*, "came as people, winking and grinning at one another over their cleverness, joined a line at a bakery selling French bread across the street from the courthouse (where the demonstration had been called). The line soon extended down the long block." The regime had played its hand perfectly.

But then, for a brief interval the next day, November 11th, there was a hitch. If only for a few hours, it suddenly appeared that all the regime's clever planning and orchestration would go for naught. From Moscow came word that at 8:30 on the previous morning—*November 10th*—Leonid Brezhnev had died. And, for all their desolation following the failure of the strike, most Poles must have been simultaneously seized by the thought—no, the absolute conviction—that Brezhnev had died not on just any random day but on the second anniversary of the registration of the independent free trade union Solidarity, and on the very morning of the called-for strike. He had died, many Poles were no doubt certain, of retrospective guilt and prospective terror.

This psychological setback might have been a serious blow to the regime, but Jaruzelski was prepared with a bombshell of his own for that very afternoon: the announcement of the forthcoming release of Lech Walesa. Even this news was handled with shrewd calculation by the authorities. On the one hand, they were throwing the masses a bone following their temperate behavior the day before; Walesa's release, after all, had been one of the public's most fervent demands. On the other hand, the circumstances leading to the release were clouded with a disturbing ambiguity—ambiguity that the regime was only too happy to play upon.

A large part of Walesa's prestige stemmed from his having refused for 11 months to negotiate with Jaruzelski in the absence of his interned advisers and colleagues. Now came word that Walesa had sent a letter to the General on November 8th (that same November 8th), two days *before* the called-for strikes, with a tone that was—well, peculiar: "It seems to me that the time has come to clarify some issues and to work for an agreement. Time was needed for many to understand what can be achieved, and to what extent, on either side. I propose a meeting and a serious discussion of the problems, and I am sure that with good will on both sides a solution can be found." A few months earlier, such a note, without a simultaneous demand for the release and the presence of his colleagues, would have been deemed capitulation. Furthermore, Walesa's prestige had grown with each passing day precisely because he had refused to appear on Polish television—something that the regime devoutly wished he would do. Every day for 11 months, the only thing the regime had been able to offer its TV viewers was *not Lech*. Now came word that he had agreed to a 45-minute interview with Polish TV, that it had been recorded, and that it was going to run that very evening—only, it was suddenly withdrawn at the last minute (maybe because of something he'd said, or because he'd worn a Solidarity pin prominently the entire time). It wasn't a question, though, of what he'd said that bothered some people but, rather, that he'd agreed to the enterprise at all—to talk to *them*.

Suspicions were rising. In silent internment, Lech had been a symbolic hero *for everyone*. Now, released—even before he surfaced in Gdansk after a mysterious two-day absence—he was once again the union leader whose authority had been dwindling even before martial law, who was thought too moderate by some, not intelligent enough by others. This was, of course, the whole point: the regime had apparently decided that at this stage Walesa was less dangerous to them outside than in detention. Once he was outside, they could begin to pelt him with difficult situations, impossible perplexities, like the Pharisees interrogating Christ—only this was no Christ, he was merely human, as everyone would soon see. For the time being, he could get away with his soft truisms ("We must win, since there is no alternative"), but at some point he would stumble. So what if, for the time being, he was still—again—proving extraordinarily careful, prudent, and clever? "We must win," he told the crowd outside his apartment that first night. "Of that there is no doubt. But you must understand that I have always felt that to win doesn't mean to overcome and destroy but to gain friends and allies. . . . I must look around in order to follow a sensible path sensibly. . . . As I said in August, if we understand each other and travel together we'll travel on a common road to victory. I promise you that I won't leave the road and the ideals that we came up with in August."

Fine, but the regime leaders knew that this wasn't August 1980—this was late November 1982, and Frasyniuk was going on trial the very next day (he'd receive a six-year sentence), and how was Walesa going to look, a few miles down the road, with all his friends in prison and himself still out? What was he going to say about *that*? And then, to spice the stew, there was always the possibility of resorting to some good old-fashioned smears. NBC reported within a week or two of Walesa's release that, according to Church contacts, who were trying to muffle the blow by leaking the story, the government had photographs of Walesa before the coup in compromising sexual situations, along with alleged evidence of purported graft. Walesa's was certainly not an enviable position; some would call it no-win. And, for that matter, he wasn't the only one compromised by his release. Where did his sudden liberty leave the leaders of the TKK? If Walesa was merely "the ex-leader of an ex-union"—as Jerzy Urban, the government's spokesman, said when he explained to reporters, as early as November 16th, why there would be *no* meeting between Walesa and Jaruzelski—what were they? Walesa, at least, had been the president of the union, they had merely been lower officials. On what were they now going to base their authority? (He apparently wasn't going to embrace them, and there was no question of their paying him a call.)

On November 27th, the TKK gave its first clue about life after the double whammy of November 10th and 11th. Citing "the completely new political situation" (Walesa's release, the Pope's scheduled visit, the likelihood of an early lifting of martial law), and putting the best possible face on what had obviously been a debacle ("This allows for the hope of at least some type of truce between the authorities and society"), the TKK announced a revocation of its October 20th call for actions in December. From the neo-Kuronesque position of a month earlier they now beat a hasty retreat to somewhere well the other side of Bujak and Kulerski. On the evening news, Jerzy Urban, asked to comment, ostentatiously declined: "The government takes a stand only on important issues, and this is of no significance whatsoever."

Meanwhile, behind the smoke screen of good feeling provided by the releasing of Walesa and the scheduling of the Pope's visit, the regime was moving quickly to ferret out any last centers of overt resistance in anticipation of the lifting of martial law. On November 17th, the psychology department of the University of Warsaw was shut down until further notice, and its dean suspended, because it had held no classes on November 10th. On the same day, the director of the Institute of Psycho-neurology, one of the capital's biggest medical-research establishments, was fired after he refused to give the names of staff members who had staged a five-minute strike there. On December 1st the regime dissolved the independent actors' association, whose members refused to the very end to break the boycott of television they had called the day after the coup. It was officially reported that a few days earlier, on November 29th, Archbishop Glemp, in his new role as head conciliator, had personally intervened, pleading with the actors "to return where you belong," to no effect, and that the government had had no choice but to dissolve the organization that was perpetuating the "antisocial and immoral" boycott.

So the way was prepared for the December 13th lifting of martial law in Poland—an action that most Western newspapers and governments seemed prepared to see as marking a return to a sort of normality, despite the fact that thousands were still in prison, the economy was still a complete joke, most of the principal features of martial law had by now been institutionalized into the civil code, and all that was really going to happen was a transfer of power from a group of Army officers, whom people had grown to hate, to the usual cabal of Communist Party bureaucrats, whom they'd hated all along, only more intensely.

And then even *that* didn't happen. When December 13th rolled around, things didn't go exactly the way everyone had been predicting. It is a measure of the precariousness with which Jaruzelski and his colleagues view their situation that—despite the virtuosity of their handling of the previous three months of challenges; despite the signals they were receiving from Western governments that a lifting of martial law would be looked upon favorably and might well meet with a concomitant lifting of Western trade sanctions; despite all their own signals that they were preparing to lift martial law—when it finally came down to it, they still felt they couldn't. The bill Jaruzelski dictated to the parliament on December 13th stipulated not the *lifting* of martial law (*zniesc*, meaning "to nullify") but, rather, merely its *suspension* (*zawiesic*, which has the connotation of something left hanging that can easily be brought back down).

John Kifner noted that week in the *Times*, "The legislation is studded with catch-all phrases assuring that any part of martial law can be imposed anywhere, at any time, and that the decisions made under martial law will be legally binding." Institutionalizing such martial-law provisions as Article 6, which empowers the authorities to make "any decision necessary to protect public security, the interest of the state and of the citizens," and specifically including provisions that would allow the dismissal of any worker who "sows disorder," the new legislation, if anything, tightened the regime's hold on power; for example, evidence obtained by wiretaps would hereafter be admissible in court—an incursion into civil liberties that the Poles had managed to fight off even during Stalinist times.

There was relatively little indication, as things developed, that military officers were giving way to Party bureaucrats—partly because the Party was still in such disarray that there was no institution to give way to. Several of the remaining internees were now being released, but the most important had already had their internment status shifted to arrest (and hence continued incarceration) or else those arrests now began to occur within days of the supposed releases. In New York, the Committee in Support of Solidarity issued a statement on December 13th claiming that from five to ten thousand people were still under arrest for martial-law violations, even though martial law was being officially suspended.

Furthermore, the regime stepped up its practice of conscripting individual activists, especially workers, into military service, without regard to age, health, or prior military service. For example, one of the new "soldiers" could move only with the help of a walking stick, because of deteriorated leg muscles; another had no fingers; a third, who suffered from stomach ulcers and was unable to eat regular military rations, was accused of thereby "lowering the combat ability of the Polish Armed Forces." All the new recruits were sent to special, remote camps, where they were subjected to indeterminate sentences at gruelling hard labor. The Committee in Support of Solidarity recently cited the existence of 22 such camps, confining as many as 8,000 men; the regime for its part could omit any mention of these prisoners in its own statistics on "martial-law sentences," since, technically, these men were only serving time in the Army.

The only tangible evidence of the suspension of martial law was the discontinuation of the taped *"Rozmowa kontrolowana"* warning ("This call is being controlled") that had preceded every telephone connection in Poland since December 13, 1981—and, what with the new wiretap legislation, few Poles believed that the regime had discontinued the practice of listening in on private conversations whenever it pleased, whether or not it chose to continue announcing the activity in advance.[34] Meanwhile, although Walesa's position semed more precarious than ever (the regime highlighted the incongruity of his freedom by pointedly refraining from releasing all three of the Solidarity officials—Andrzej Gwiazda, Jan Rulewski, and Marian Jurczyk—who had challenged him for the union's top post at the convention back in October 1981), the union president still retained a substantial degree of authority. On December 16th, it was the regime that ended up appearing weak, frightened, and foolish as its representatives abducted Walesa from his home and drove him in circles for eight hours along the ring road surrounding Gdansk, so as to prevent his appearing at a rally commemorating the twelfth anniversary of the Gdansk massacre, the second anniversary of the dedication of the Gdansk monument to those martyrs, and, incidentally, as everyone realized, the first anniversary of the massacre of the nine miners at the Silesian coal mine of Wujek during the first week of martial law. "I felt *dizzy*" is what Walesa said the next morning when Western reporters asked him about the experience, although it was not immediately clear if he was referring to the drive or the history.

In any case, he had managed to outwit the regime by contriving the release of his statement to Western reporters two days earlier (and hence the broadcast of large parts of it back into Poland via the BBC and Radio Free Europe, so that it might easily have been picked up over the radio in that car circling Gdansk). By month's end, the regime was countering with, of all things, a disinformation campaign linking Solidarity with Italy's Red Brigades (perhaps in response to the rising chorus of Western allegations concerning Bulgarian and KGB involvement in the assassination attempt on the Pope and with those same Red Brigades). The deadlock seemed to resume, both sides having merely descended a few notches. I was reminded of something that a Polish professor had told me sadly two months earlier in Warsaw: "It doesn't matter how clever the underground is, it will lose. And it doesn't matter how clever the regime is, it will lose. Poland—Poland always loses."

Archbishop Glemp's behavior throughout martial law, and especially during the autumn of 1982, dismayed many people, both inside and outside the Church. On December 8th, for example, he was confronted by a group of at least 200 Warsaw-area priests in an audience that one participant described as "very stormy, difficult, and painful." The priests were particularly troubled by Glemp's recent call for the actors to end their boycott. "It was an appeal against the people," one priest charged bitterly. "We are under occupation. If [actors] had performed in response to such an appeal under Hitler's occupation, they would have been called collaborators and traitors." Another priest cautiously echoed these feelings: "The question has been asked: Are we not collaborating? The aim seems to be this—the Pope's visit as the price for the Church's consent to liquidate Solidarity. We are deeply concerned about Your Excellency and about Poland."

Part of the problem with Glemp's approach, according to his critics, has been one of tone and emphasis. Although in his sermons Glemp often spoke of the pain and confusion of the nation, he usually avoided assigning blame, or at any rate fudged the question, as if the malaise were some organic illness afflicting the entire nation, and not a persecution carried out by one specific segment of the nation (the representatives, at that, of another nation) against everyone else. By continually counselling Christian equanimity and forbearance, he seemed to many Poles to be denying the validity of their anger and resistance. In one sermon, he commented that the Cross, and not the V sign, was the true token of Polish identity. A few weeks later, in late August, addressing a crowd of several hundred thousand pilgrims gathered at Czestochowa to celebrate the six-hundredth anniversary of the founding of Jasna Gora, the monastery that houses the Black Madonna, he was confronted by a sea of raised arms, each with two fingers spread in conspicuous defiance.

"We must avoid involving the Church in an atmosphere of struggle among social groups," he said on another occasion. "Indeed, the Church has enemies and will continue to have them, but it never wants to destroy them, since the Church embraces its enemy with love and wants to convert him." Whenever Glemp cited the commandment to love one's neighbor or insisted on the need to avoid spilling blood at all costs, he seemed to be aiming his words more at those who were contemplating taking part in a demonstration than at those who were going to be ordering the shooting. By contrast, Bishop Ignacy Tokarczuk, in a homily at Jasna Gora monastery on September 5th, took the same theme and turned it around: "Today, we are addressing ourselves to everyone, including those brothers who beat us. Yes, they are our brothers, whether we like it or not, for they are of the same nation. Brother, do not beat your brother: do not raise your hand against your sister if you wish to continue to belong to the nation! Do not hide behind orders!"

While Glemp kept invoking the example of the Virgin Mary, who endured the agony of her son's crucifixion in deep silence and prayer and who herself could offer the oppressed a solace somehow more profound than any resistance, Tokarczuk instead summoned the example of a young Austrian soldier named Schimek, who during the Second World War had refused to participate in the execution of a Polish Freedom Fighter—a defiance for which he was himself shot by the Nazis. Glemp kept saying that human life was the highest value, and hence confrontation was to be avoided at all costs; Tokarczuk, while starting out from the same premise, seemed to take it a step further, or, rather, to apply it to the actual situation as it existed in Poland in 1982— counselling the Army and the ZOMOS not to follow orders, not to shoot. For Tokarczuk, that was what being Catholic had to do with being Polish. "Beloved," Tokarczuk preached at a different point in the same homily, "we are faced with an obvious principle confirmed by contemporary history even on the world scale: blind and brutal force, be it even the greatest, is incapable of solving anything, it can only complicate the situation further and make it more difficult. Beloved, I do not wish to offend or irritate anyone, but I am speaking on behalf of the Church. Jesus Christ told the Church, 'Go forth and proclaim the truth.' Thus, we have shoemakers, and their task is to make good shoes; we have farmers, and their task is to produce bread; and we have the Church, and its role is to be the teacher of the truth and the defender of the oppressed." Although he was by no means advocating an uprising, he was bearing witness, in a way that Glemp often seemed to shy from.

Tokarczuk spoke of an attempt by workers in Przemysl, the small-town seat of his own bishopric, to hold a peaceful rally the previous week, on August 31st, how workers were moving toward the cathedral when "suddenly the beating started. They were beaten in a horrendous manner. Not infrequently, people who had nothing to do with the peaceful protest were beaten up. One man—this really happened—was on his way back from his allotment. He was in the suburbs and in his bag he had vegetables. He was attacked and beaten up and struck to the ground: and this man, wiping the tears from his eyes called out, 'Not even Hitler would do this. What are you doing to me?' "

"This is how we wish the Primate would speak," the pastor of a small parish just outside Warsaw told me one afternoon. "Like Tokarczuk, who knows that the Church must above all speak and *be* the truth." Like many at the base of the Polish Catholic Church, this pastor was considerably more radical than his leader.

Glemp's behavior, however, arises directly out of the contradictory situation of the Catholic Church in Communist Poland. As the centuries-old expression of Polish national identity in the face of a continuous history of occupations, partitions, and repressions, the Church must both constantly express that national identity and survive to express it another day. Its institutional requirements—those of sustaining some sort of modus vivendi with the authorities—are therefore often at odds with its vocational requirements, which consist in expressing resistance to those same authorities. This basic contradiction has been heightened since the imposition of martial law as the vast network of parish churches has come to constitute the principal social institution ministering to the immediate material needs of the prisoners, those laid off from work, their families, and, for that matter, the community in general. The higher levels of the Church have to shield the lower levels from the anger and retribution of the authorities, so that the parishioners and parish priests can continue their work, but they have to do it in such a way as to avoid completely alienating the very people whose activities they are attempting to shelter. It's an extremely delicate assignment, perhaps an impossible one. At any rate, during my visit to Poland I found few Poles who were satisfied with the job Glemp has been doing.

Criticism of Glemp often takes the form of unfavorable comparisons and wishful fantasies. I must have heard the same sort of comment two dozen times: "If Cardinal Wyszynski were still alive, he wouldn't let them get away with this," or "If Karol Wojtyla were still Archbishop of Krakow, Jaruzelski would think twice before trying that." The Poles prefer to frame a situation that is basically one of internal contradiction as a problem of character—of personal strength and spiritual virility. Glemp, many figure, is simply inadequate to the task, in a way that Wyszynski and the future John Paul II were not. Comparisons of this sort, however, are delusionary—indeed, precisely the sort of delusions that so often cloud clear thinking in Warsaw these days.

Poles today like to forget the fact that at the height of the Gdansk strike in August 1980, well before the government acceded to the key demand for independent free trade unions, Wyszynski himself had urged the workers to give in and return to work. (They even managed to forget that incident as it was happening: John Darnton, the *Times* correspondent who was in the shipyard at the time, tells a story about how an auditorium full of workers listened to the Primate's comments in a broadcast over the state radio and then fell into a nervous, hushed silence, which was only broken when one of the workers stood up and shouted, "There, you see, the Primate is with us!" at which point the hall burst into thunderous applause.) Poles likewise avoid the fact that it was John Paul II who chose Glemp for this assignment, and presumably chose him over others for precisely the qualities of circumspect intelligence, careful meekness, and diplomatic tact which he has been displaying. More recently, people tried desperately to ignore the fact that when, on November 8th, Glemp cut his deal with Jaruzelski he had just returned from ten days of meetings at the Vatican, and that John Paul II must have personally approved, if not dictated, every nuance of the impending agreement.

Furthermore, who is to say that, given the limited possibilities in Poland today, this strategy will not in the long run prove the correct one? In effect, Glemp has decided that this is not the time for an underground mobilization leading to a general insurrection. ("We want to show ourselves strong and mature," Glemp said in a homily at Jasna Gora in September. "But this hunger for heroism is sometimes reminiscent of a desire to don heavy armor when in fact we are weak. The armor is heavy, and we are exhausted, and it is not prudent to don such armor for the fight. We must be aware of the reality of force.") Perhaps he feels that the greatest service the Church can currently provide is to effect the earliest possible return visit by the Pope, with all the boosting of morale and the possibilities for subsequent organizing which such a visit could entail. Perhaps he is right. On the other hand, skeptics will say that the principal concern of the Polish Church has always been its own institutional survival, which it only too conveniently equates with Polish national identity. Anyway, many people will believe in the Pope's June visit when they see it.

It is in any case interesting to note that the very thing that makes a continuous tradition of resistance possible in Poland—the universal attachment to symbols—can be turned against resistance. The election of a Polish Pope, John Paul II, can catalyze a movement. The detention of a single hero, Lech Walesa, can symbolize repression and summon forth defiance. But, by the same token, the regime can fob off the masses with the release of a Walesa or the promise of a visit by the Polish Pope without having to offer *any* substantive changes. Poles do tend to learn from the failures of their rebellions: they tend not to repeat strategic errors. Perhaps they will learn something from this.

Even in October, when the end game had yet to be played out, things were very gloomy, and few of those I spoke with in Warsaw imagined that the November 10th demonstrations, for example, had any chance of success. "Time is on the side of the regime," one screenwriter observed. "At least in the short term, it has all the cards. Increasingly, the underground leadership will be forced into the margins." Over and over, I had the same conversation: each new friend and I would rehearse the various double binds (Solidarity's, the regime's), contemplate the seemingly inexorable downspiralling of the economy, the inability of the government to act, its ability to prevent the workers from acting, and then I would ask "So what do you think will happen?" and the friend would sigh and say, "A miracle." I must have got that answer a dozen times, from college students, writers, engineers, taxi-drivers, other work-ers—sometimes ironic, sometimes in dead earnest, sometimes wistful, sometimes forlorn. A miracle.

One afternoon, I was talking with a village priest, a fairly radical, longtime activist. When our conversation came to its dead end, like all the others, I asked, "So what do you think is going to happen?" He leaned forward and quietly said, "A miracle," rolling his eyes toward Heaven and smiling. I wrote the word down in my notebook and then leaned forward and asked, "Like what?" He leaned even closer, his face now a mixture of anticipation and serenity, and whispered, confidentially, "The Third World War."

As the days passed, this remarkable exchange faded to commonplace. In Poland, it was another answer I heard repeatedly. The Third World War seemed imminent to everyone, and yet imminent in a strangely irreal way. "This is the Soviets' last chance," I was told. "They must fight now or fall hopelessly behind. So they will fight." Several Warsavites looked upon the thaw in Soviet-Chinese relations as an important sign that the Soviets were preparing for a European war. People often talked to me about how things would look in Poland after the war, and I gradually realized what made their tone seem so strange: they all took it for granted that there would be an after-the-war. "Of course, there will be suffering," one student acknowledged. "But those who survive will be better. The evil will have been bled out, and the strong and the good will survive to build an independent Poland." "The *Wojna Narodow*—the War of Nations—is a traditional longing among the Poles," the sociologist Jad-wiga Staniszkis explained to me. "For centuries, we've believed that we would achieve independence through a war fought out between our vari-ous oppressors—one in which they would all lose and we would survive. This was, after all, our experience in the First World War. And many Poles hope for something similar today."

When they envisioned this Third World War, I took to asking, did they imagine nuclear bombs falling on Poland? No, I was repeatedly told. Many of my informants had vague fantasies of tank battles, in the manner of the Second World War, being fought out on the border be-tween East and West Germany, with an accompanying insurrection in Poland. The nuclear threat, a frequent theme of government propa-ganda, was for that very reason largely dismissed. (Before the coup, Kuron had tried to convey the complete rupture of people's faith in government pronouncements by saying, "If atomic bombs were falling right now on Warsaw and the government said so, the people wouldn't believe them.") Those whose thinking about the war did include nuclear weapons tended to exclude them from their prognoses of the fate of Poland. "For once," a former Solidarity activist, a highly intelligent young woman, assured me, "for once, Poland will be given a bye. The missiles will sail over us in both directions, but we will be left unscathed. We won't be targets."

As she was talking, I was reminded of something that Neal Ascherson had told me in his office at the *Observer*, in London, a few weeks earlier: "The Poles have this tremendous millenarian streak in them, and hence they have a certain soft spot for woolly, divinely inspired prophets and prophecy. During the Gdansk strike in August 1980, for instance, a smudgy typescript of the recent vision of a Baltic Coast prophet was making the rounds. People would huddle together, pore it over, and talk it up. Over several dense pages of wildly florid language, much of it derived from the Book of Revelation, this man had detailed a prophecy that included Leviathan and Mog and the Four Horsemen and a global nuclear war, the heat from which was going to melt the ice caps, drowning Europe in the rising seas—and Poland, Poland alone, was going to emerge unflooded to fulfill its destiny as the breadbasket for the survivors on the European archipelago."

Well, neither of us much expected the ice caps to melt anytime soon, but we were both sure that if they ever did, it would certainly not be low, flat Poland that would survive unflooded. Similarly—and this is what I told my activist friend—I don't put much stock in scenarios of limited nuclear war, but if there ever is one, I suspect that it will be limited to the two Germanys and Poland: to the scene, that is, of those tank battles and the low, flat routes of resupply.[35]

"Perhaps you're right," she concluded, sighing. "But it's strange. Things are so bad that people here are almost longing for it."[36]

Still, all these millenarian considerations aside, there *is* something metaphysical about the movement of history in Poland. If the word "miracle" rankles, the word "moment" is nevertheless unavoidable. People in Poland are always waiting for the Right Moment. "This just wasn't the right moment," a shipworker said bitterly, leaving the Gdansk shipyard after the collapse of the two-day strike last October. Unless the moment is right, extraordinary people seem doomed to fail; when the moment is right, it seems, ordinary people can't help excelling. Or, rather, ordinary people become imbued with extraordinary qualities—courage, character, and *solidarity*. It's not the sort of thing that can be precisely calibrated in advance, the way a given effect can be predicted as the outcome of a convergence of necessary causes. There were, for example, countless economic, sociological, and historical factors that contributed to the upsurge of Solidarity in August of 1980, and in retrospect we can catalogue many of them—many were the result of years of dogged preparation and planning by seemingly marginal activists, and it would not have happened without that prior work—but anyone who was there will tell you there was something more: the Moment was Right.

No matter how much and how effectively the regime bears down on the mass of workers in Poland, how well it undermines and confounds their sense of dignity and cohesion, the Moment is somehow always there, in the mode of the immediately potential. "Sometimes we forget how close engagement is to exhaustion," a Polish friend told me one afternoon, rousing himself from the gloom into which our conversation had thrown him. "It's a mistake to imagine that a beaten-down and apparently defeated class can't *suddenly* emerge defiant and fierce, with a fierceness brought on by precisely the things that were making it exhausted."

In an article in the September-October 1981 issue of *Encounter*, the Polish sociologist Jan Rozinski (writing under the pseudonym Casimir Garnysz) dubbed the mass of Solidarity, the majority of its ten million onetime dues-paying members, "the Golem." He wrote:

> As in all movements and revolutions, the mass [of Polish workers] drifts and then, when mobilized, pushes forward with all its might. . . . Today it listens to clandestine Solidarity radio programs when notified about them, blinks its lights on and off [in windows] when asked to do so, reads the underground press, and takes part in street demonstrations when informed of time and place—or, more likely, watches them pass from the sidewalk, cautiously flashing a V-sign. . . . Strongly attached to religious and patriotic symbols, the Golem group, whose nationalist sentiments run very deep and which is much less given to cool analysis, appears more inclined toward romanticism. This inclination, however, erupts only at times of mass mobilization and is simultaneously checked by down-to-earth practicality. Occasionally frightened by its own potential might, this group wants peace and security at the same time it wants to struggle for change, a struggle which is risky and threatening to day-to-day existence, however pitiful it might be. The massive show of force by General Jaruzelski [and his colleagues] has checked the Golem group, but cannot control it for long. . . . At the first opportunity they will close factories and offices and rejoin the active struggle.

Another way of defining the Moment is the sudden, simultaneous perception of opportunity by everyone in society. For a few hours on October 11th, it seemed that the Moment was at hand. Furious over the delegalization of Solidarity a few days earlier, the shipyard workers in Gdansk, who had always thought of the union as somehow especially theirs, spontaneously went on strike. All over Poland, people looked to Gdansk. (Poles today identify the Moment with the behavior of the workers at the large enterprises—the shipyards along the Baltic Coast, the steel mills outside Warsaw and Krakow, the coal mines in Silesia, the tractor works at Ursus. "What I think on one day or another is finally almost irrelevant," a worker in Warsaw's relatively small, thousand-man central-heating plant told me one evening. "It's what the workers at the big factories think—what they do. We can only follow their lead.") But October 1982 in Gdansk proved an aborted replay of August 1980. Back in August, too, the young workers led the walkout, urging their older colleagues on. Then, too, the older workers had been on the verge of buckling—indeed, had buckled a few days into the strike and were calling it off. In August, the Moment did not occur on the 14th, the day the occupation-strike began, but, rather, on the 16th, the day the younger workers persuaded the older ones to stick it out—not to settle for light-weight concessions, such as pay raises, but to hold out for an independent, self-governing trade union. *That* is the moment that did not recur on October 11th.

But no one doubts that it will recur at some point—if not next year, then two, five, ten years hence. If for no other reason, this seems likely because of the by now compelling fact of its cyclical recurrence through-out postwar Polish history—1944, 1956, 1968, 1970, 1976, 1980. Referring to this sort of certainty, Rozinski noted in *Encounter*, "The generals and the Party moderates know this, just as they probably know how little they have to offer a resentful people whose initiative and hopes they are attempting to crush."

With this last phrase, Rozinski touches on the phantom prospect of "Kadarization." The optimists in the current regime are hoping that they will be able to match the record of Janos Kadar in Hungary. Following the brutal suppression of that country's 1956 uprising, Kadar, the new Communist Party leader, was able to move quickly, deploying increasingly innovative market mechanisms to raise the standard of living and the quality of life for average Hungarians. Even apart from the fact that Hungary's economy has itself begun to stagnate recently—a development that throws some doubt on the ongoing quiescence of the Hungarian body politic—Jaruzelski has little chance of emulating Kadar's achievement in Poland. To begin with, Kadarization would require decentralization of a kind that would threaten the only civilian con-stituency Jaruzelski has left—the *nomenklatura*, the middle-level ap-paratchiks and bureaucrats, who, having just fended off the barbarians attacking from below, are not about to succumb to any creative tinkering by the precarious generals above. Jaruzelski relied on the vested interests of this surprisingly large group to buttress his coup; they still have the power to stage a "management strike" if those interests are threatened, and to destabilize things so badly that Jaruzelski would fall.

The generals can't have it both ways—a centralized monopoly of power and a decentralized liberalization of the economy. (What would happen if, for instance, one enlightened administrator at a decentralized factory started giving his workers more say in their own affairs, and then the fellows at the next factory started demanding the same rights?) Besides,

Poland in 1982 is not Hungary in 1956. For one thing, the world in 1982, mired in deep recession and tending, possibly, toward something even worse, is not the world of 1956, well into the boom of reconstruction, industrialization, and trade expansion which followed the Second World War. And, of course, Poland's current internal economy makes everyone else's look positively bullish. "Face it," I was told by a Western diplomat. "By every conceivable index, this country is bankrupt. That means: Shut the lights, close the doors, board the windows, *everybody go home*. Now, that doesn't happen, partly because we don't know how that should happen—what you do if a whole country, and especially an industrialized country, goes bankrupt. But I'll tell you one thing: you don't just turn things around any time soon." Poland's sole short-term chance for economic improvement—increased production and export, for hard currency, of Silesian coal—has run up against the world oil glut and a consequent tailspin in coal prices. (The regime expends tremendous authority to get the angry miners to work Saturdays, and thereby achieves the predictable increase in coal production, but it all goes for naught: the expected rise in hard-currency revenues is cancelled by the fall in prices.) As Aleksander Smolar observed in Paris, "all that Jaruzelski can offer the Poles is Churchill's 'blood, toil, tears, and sweat,' without his horizon of hope and eventual triumph."

The historian in Warsaw who had recently been released from internment phrased it this way: "After 1956, Kadar basically said to the Hungarians, 'Keep out of politics and I'll give you bread and butter.' But in Poland today where is the bread and where is the butter? Jaruzelski has barely enough bread and butter to feed the police, the Army, and the miners."

A Warsaw academician told me dispiritedly, "What the delegalization of the union was about was taking all hope away, and you can't take hope away from people when it's all they have and you have nothing else to offer."

"The deep underlying economic and social causes which generated Solidarity" are still there, Rozinski concluded in his *Encounter* article. "These causes are as irremovable as the causes of the bourgeois revolutions in Europe a few centuries earlier."

And so Poland moves inexorably toward its next Moment. Perhaps it will erupt this time in the mining region. Although the miners are among the best-paid industrial workers in Poland, their working conditions have become atrocious, especially since the reimposition of the six-day week. Miners complain that there is insufficient time now to repair faulty equipment or to reinforce sagging mine shafts. On June 18, 1982, ten miners were killed in an explosion at the Dymitrow mine, in Bytom, Silesia. Less than a month later, on July 8th, at the same mine, two more died in another accident; on October 6th, six more died; and then, on November 28th, still at the same mine, eighteen miners were killed and ten seriously wounded. Thirty-six deaths in one mine in four separate accidents in less than six months—and that, according to official statistics.

Following the June 18th accident, a local underground newsletter related what happened: "The roof fell. The sequence of events was as follows: A group of miners engaged in the construction of a ventilation shaft noted that the percentage of methane was at least half again as high as the permitted norm, threatening an explosion. The measurement was reported to the military commissar, Colonel Plucinski, who, however, refused permission to suspend work and threatened those who abandoned work with a court-martial. [All the Silesian mines have been militarized.] The miners had no choice but to hope for a bit of luck. The explosion followed." After that first accident, experts estimated that the mine should have been closed for safety reasons at least six months earlier, but the commissars, under tremendous pressure to produce coal for hard-currency export, ignored advice that this be done. The *Economist* recently reported that, according to official statistics, 65 miners died in Polish mines during the first quarter of 1982 alone.

Or perhaps the Moment will occur as an inadvertent or semiadvertent side effect of squabbling among the ruling cadres. There are hard-liners inside the bureaucracy and the higher Party apparatus who are fed up with Jaruzelski's relatively "moderate" line and, perversely, are encouraging the sort of confrontation that might sweep him from, and them into, power. Tadeusz Grabski, the former Party chief of Konin province and a former Politburo member, who is now not even a member of the Central Committee, circulated a poison-pen letter prior to a recent meeting of the current Central Committee. As quoted in London's *Uncensored Poland News Bulletin*, the letter began "What ever happened to the hopes we had for martial law?" and continued, "The forces of the counter-revolution have not been defeated. On the contrary, they have succeeded in forming powerful underground structures capable of threatening the security of the state. The Party has not been reconstructed. On the contrary, it has sunk into a deep coma and is suffering progressive atrophy. . . . The majority have lost their sense of being members of a Marxist-Leninist party."

In London, Neal Ascherson described for me the way "some of these guys are actually hoping for a general strike, trying to provoke one, as a way of eventually taking power themselves."

Why, I asked, would *anyone* want to become leader of contemporary Poland?

Ascherson paused for a moment, considering the riddle, and then smiled and said, "Well, I mean, there you have it, don't you? *Ambition pure.*"

At any rate, one of these clever conspirators may actually get his wish

—a rebellion—although it is by no means clear that once it starts he'll also get his way.

Or perhaps the Moment will erupt at some point when the Soviets seem bogged down elsewhere: in a border war with China; during a new insurrection in Rumania or Czechoslovakia or in the Ukraine; with labor troubles of their own; or during an upsurge of tensions along the frontier between the two Germanies. (Western experts who shudder at the high numbers of Warsaw Pact tanks in Eastern Europe, extrapolating from these concentrations the imminent threat of a Soviet invasion of West Germany, fail to realize that at the first hint of such an invasion most of the Polish nation would almost certainly launch a rearguard insurrection of its own—one that would start out with the destruction of all the rail links crucial to resupply.)

Assuming that one way or another, at one time or another, things do start up again, it's difficult to imagine how the Moment will play itself out. One asks the people of Warsaw about it ("So what will happen, what will it be like?"), and if their fantasies about a Third World War are fluky and odd and not quite tethered, their forebodings about the next uprising are dark and pervasive and, possibly, more realistically grounded.

"It's frightening to think where the next round of strikes will lead," the former Solidarity activist told me after we had moved on from our consideration of nuclear war. "Because it sure as hell won't lead to the signing of any agreements. Nobody's ever going to be satisfied with that again—especially after October 8th, with the parliament's bill delegalizing Solidarity. Before that, when Solidarity was merely under suspension, one could imagine a strike with suspension of the suspension as its principal demand. But not anymore. What's going to happen when there's a general strike and we once again feel our strength? We will strike for revocation of that bill, of course, but we will also be demanding revocation of the parliament that passed it and of the government that broke its signed word. In other words, our first demand will be for free elections. And with that kind of demand, right away you're in pretty deep. Very deep." She paused and shook her head slowly. "There's such a lot of hate now. Before, during Gierek's time, there was contempt for the Party, or ridicule." (I was reminded of a joke I'd heard a few times back in 1981: In Poland today, a person can be honest, or intelligent, or a member of the Communist Party—in fact, *any two*, just not all three at the same time.) "But now it's hate. Each time they humiliate us, each time they foil a demonstration, parade an arrested leader before their vile cameras, or leave another murdered victim, it leaves a legacy of hate, and something new—an itching for revenge."

On August 31st, in the copper-mining town of Lubin, in southwest Poland, during demonstrations commemorating the second anniversary of the triumph at Gdansk, the ZOMOS opened fire, killing three people.

The September 14th issue of that region's underground bulletin, *Solidarnosc Zaglebia Miedziowego,* included eyewitness accounts of the shooting. One of them read, "Our children were on their way to school. T⁻ saw, they heard, they know. This knowledge is forever. The town is of people, and most of them were at the scene of the carnage."

"Next time, people will be much less willing to compromise," the historian who had recently been released from internment, a soft-spoken, thoughtful man, told me. "Things will be much more dangerous. What struck everyone last time was that the revolution avoided *even one drop of blood.* This instinctive political restraint will be much less probable. And here is why I am a pessimist: *nobody* will be able to control the crowd. In this sense, we live under a volcano. Do you know the phrase 'the fire next time'?"

"Delegalization was a mistake," a distinguished academician told me one afternoon as we sat in a small park. "But it was one that they had to make. By 'they' I mean the middle apparatus—Milovan Djilas is right, they are a 'new class.' They were frightened by the 16 months of Solidarity, and humiliated. And they will never again deal with Solidarity —or Solidarity with them. That is the collision ahead." He took his two fists and slowly brought them together in a grinding motion and then shrugged and looked at me sadly.

A few days later, I was standing at a window on the tenth floor of one of the many mass-produced, gray-flanked apartment buildings that dot the suburbs of Warsaw. I was talking with Roman Laba, the American Fulbright scholar who had been in Poland for some time. From that small, cramped apartment we could look out upon several similar buildings and, between them, in their shadows, a profusion of modest single-family houses with little gardens and high fences—the dwelling places, in most cases, of the "new class," the middle-level bureaucrats. "The apparatchiks worry about the fire next time, it worries them silly," Laba said. "They know that when the time comes Jaruzelski and Rakowski and Urban and Grabski will board helicopters and hightail it to Moscow, and they'll be left here, in their little villas, surrounded by these apartment buildings full of seething workers."

His words reminded me of "Those Men, So Powerful," a poem that the fine young Polish writer Stanislaw Baranczak, now an émigré professor at Harvard, wrote in the early seventies. It begins (in the translation of Magnus Jan Krynski and Robert Macguire):

> *Those men, so powerful, always shown*
> *somewhat from below by crouching cameramen, who lift*
> *a heavy foot to crush me, no, to climb*
> *the steps of the plane, who raise a hand*
> *to strike me, no, to greet the crowds*
> *obediently waving little flags, those men who sign*

my death warrant, no, just a trade
agreement which is promptly dried by a servile blotter . . .

And it concludes, a stanza later:

always
you were so afraid of them,
you were so small
compared to them, who always stood above
you, on steps, rostrums, platforms,
and yet it is enough for just one instant to stop
being afraid, or let's say
begin being afraid a little less,
to become convinced that they are the ones,
that they are the ones who are most afraid.

"There will be hangings," another writer told me, almost matter-of-factly. "One of the most popular parlor games in town these days consists of trying to come up with a list of the first ten to go. The list changes from week to week, although Urban has had a lock on the top slot for sometime now. People suspected of being informers or secret police, people who have been ruining the lives of our friends and neighbors—they're going to be in a lot of trouble."

Of course, any uprising on the border of the Soviet Union which descended into mass hangings of local Communist Party officials would itself be in a lot of trouble very quickly. Kuron wrote in his first prison article, "The dying of the Empire has begun. But it is still capable of a bloody settling of accounts with Poland." And this is a prospect that obsesses the underground leaders of Solidarity, Church figures (especially Glemp), and, for that matter, to varying degrees at various times, just about everyone in the society. This is why, despite continual rebuffs, the underground continues to plead for negotiations with the regime, for compromise and conciliation. And it accounts for the strange double message that pervades most of Solidarity's underground literature these days—the language of battle laced with the language of compromise. The more the government ignores the underground's call for conciliation, the more militant the underground's response becomes, and, the implications of such militancy being so frightening, the more urgent becomes its simultaneous pleading for conciliation.

"The dramatic alternatives with which this strange war began are still open," Jacek Kuron wrote in September 1982, in "What Next," his most recent manifesto from prison. "Either it will be possible to create the conditions in which the people will feel that they have a say in the running of the country or there will be a bloodbath." After pointing out that up to this time Poland has been "saved from civil war by the trust the society puts in Solidarity," which "works like a parachute," he goes on to suggest that there are only two ways left in which "the society could become a partner in running the country." In the first version, which he calls Variant A, "the authorities wholly or in part agree to enter into a genuine agreement with the society, represented by organizations independent of the Party and the state—that is, first and foremost, Solidarity." Kuron goes on to enumerate the various elements of such an agreement. Since that scenario seems progressively less likely, the second version, Variant B, becomes a sort of last hope: "The authorities will provoke a social outburst which will sweep them away. There would still be a chance to avoid Soviet intervention, provided all the institutions that enjoy social trust quickly take responsibility for the situation. They must also immediately form a national government with the people who have authority in the society and who at the same time will not be regarded by Moscow as troublemakers. The government should at once declare its intention of respecting the Polish national alliance with the Soviet Union, and begin to carry out the tasks described in Variant A."

Kuron is not alone in thinking along these lines today. One writer, a respected political theorist, put it this way: "There is an old Polish story about a priest who is dying, and they ask him if he would like another priest to come attend him in his final hours. 'No,' he replies. 'Why should I talk with a servant when soon I shall be speaking with the Lord?' Next time, assuming we can keep the initial uprising from immediately descending into anarchy, we won't even bother dealing with the servants— the Polish government or local Communist Party officials. We will demand to speak directly with the Lord. And—who knows?—perhaps the Russians *will* come and talk. Certainly they don't want to have to come in here with their Army—they know how horrible that would be for them as well as for us." That, it occurs to me, is also one of the things 1980 and 1981 were all about.

The longer the situation persists in this "precarious negative equilibrium," as Aleksander Smolar calls it, the more furious the Polish people become, the more thirsty for revenge, and yet, also, the more time they have to think about how horrible the consequences would be if they ever did descend into that kind of bloodbath—what the underground bulletin in Wroclaw recently referred to as "the Salvadorization of Poland." It's hard to say whom time is playing for in Poland these days: it may yet turn out that its passage has been allowing a further deepening of the political maturity and the sophistication of an already very wise and long-suffering society.

"I will surely be silenced for some time to come," Adam Michnik wrote in concluding an early article he smuggled out of Bialoleka prison, "and that is why I would like to greet my friends, especially those being sought by and struggling against the regime, and wish them enough courage and strength to walk across the empty darkness between despair and hope, and enough patience to learn the difficult art of forgiving."

June 1983: Pope Paul II blesses the throngs gathered at the Jasna Gora monastery in Czestochowa. Despite over a year and a half of martial law, Solidarity banners and fingers raised in the V-sign still greet him at every stop on his eight-day pilgrimage. (*UPI*)

EPILOGUE

———— + + ————

September 1983

"PLEASE ABANDON HOPE," the voice of the police commander intones in a recent poem by the émigré Stanislaw Baranczak. "I want this square, this brain, this country cleared of hope, so it will be pure as a tear."

And yet, the situation in Poland today, almost a year since my last report, remains cloudy grey: the Polish tear is anything but clear. Late this past May, speaking before the long-delayed meeting of the Party Central Committee, General Jaruzelski boasted that "The party is now better prepared to carry out its tasks and much stronger than a year ago." But the back-up report from the general's governing politburo "obliquely conceded," in the words of the *New York Time*'s correspondent John Kifner, "that the party was still having trouble winning the support of, among others, workers, peasants, intellectuals, and young people" (June 1, 1983). Who else, one wondered, was there?

The regime had not, for example, been able to undermine the intelligentsia's persistent identification with the aspirations of the workers; as if to underscore this failure, the authorities were having to dismantle virtually all of the country's professional organizations—banishing the actors' association, purging the filmmakers', abolishing the journalists' and artists' and writers'. After more than eighteen months the authorities had yet to convert a single major sector of society, let alone any significant public figures. Everywhere, seemingly, they were being met with a sullen, defiant silence.

Worse yet, the economy, although stabilized, remained a hopeless mess. "Grave, but stable," went the joke: "Yes, dead." Of all the debtor nations, the *Washington Post* reported on May 15, 1983, in a survey of the international debt crisis, "Poland has the worst prospects for regaining solvency." Lack of spare parts, pervasive shortages, impossibility of tapping into fresh lines of credit—nothing had changed. Managers seemed paralyzed, unable to determine at any given moment how long any newly announced policy scheme would last, hence unable to chart long-term plans. The central authorities, for their part, most of their attention focussed on their ongoing skirmishes with the opposition, were unable to project leadership in the area; and the stratagems of repression themselves were often undermining recovery. I heard a story about one of the most prestigious scientific research institutes in Warsaw. The faculty consists of approximately 50 staff members, one of whom, a renowned physicist, had been interned for most of the first year of martial law. After he was released, he reported back for work, only to be informed he'd been fired. A petition protesting the firing was drawn up and quickly signed by 47 of the institute's staffers. The only three people who declined to sign were two janitors and one nondescript lab associate who had no professional standing whatsoever. A few weeks later, the director of the institute was demoted, for allowing the petition to get started, and two of the senior scientists, chosen apparently at random, were fired. The man appointed to be the new director, of course, turned out to be the one nondescript lab associate who hadn't signed the petition. This sort of charade was being repeated at enterprises throughout the country. It was an effective way of spreading fear, but no way to get the economy moving once again.

Despite the inordinate amount of the regime's efforts being directed into propaganda, its record even there was at best mixed, careening bizarrely from the savvy to the hapless. Of the latter variety, one particular preposterous example proved to be the fiasco of the Ghetto Memorial ceremonies. Certain elements in the regime hoped to take advantage of the fact that April 1983 would mark the fortieth anniversary of the heroic, doomed Uprising of Warsaw's Jewish Ghetto against the Nazis. Expecting to defuse prior imputations of anti-Semitism and at the same time to garner a certain amount of de facto recognition from at least some sectors in the West, the regime sent out thousands of invitations for a week of major ceremonial functions. Dr. Marek Edelman, a prominent cardiologist from Lodz who is the last surviving leader of the Ghetto Uprising still living in Poland, pointedly declined to join the official honorary committee. Early in February, in one of the first indications that things might not go as the authorities were hoping, Dr. Edelman released an open letter, saying, "Forty years ago we fought not only for our lives. We fought for life in dignity and freedom. To celebrate our anniversary here where social life is dominated throughout by humiliation and coercion would be to deny our fight. It would mean participating in something contrary to its ideals. It would be an act of cynicism and contempt. I shall not participate in such arrangements or accept the participation of others, regardless of where they come from and what they represent" (*Uncensored Poland News Bulletin*, March 25, 1983, p, 32).

Nevertheless, 1200 Jews from Western Europe, the United States, and Israel did decide to attend, feeling perhaps that the significance of the occasion far transcended the momentary vicissitudes of intra-Polish politics. (The *UPNB*, commenting on the incongruity of their decision, pointed out that "Very many prominent Polish leaders trace the beginning of their careers, or at least important turning points, to the anti-Semitic purges of March 1968. We would only remind our readers that several weeks after the March 1968 events the very same Polish authorities responsible for the anti-Semitic campaign organized commemorations of the twenty-fifth anniversary of the Warsaw Ghetto Uprising." May 6, 1983, p. 19.) On the 17th of April, two days before the beginning of the official ceremonies, Solidarity held its own rally at the Ghetto Monument, drawing a crowd of several hundred. A letter from Dr. Edelman was read. He was unable to attend personally since his home in Lodz had been surrounded by state security agents who'd felt it necessary, in their words, "to protect the doctor from danger." Janusz Onyszkewicz, the former national spokesman for Solidarity who'd only been released from internment four months earlier, also delivered a stirring address, at the end of which he was detained and slapped back into prison. The next day, the 18th, Lech Walesa left Gdansk by car headed for Warsaw where he intended to lay a wreath at the Ghetto Memorial; instead he was stopped by police en route, questioned for nine hours, and then sent back to Gdansk.

The next day, at the official ceremonies, the 1200 foreign Jews were scandalized when a group of PLO representatives joined the ceremonial march and laid their own wreath at the monument, pointedly comparing the situation of the besieged Jews in Warsaw in 1943 to that of their own confederates in Beirut the previous summer. Things weren't helped at all later in the day when General Jaruzelski at an intimate cocktail party was heard to offer a toast in which he said he hoped his guests had found the hospitality in Warsaw to their liking, that they should now be able to go home and tell everyone that there was indeed no anti-Semitism in Poland, adding that he particularly hoped his American

Jewish guests would now feel it appropriate to go back and persuade the bankers and government officials in their country, over whom, as everyone knew, they exercised so much influence, that . . . and so forth. During the next few days most of the Israelis and the delegates from the World Jewish Congress cut short their stays and departed in protest. So much for that propaganda coup.

Meanwhile, for all its success during the previous November in upending the TKK's call for a general strike, the regime had clearly failed in its attempts to follow through with a thorough eradication of the underground. On the contrary, the TKK appeared to have rebounded nicely from its humiliation. "It was precisely November 10th that became a turning point for the union," Zbigniew Bujak, the Warsaw representative of the TKK told an interviewer in the May 26 issue of the underground journal *Tygodnik Mazowsze*. "It became clear that the idea of organizing a general strike could not succeed. People realized that in our situation it was a daydream to attempt to build a structure that could initiate and conduct such a strike. . . . Those who are active today have a better sense of reality. They have matured. Working with them is much easier and more effective; there are fewer conflicts now."

The regime was able to announce almost daily seizures of printing equipment or radio transmitters, but this didn't seem to matter: underground journalism was one of the few enterprises in the country whose productivity seemed to be evincing a ceaseless upward curve. Meanwhile, on December 31, 1982, on the very night of the suspension of martial law, the electronic gremlins of the underground were able to pull off one of their sweetest stunts, broadcasting buoyant messages of solidarity right into the cells of the political prisoners in Warsaw's most heavily secured detention center from two huge loudspeakers atop an apartment building across the street! The fact that significant portions of the underground had managed to stay hidden for over a year and a half was in itself significant. "After the Second World War," Bujak pointed out in his interview, "in similar conditions, attempts to create an effective conspiracy failed. Prior to December 1981, hiding meant a tunnel with no exit. It entered nobody's mind to go into the underground. Today, if following a setback, one has a choice of going into prison or going into hiding, the choice is simple. This is a great achievement of the last year and a half. Now, everyone who wants to be active and cannot do it aboveground has the possibility of hiding, and furthermore, he knows it can be done and knows how to do it. This is a fact that now hangs over the authorities."

Relatively few of the regime's opponents spent all of their time underground. But those few who did shone out as a continuous symbol for everybody else. Furthermore, many people enjoyed a quasi-open existence somewhere in between, reporting to work, for example, living at home, but carrying out errands on the side, setting up Flying University classes, distributing aid to families of prisoners, collecting dues, and so forth. (According to the May 7, 1983 issue of *The Economist*, "About 10–15% of Solidarity's members—about 40% in the larger factories—apparently still pay their union dues." According to Andy Tymowski, writing in *Poland Watch #3*, the Gdansk Region Coordinating Commission's recent annual accounting statement for the calendar year 1982 claimed dues collections of 6.1 million zlotys, of which 2.5 million were paid out as benefits to those arrested or fired, and their families, including 50,000 zlotys for vacations for the children of internees; 2.25 million went for publication expenses; and only 250,000 zlotys were lost due to the confiscation of supplies.)

The most prominent figure in the Polish opposition spent virtually none of his time underground. Lech Walesa utterly dashed the expectations of the authorities who were convinced last November that they were releasing him into a hopelessly no-win situation. The man has not made a single wrong move. His public utterances blend a calm, sage sense of perspective with a biting, ironic tone of defiance; and his public actions since his release show that he has in no way lost his uncanny sense of political timing and possibility. For the first several months following his release, he projected a moderate line in his conversations with Western reporters, saying that he agreed with the TKK but seldom actually resorting to their stronger rhetoric. Just when the gap between the two approaches was beginning to seem problematic, in mid-April 1983, Walesa suddenly disappeared from view, reappearing a few days later to announce that he'd just held a series of secret coordinating meetings with the TKK itself! The single-most-watched man in Eastern Europe, in a state in the very grip of martial law, manages to elude his surveillants and hold a colloquy with the single-most-sought-after group of gentlemen in the entire country, and then has the nerve to reemerge, bragging about it! The authorities were reduced to a Keystone frazzle. Finally, partly to be able to keep closer tabs on him, they acceded to his demand that he be allowed to resume work in the Gdansk shipyard (a prospect they naturally weren't too crazy about).

Within weeks of his renewed employment, Walesa announced that he was exhausted and would be taking a vacation during the summer. The regime offered him four weeks in August, delighted that they'd be rid of him during the coming strike-anniversary season. Walesa declined, saying he'd rather take the four weeks in July. When the authorities said No, he went ahead anyway, returning to work on August 1st, wearing a Solidarnosc T-shirt. The regime, fretful of the consequences of firing him at the very outset of the anniversary month (and aware that he'd threatened, if fired, to actually go and join the underground) capitulated to his whimsical challenge. "He is just the former leader of a former trade union; he is a nobody, nothing special," Jerzy Urban, the government spokesman, kept insisting whenever Western reporters would bring up the subject. And yet it was Walesa himself who exposed the absurdity of Urban's refrain in an August interview with the Italian weekly *Gente*. When he had been a leader of a powerful union, he said, the authorities had treated him as a common man. Now the authorities kept insisting he was a common man but did not treat him like one. He pointed out that he was being followed constantly, even to the lavatories in the shipyard. The claim that this was done for his own protection he dismissed by pointing out that the security agents only checked the identity papers of people who came to see him *after* the meetings had taken place. He then related an amusing incident in which the manager of the shipyard had chased away the security agents assigned to shadow him, thinking that they were "undesirable elements" attempting to make contact (*UPNB,* August 19, 1983, p.18). All the while Walesa maintained his firm insistence that eventually the regime would have to resume the dialogue. "Sooner or later, they will have to talk to us," he affirmed one day. "If we're no longer here, they'll talk to our children."

And yet, for all that, these few glimmers of continuing defiance cannot be merged to form anything resembling a bright picture. True, the regime has failed to obliterate all opposition: the TKK persists, certain elements of an underground society have been consolidated, Walesa continues to befuddle the authorities. They have not been able to achieve victory, "clear as a tear." But neither has the underground been able to sustain any clear sense of hope. The failure of November 1982, for all its silver lining, still cast a dark, dark shadow over the Polish people—especially during the first six months of 1983. I sensed this in everyone I spoke with. For one thing, there were increasing numbers of people to speak with, émigrés arriving in New York who'd at one time been middle-level activists in the union and who had finally given up (the regime offered them an out, and despite terrible feelings of guilt, they took it). Furthermore, there was the growing incidence of internal emigration which showed through much of the correspondence I was receiving. People were retreating, for the time being at least, into their private concerns. This was partly because public space had become so poisoned—suspicions of informers and treachery abounded, and everyday corruption was growing exponentially. But it was also because people were coming to realize— and this realization perhaps did not fully dawn until the November debacle—that any resurgence of Solidarity was going to be a question of years, maybe even of decades, certainly not of months. Oddly enough, this phenomenon of internal emigration was perhaps most clearly revealed in a renewed baby boom. (From June 1982 through June 1983, according to a U.S. Census Bureau report abstracted in the August 31st *San Francisco Chronicle,* Poland showed both the highest total and the highest rate of population growth of any of the major countries in

Europe. West Germany at 61.5 million was down 95,000. Italy at 56.3 million was up 79,000. Britain at 56 million was up 2,000. France at 54.6 million was up 251,000. Spain at 38.2 million was up 216,000. And Poland, at 36.5 million, was up 329,000!) But this was no longer the baby boom of joy and expectation which had immediately preceded the upsurge of Solidarity and then persisted through the union's first six months. Rather, it was a baby boom of spiritual deflation. "I am having a baby now," one correspondent wrote me, "because this is the only sphere in which I can still find any meaning in the world. Nowhere else any longer can I sense that what I do or feel could make a difference." Yet children themselves, in other letters, seemed sources of despair. "At first," wrote another friend in a letter smuggled past the censors, "watching the children playing ZOMOS was somewhat heartening: you knew the spirit had been passed on. But months have passed and they don't stop. They play state-of-war and standing-in-line and you realize with horror that this is the only childhood they are ever going to have." It's one thing, furthermore, to see the country's economic collapse as a factor guaranteeing the regime's continuing inability to gain the confidence of the people. But it's another to realize that this-is-it, this is the economy you and your children are going to have to be living with for the next decade at least. And that this gutted, grey shell of a cultural life —for slowly the regime has been asphyxiating the once vital, independent enterprises of film, theater, art, and literature, and the underground can only take up so much of the slack—this is the kind of culture you'll be living with for years. . . .

People during the first half of 1983 hadn't lost hope completely, but they'd completely lost the fantasy of immediate hope.

It was against this backdrop that the Pope's promised June visit took on growing significance. In its issue of April 7, 1983, the Warsaw underground weekly *Tygodnik Mazowsze* published an article entitled "Waiting for the Pope" whose author concluded with the hope that John Paul II's 1983 visit would help "enable people to break through the barrier of despair, just as his 1979 visit broke through the barrier of fear" (*UPNB*, May 6, 1983, p. 18). And it was clearly with this motive at least partly in mind that the Pope left the Vatican on June 16th for his eight-day pilgrimage. On the eve of the trip, he commented on how the journey was to take place "at this sublime and difficult moment for my homeland." (Maybe you'd have to be Polish, maybe you'd have to be a Polish pope, to even consider using that word "sublime" in this historical context!)

The trip included public masses conducted before huge throngs in Warsaw, Czestochowa (the site of the Jasna Gora monastery whose six-hundredth anniversary in 1982 was the ostensible occasion for this slightly delayed pilgrimage), Poznan, Wroclaw, Katowice, and Krakow. In Warsaw the Pope shared a podium with General Jaruzelski during greeting ceremonies which were broadcast live throughout the country. In Krakow, the two held a surprise second meeting at the end of the trip. In between, the Pope beatified three historic Polish Church figures, bringing them a step closer to canonization and sainthood. In Nowa Huta, the onetime model socialist (*i.e.*, atheist) steeltown outside Krakow, the Pope consecrated a great church, dedicated to the memory of Maksymilian Kolbe, the Polish friar martyred at Auschwitz whom John Paul II had canonized the previous year. (This is the second church in Nowa Huta: the erection of the first one, dedicated to Mary Queen of Poland, after a twenty-year struggle, had been one of the most visible achievements of John Paul II in his prior incarnation as the Archbishop of Krakow.) And on the last day of the visit, at a remote retreat high in the Tatra mountains south of Krakow, the Pope even held a special private audience with Lech Walesa.

The Pope's homilies and addresses throughout the pilgrimage were remarkable both for the force of their eloquence and for the intensity of the response they inspired in the crowds who heard them. From the outset he minced few words in his allusions to repression. "I ask those who suffer to be particularly close to me," he said at the airport the very first day. "I ask this in the words of Christ: I was sick and you visited me. I was in prison and you came to me. I myself cannot visit all the sick and all those in prison [the crowd gasped], all those who are suffering. But I ask them to be close to me in spirit, to help me, just as they always do. I get many letters bearing witness to this spiritual closeness, particularly in recent times." Furthermore, this pope whose first visit had in part inspired the upsurge of Solidarity now reaffirmed and ratified the movement's principal themes. In his homily at Katowice, he insisted on the moral dimensions of the struggle for workers' rights: "The working man is not just an instrument of production but a subject, an autonomous individual within the production process. . . . Man through his work becomes the veritable master of his workshop, of the work process, of the products of work, and of their distribution. He is also ready to make sacrifices as long as he feels himself to be genuinely influencing the just distribution of the products made along with others. We appeal to Mary as the mother of social justice for these principles of social order to assume genuine form in the social life of our soil."

But many of his most profound passages were more immediately pitched to the current mood of spiritual exhaustion afflicting the country. In Krakow the Pope celebrated "that strength which is more powerful than any human weakness and more powerful than any situation, even the most difficult, not excluding the arrogant use of power. I ask you all," he went on, "to call these weaknesses, these sins, these vices, these situations, by name, and to fight against them constantly—not to allow yourselves to be swallowed up by the wave of immorality and indifference." And at Jasna Gora, in an address at a special mass for Polish youth, more than a million of whom swarmed about the vast grounds in front of the monastery, he used a meditation on the monastery's motto, "I watch," as an occasion for the reaffirmation of first principles: "I watch: how beautiful it is that this word is found in the call of Jasna Gora. What does it mean, 'I watch'? It means that I make an effort to be a person with a conscience. I do not stifle this conscience and I do not deform it; I call good and evil by name, and I do not blur them. I develop in myself what is good, and I seek to correct what is evil by overcoming it in myself. 'I watch' also means 'I see another.' I do not close in on myself, in a narrow search for my own interests or my own judgments. 'I watch' means: love for one's neighbor. It means fundamental human solidarity." With the Pope's enunciation of this last word, the throng erupted into tremendous applause.

Evaluating the significance of the Pope's visit in the weeks after his departure, the editors of the underground bulletin кos (No. 35) concluded that "the most obvious and important" result of the pilgrimage was the fact "that in the course of this historic meeting of the Pope with millions of Poles we have again become visible to ourselves and others, that we have regained our voice and are able to stand straight again. A year and a half of terror have failed. We have become self-determining subjects again, something quite extraordinary in a totalitarian state. We should no longer consider ourselves to be the objects of political bargains being worked out above our heads." The authors of this evaluation struck on something very important, the way in which Solidarity was made to live again through the very massing of the crowds and the momentary freedom provided within the contours of the mass—the banners, the buttons, the V-signs, the ostentatious applause—and the way in which the epiphany of that solidarity had everything to do with a renewal of subjectivity. But the question is, what was the character of that renewal? Back in 1979, at the time of the Pope's first visit, Poles discovered themselves in those crowds, discovered a sense of power and possibility and subjectivity—subjectivity with a horizon, a future. From the papal masses of 1979 to the mass strikes of 1980, there was a direct trajectory. But that sort of horizon—a horizon in which subjects can imagine themselves becoming agents, actors on the plains of immediate history—is precisely what was missing from the papal masses of 1983. And it was missing partly because John Paul II didn't intend to project it there.

This was the facet of the papal pilgrimage that was most frequently misread by Western correspondents on the scene. Over and over again we were told about crowds bursting into applause at the slightest mention of the word "solidarity." We were shown seas of hands raised in the V-sign. The whole trip was covered as if it were some giant traveling pep rally for Solidarity, and in turn a huge propaganda defeat for General Jaruzelski (who was said to have "disastrously miscalculated" the outcome).

When, midway through the pilgrimage, the Polish Church issued a statement criticizing the Western media for their obsessive over-emphasis on the political and supposedly antisocialist connotations of the Pope's visit, there was a good deal of smug snickering among Western correspondents who quickly convinced themselves that the statement was merely a crafty bit of diplomatic subterfuge. (The Church, it was said, deployed the word "moral" the way Solidarity used to deploy the word "social," as an ironic equivalent of "political.") But the Church's statement was more than just diplomacy. The criticism was justified: much of the Western reporting was indeed missing much of what was actually going on.

This is one reason everyone was so taken aback a few days after the Pope's return to the Vatican by the stunning editorial in *Osservatore Romano* by Father Virgilio Levi which praised the heroic sacrifices of the Poles but then called on Walesa to stand aside now for the sake of "national reconciliation." Levi resigned in the subsequent furor, but the sentiments expressed in the editorial were never clearly repudiated by the Vatican. And although Levi's specific counsel to Walesa may have overstated the Pope's position, much of the rest of the editorial was in line with what the Pope had been saying all along. (It is particularly noteworthy in this context that the Vatican never did release any photographs of the Pope's meeting with Walesa, these being the very images Poles had for months been longing to see and to frame for display in their living rooms.)

On the eve of his journey, John Paul II had addressed a crowd of 35,000 people gathered in St. Peter's Square, praying that "this pilgrimage may serve truth and love, freedom and justice, that it may serve reconciliation and peace." A close reading of all the texts from all his Polish addresses shows that the Pope hewed pretty much to those proportions—calls for truth freedom and justice, yes, but also, and always at the same time, for love, reconciliation and peace. His was hardly a battle cry for immediate revolution.

Daniel Singer, in an article in the September 3, 1983, issue of *The Nation*, is even more emphatic in making this point: "Upon detached reading, the Pope's speeches yield different meaning from those the crowds cheered. He invoked the Gdansk agreements. So does the government. He called on the Virgin Mary to protect suffering Poland and exhorted Poles to stick to their moral principles. Spiritual resistance does not bother the regime, which does not want to be loved but simply tolerated as a lesser evil. And consider the political advantages [the regime] derived from permitting this pilgrimage! If the Polish Pope can shake hands with Jaruzelski, why can't Reagan or Thatcher? . . . The leaders of Poland could paraphrase the Huguenot Henri IV's dictum about Paris: Power in Warsaw is worth many a mass. Only one cannot say such things so crudely in public. Father Levi was dismissed at once for forgetting the art of Jesuitical circumlocution."

Many observers failed to understand that after a certain point, huge throngs were *in Jaruzelski's interest*. Of course, he would have preferred it if only a few hundred people had shown up to greet the Pope at the Krakow rally. But as long as there were going to be more than that, it was better that there be 2 million than 20,000. Now he could turn to his hard-line rivals in the Polish Communist Party, or to his dubious overlords in the Kremlin, and say, "Look, you keep telling me these folks are longing for a return to socialism, or that normalizing them should be easy, but I've got to tell you, I don't see it. You've got to give me more room to maneuver." Furthermore, Jaruzelski scored propaganda points both through the relative dignity of his welcoming speech to the Pope at the outset of the trip (his identification of himself, like John Paul II, as a loyal son of Poland) and even more through the very fact of his second meeting at the conclusion of the pilgrimage. Joseph Kraft in a *Washington Post* op-ed piece on June 23rd, struck precisely the chord the regime intended when he wrote, "If the Pope comes off as magnificent, Jaruzelski also emerges as a considerable figure. The two men define the narrow range of choice open to those with real stakes in Poland."

Furthermore, if one examines the calculus behind Jaruzelski's decision to let the Pope come in the first place, one quickly realizes that the general had already reaped many dividends before the Pope even set foot on Polish soil. It was in large part the announcement of the upcoming visit on November 8th that sealed the sorry fate of the TKK's November 10th strike call. After that, continuous anxiety about upsetting the chances for the Pope's visit served to temper public response throughout the next seven months, no matter how provocative the regime's actions (and this was a period when all sorts of repressive post-martial-law legislation was being set in place). Indeed, in general, the regime was cleverly able to redirect all public discussion during those seven months away from substantive political questions and back toward relatively safe symbolic longings.

Meanwhile, the meetings themselves between the General and the Pope were by no means empty affairs. Substantive negotiations were taking place. The Pope no doubt was further consolidating the position of the Church. (The period of martial law, for example, has seen an unprecedented increase in new church construction in Poland, so much so that even some close allies of the Catholic hierarchy are beginning to find the spectacle a bit unseemly in a country with as severe a housing shortage as Poland's.) In addition the Pope and the General were finalizing plans regarding an earlier initiative of Cardinal Glemp to form a multi-billion-dollar, Church-directed development bank to assist Polish agriculture, an institutional arrangement unprecedented in prior communist-bloc practice. The General, for his part, was pressing his own concerns. We may never know the exact content of those negotiations, since we are dealing with two fanatically secretive institutions. For that matter, any deals arrived at may have fallen through in the meantime. But one wonders, for example, whether the Pope was enticed to go along with a lifting of martial law and a partial amnesty in exchange for the Church's relative silence in the event of the prosecution of the KOR and Solidarity activists. There was considerable speculation in this regard at the time, and it was known the Church had never had much use for the distressingly agnostic KOR.[37] In any case, no matter what was negotiated, the bilateral character of the talks was perhaps their greatest significance: here once again were the Church and the regime, deciding the fate of Poland, with that annoying upstart Solidarity conveniently out of the picture.

The meetings between the Pope and the General were not, of course, the true focal point of the trip. The meetings between the Pope and the Polish people were always fundamentally more important. And I say this even though I can't agree with the contention advanced by the editors of KOS that the Pope's trip succeeded in reinstilling a sense of subjective solidarity in the Polish people. True, the Pope's visit needs to be interpreted in terms of the continuous struggle to retain a sense of Polish subjectivity in the face of the regime's attempts at objectification (or, as they'd call it, normalization). And, in his own way, this is precisely what the Pope was trying desperately to do. But John Paul II was no longer advancing the notion of subjectivity through Solidarity. Rather, during that week in Poland, he behaved almost like a father tucking the children into bed and explaining to them the moral of the story: Yes, children, you've had a very, very busy day, and you were very, very good. All the things you wanted were correct, and the authorities were very mean and nasty to treat you like that. But remember, this is Poland, and Poland always suffers, and when Poland suffers, what do good Poles do? We return to the womb of our Catholic belief. A reconfirmation and rededication to our Catholic faith will see us through this sorrow, just as it has all the others before.

When the Pope said lower-case "solidarity," he meant *lower-case* solidarity. Subjectivity was to survive the coming dark time not through a return to Solidarity—to mass actions and direct confrontations—but rather through refortified individual faith. Subjectivity would persist, for the time being, in the safe harbor of the Church.

This sort of message was particularly evident during the ceremonies in Krakow, where before two million rapt listeners John Paul II beatified two Church figures who fought in the failed 1863 insurrection against the Russians. According to the *Washington Post* (June 23), "The Pope praised the two—Father Rafal Kalinowski and Brother Albert Chmielowski—for their service in the attempted revolution, saying they fought for their compatriots out of love and were inspired 'by heroic love of the homeland.' But he added that participation in the uprising was only 'a stage on the path to holiness.' His stress was on what came afterward. For Kalinowski, who joined the Carmelite Order, it was teaching. For Chmielowski, who founded the Albertine branch of the Franciscans, it was artistic activity." The two beatified Churchmen were to be seen as saints for the long haul, for times of adversity. An engineering student from Gdansk Polytechnic quoted by the *Washington Post* (June 17) grasped the point precisely: "Just as in the insurrection of the last century, what was created has been destroyed. Kalinowski's example shows us how we can start all over by changing ourselves from within."

"Yes," John Paul II counselled a few weeks later, "accept that it is thus, not by a more or less blind resignation but because faith assures us that the Lord can and wants to draw good from evil." He was no longer in Poland, but rather at the invalids' shrine in Lourdes, France, on his first pilgrimage since his return. "If the Lord wants to draw good from evil, it is that He invites you also to be as active as possible, despite sickness, and if you are handicapped to take yourself in hand with the strength and talent which you have despite your infirmity." I quote this passage because it echoes so exactly the counsel John Paul II was offering his Polish compatriots a month earlier. My point is that despite the rousing applause at the key words and the sea of upraised V's, John Paul's was an apolitical message: it was not a call to immediate action but rather a homily on how to live in the meantime. "The only road that leads to victory," he proclaimed a few weeks later in Austria, at Kahlenberg, the hill outside Vienna where 300 years ago the Polish King Jan Sobieski launched his successful assault on the encroaching Turks—"the only road that leads to victory and the regaining of lost freedom is through internal conversion."

I want to be clear here. Unlike Singer, I am not necessarily criticizing the Pope's approach. The Pope's may be a reasonable course, given the actual configuration of obstacles in the present situation. But it's important to describe what he was actually doing. On his first evening in Warsaw, at a mass in honor of Cardinal Wyszynski, John Paul II invoked a passage from Slowacki, the great visionary poet of the Polish nineteenth century: "I go down on my knees now in order to rise up a stronger worker through God. When I get up my voice will be the voice of the master. My cry will be the cry of the homeland." These lines epitomized the Pope's entire message: Now was a time for bowing down in humility, for purification and rededication to first principles. Later, perhaps, would come the rising up. In a post-pilgrimage interview, the TKK's Warsaw representative, Zbigniew Bujak, asked for his view on the impact of the Pope's visit, replied, "We accept the teaching of John Paul II as the basic inspiration for our life, for our work and struggle. We shall spread them and we shall always go back to them." And this was indeed the major lasting significance of the Pope's visit: he had set guidelines and signposts for the future. For the next 50 years, no matter what else happens, Poles who were only children today will recall that this particular moral precept was enunciated at that particular spot. The teachings will be indelible. These people will be all the more difficult for future regimes to repress. Their subjectivity will be anchored in those words and those moments. This sublimation of subjectivity is what the Pope was accomplishing in Poland. But he certainly wasn't calling for any immediate revival of Solidarity.

It's necessary to comprehend that distinction if we are to understand what followed. During the spring leading up to the Pope's visit, many commentators in the West, and I include myself, were predicting serious problems for the regime in the wake of the pilgrimage. For seven months, the regime had masterfully used anticipation of the visit to defuse public restiveness. This was the one big carrot the authorities were endlessly dangling before the masses. But once the visit was over, we wondered, what other carrots would the regime be able to offer? How would the authorities be able to cope with a population which had once again recognized the power of its own numbers? With all the anniversaries of August still looming up ahead, many of us were predicting a fairly hot summer.

But this basically failed to materialize. Instead the regime immediately began claiming the success of the Pope's visit as its own. Precisely because the Polish people had shown such "responsibility" and "restraint" during the visit, the authorities now said it was going to be possible to completely lift martial law on July 22nd, the official National Day (anniversary of the 1944 manifesto announcing the formation of the Lublin Committee, forerunner of Polish communist rule). Thus began another charade, largely intended for foreign consumption and patterned virtually exactly after the shenanigans of the previous December, when "suspension of martial law" and release of internees was preceded by a parliamentary session inculcating many of the worst features of martial law into the country's civil code. This time, the lifting of martial law and a limited amnesty for selected prisoners was preceded by a parliamentary session in which repressive statutes *which hadn't even been part of martial law* were slotted into the civil code. Among other things, the new legislation provided for up to three years' imprisonment for anyone "active in an organization which was disbanded or outlawed and which still operates illegally." (Prior to this, although particular acts were liable to lead to prison, mere membership in the various institutions of the underground society was not prosecutable.) Workers at key industrial plants were forbidden to resign from their jobs with less than six months' notice, which was probably a good (or, at any rate, necessary) thing, because now their managers were going to have the right to increase their work week without extra pay whenever production quotas went unfilled. Students would be subject to expulsion for even belonging to any association other than those approved by the regime. As Lech Walesa told a group of reporters, "I would rather have martial law than this."

The TKK responded with fresh calls for actions to protest the new laws and to commemorate the various strike anniversaries. A work slow-down was slated to begin in the Gdansk shipyard on August 23rd and continue through the 31st, the actual anniversary of the 1980 accords, on which day the TKK was also calling for a two-hour nation-wide boycott of all public transportation facilities. However, in another case of *déjà vu*, whatever momentum the underground might have been building was undercut when on August 21st the regime managed, with once again perfect timing, to bag another clandestine leader. Bag him, or something. For there he was on national television—Wladyslaw Hardek of Krakow, one of the five founding members of the TKK—claiming that he'd come to recognize the futility of further clandestine action, that the struggle was not worth the shedding of any more blood, and that he was therefore turning himself in voluntarily. The entirely voluntary nature of the surrender was subject to question: his eyes were glassy as he read his statement from a typed sheet in an uncharacteristically monotone voice. Still, everyone from Walesa on down was shocked and shaken to see him there: he'd participated in the TKK's most recent call just the day before.

The effectiveness of the subsequent slowdown at the shipyard was difficult to gauge—production in the yards had been way below normal for months owing to a lack of spare parts and dismal worker morale—so that it was probably not a terribly good tactic to try in the first place. As for the transportation boycott, the authorities were ridiculing its significance even in advance: Mieczyslaw Rakowski, the deputy prime minister, in a rather grim meeting with workers inside the Gdansk shipyard on August 25th, told them that "a walk in Poland's sunny late summer weather" might do them some good. As it developed, the transportation boycott met with mixed results around the country, effective in some places, less so in others. Meanwhile, the August 31st anniversary also saw demonstrations in cities throughout the country—the biggest featuring about 10,000 marchers in Nowa Huta—but these were in general considerably smaller than those a year before. Things were winding down.

In retrospect the immediate impact of the Pope's trip became all the clearer. Far from focussing the country's energies for a summer of defiance, the sheer emotional intensity of the June visit seemed to have drained most Poles of any further will to struggle, at least overtly, at least for the time being. The Pope may have succeeded in planting seeds of persistent hope and continuing subjectivity in the loam of Polish history, but it would probably be some time before they would flower into renewed political action. In the meantime, Walesa and the TKK and their allies, faced with the waning effectiveness of their various tactical approaches (strikes, demonstrations, slowdowns, boycotts) were having to retrench and come up with a strategy for the longer haul. The regime, for its part, was hardly closer to gaining the allegiance or the productive enthusiasm of its subjects. Following a summer which had started in epiphany and ended in exhaustion, the Polish stalemate had once again resumed.

As I look back over these pages now, putting this book to bed late in the summer of 1983, I am beginning to entertain my own revisions. Or rather, issues which were muddy for me as I compiled my reports, in the passion of witness, are now becoming clearer; or at least the existence and the contours of certain questions are becoming more evident. Through most of my reporting, for example (and even up to this point in this epilogue), I focussed on the challenge, the promises, and the flaws of the Solidarity movement and its afterglow (the fragile persistence of "subjectivity"). I did relatively little reporting about The Other Side, about that segment of Polish society which opposed Solidarity, except in terms of *how* it opposed Solidarity. I tended to lump the many strands of that opposition together and spoke of the forces of repression as if they were uniform, and uniformly evil. I was hence particularly ill-equipped, for example, to evaluate Jaruzelski's claim that he acted as a patriot, saving Poland from both a civil war and from a considerably sterner repression.

In this failing I was perhaps reflecting a parallel lapse in the analysis advanced by Solidarity's own theorists. A few weeks after my reports on "The State of War" appeared in *The New Yorker*, I received a thoughtful letter from David Ost, an American Fulbright scholar who'd recently returned from several years in Poland (his own reports on Solidarity and martial law for the journal *In These Times* have been consistently among the best). He wrote:

> It's of course a very odd country and period when supporters of the status quo are afraid and embarrassed to speak *privately*. Nevertheless, they are certainly there and have to be reckoned with. I remember thinking before I went to Poland that I hoped I could make contacts with the "opposition." After being there six months, I was making feverish efforts only to find someone loyal—a real "*kolaborant*"! In Polish society it's really the *government* and its

forces that lead an underground existence. That is to say, in few social circles is it acceptable to speak positively on their behalf. Nevertheless, such people and groups are by no means insignificant —something Solidarity of course tended to forget. You know by far the weakest aspect of the whole rich expansive culture created by the Polish opposition since 1976—including the Flying Universities, underground newspapers, and the breathtaking civil society created from below from August 1980 through December 1981 and even after—the very weakest part of all of this was an analysis of the government. The word itself is indicative, *wladza*: power, authority. The category is a sociologist's nightmare! It could be studied— especially after August 1980—but no one in the opposition seriously did so. I'm convinced that this is a main reason the new opposition today finds itself in such a crisis: they *still* don't know whom they're dealing with, and they don't really try to find out. The Myth of the Unified Society is much more comfortable. Only slowly do they realize that it's much too comfortable.

The Myth of the Unified Society is all tied up with the Myth of the Society Unified Against the Puppets of an Outside Power. And it was this myth which was forcefully addressed a few weeks later in another letter, this one from Poland—faint red type on the thinnest of onionskin—a quirky critique I received from a young man I'd chanced to speak with for only a few moments in Warsaw during my October visit but who had now happened to come across my new articles (several copies of *The New Yorker* were apparently already circulating in Warsaw.) He took exception to my characterization of zomos as reincarnated Nazis. "It is natural," he wrote, "that those who are active against the government see themselves in the long line of Polish conspirators, and even some in the wider public sometimes see them this way. But it is a quite insignificant part of the population who see Jaruzelski's troops as successors of the Wehrmacht—the zomos, after all, are also conscripts, part of them. The conspirators and their propaganda apparatus make great noise about this analogy, but this has in fact been their error. It gave short-term advantages, but in the end it caused their defeat. This is because Poles may joke about the Crow, but they are fully conscious of the fact that on the other side are Poles as well. The failure by the conspirators and their passive supporters to understand that the antagonists are bone of their bone, flesh of their flesh, sons of this country is the principal reason of their weakness." I describe this man's comments as "quirky" because I have in the meantime checked and doublechecked. Everyone I speak with—émigré Poles, visiting Poles, returning journalists —confirms my initial impression as to the pervasiveness and the power of the Nazi analogy. Still, he has a point, and his intuition as to the "Polishness" of the forces of repression has a certain power of its own.

197

With the passage of time and the blessings of perspective, many Western reporters are beginning to entertain parallel revisions. Richard Spielman, a junior scholar at Yale University's Center for Russian and Eastern European Studies who travelled extensively in Poland during Solidarity time, has made a particularly strong case for a revisionist view of Jaruzelski's role, and the need for careful distinctions, in an article in the Winter 1983 issue of *Foreign Policy*. "On December 13, 1981," he writes, "Jaruzelski's interests and those of the Soviets became fatefully congruent; but they are not now, nor have they ever been, identical. Jaruzelski long resisted internal and external pressure for a repressive solution. Moreover, his postcoup politics are demonstrating why ruling communist parties have reason to fear potential Bonapartes in their ranks. His coup has been a catastrophe for the Polish Party apparatus. No individual—not even Solidarity leader Lech Walesa—has more seriously considered dissolving a communist party in power than Jaruzelski. Yet the West remains indifferent to this fact" (p.28). A few paragraphs later, fleshing out this assertion, he reviews the history of developments inside the ruling circles prior to the coup, the conflict between moderates (such as Jaruzelski, Rakowski, and Urban) on the one hand, and hard-liners (such as Olszowski, Grabski, Kociolek, and Moczar) on the other, and concludes:

> So severe was the struggle between Jaruzelski and his inner-party foes that there is credible speculation that the apparatchiks were planning their own coup for late December 1981 when Jaruzelski was to be in Moscow for Brezhnev's birthday. This group had previously and unsuccessfully tried to grab power in a similar fashion on March 19, 1981, when Kania was in Budapest and Jaruzelski was in Katowice meeting with regional Party officials. Based on this analysis, some have even gone so far as to suggest that Kulikov [the Soviet general who on a visit to Warsaw in late November 1981 has generally been suspected of carrying instructions from the Kremlin in anticipation of the coup] came to Warsaw as a representative of the Soviet army—perhaps as anti-Party as its Polish counterpart, for identical reasons—in order to warn Jaruzelski.

That last bit of speculation seems far-fetched, but Spielman's general argument that Jaruzelski was shielding Poland from the full weight of Soviet wrath as expressed through the machinations of the Kremlin's local vassals, seems increasingly plausible. Adam Michnik, of all people, writing early in the summer of 1983 from the prison cell where he was still awaiting his KOR trial, seemed to echo Spielman's analysis:

> Let us go back for a moment to the events of eighteen months ago. All interpretations of that December night, my own included, were focussed on the structural conflict of the apparatus with

Solidarity. We saw the coup as a desperate act of self-defense of totalitarian power against an organized society that was reclaiming its right to be a free agent. It was indeed that, but it was something more besides. The ruling team was also threatened by a coup organized by the Party hardliners. They were to overthrow Jaruzelski, as they had earlier overthrown Kania, at the next plenary meeting of the Central Committee. And there are many signs that the hardliners had the full blessing of the Soviet leaders, who were quite willing to use their troops to "come to the aid of Poland in need" (*Uncensored Polish News Bulletin*, July 29, 1983, pp. 20–21).

Meanwhile, relations between the commissars and the apparatchiks since the coup could hardly be described as uniformly cordial. Even with the lifting of martial law this past July, military men still hold key posts in the civilian economy, partly because of the party's continuing weakness (the party has lost a full quarter of its members since August 1980, and its ranks are still thinning by as many as 5,000 resignations per month), but especially because, in the words of John Kifner, "many of the military men who [in the years before the coup] lived a life separate from much of the rest of society . . . were appalled at what they found when they took over" (*New York Times*, September 17, 1983). One general quoted by Kifner compared the condition of workers in most factories unfavorably with those of his recruits during their basic training. He was astonished and chagrined at the corruption of many middle-level managers and at their complete indifference to the sorry plight of their workforce. According to this general, over 650 managing directors of important enterprises have been removed, along with 200 city and local officials. Even though most of these removals have merely resulted in lateral transfers and there have been very few outright prosecutions, still, none of this can have endeared the generals to the *nomenklatura*.

Charles Gati, a senior fellow at Columbia University's Research Institute on International Change, contributed a piece to the June 5, 1983 Outlook section of the *Washington Post*, entitled "Poland's Jaruzelski is not the Kremlin's Stooge," in which he amplified on some of these themes, pointing out that in the months since the coup, the Soviet leaders have been far from uniformly enthused with Jaruzelski's performance: they find him too tolerant of the underground, the Church, free discourse, etc. Consequently, "Soviet economic aid to Poland has been remarkably meager, especially when compared to Soviet aid to Hungary after 1956 and to Czechoslovakia after 1968." He analyzes the then-recent flap, when the authoritative Soviet journal *New Times* publicly attacked *Polityka*, the moderate Polish journal edited by Jaruzelski's deputy prime minister Rakowski, accusing it of "having lost its bearings," of being an apologist for Solidarity, of proclaiming Lech Walesa "the Spartacus of our time," of trying to make Poland "a land of pluralism" instead of socialism, and of "deliberately trying to disarm the party." The paradox, Gati thus concludes, "is that while most Poles contemptuously dismiss the limited freedoms offered by the Jaruzelski regime as 'too little, too late,' the Kremlin, or at least those in the Kremlin who inspired the *New Times* article, seem to regard them as 'too much, too soon.' "

Clearly, a more complex and variegated account of the Polish ruling class—its factions and their separate ambitions, both during and after the Solidarity period—is called for than the one I have offered in these reports. This is perhaps an account which cannot yet be fully written: it may be decades, if ever, before the relevant papers and archives are released to the scrutiny of historians.

Yet at another level, at the level of moral action, at the level of persistent subjectivity, at the level of how one is to behave in the present if one is a Pole who was once a follower of the independent trade union Solidarity—at that level perhaps, one already knows everything one needs to know. I am reminded of the tenth segment of Baranczak's seventeen-part "The Restoration of Order," composed in exile in Cambridge, Massachusetts, from December 1981 through July 1982:

> *According to unconfirmed reports, that figure*
> *behind the plexiglass shield may at heart*
> *be well-intentioned, the voice barking the command*
> *"Fire!" may have something else entirely*
> *in mind, that tank crashing down the gate*
> *may be opening up some new perspectives,*
> *the club coming down on the man on the ground*
> *may be a barrier protecting him from something far worse,*
> *let's not jump to conclusions, let us be*
> *objective, everyone deserves a chance.*[38]

Michnik in an interview somehow smuggled out of prison as recently as August 1983 likewise reflected on this theme. After he'd been reviewing some of the careful distinctions between factions in the ruling order which he'd already delineated in his open letter of earlier in the summer, he was bluntly asked if he didn't then admit that Jaruzelski was the lesser evil after all. "I am farthest from such thinking," he replied:

Jaruzelski defends the chair coveted by, let's say, Olszowski. What have we to do with this? One should understand the struggle taking place within the apparatus of power, but one should not vest the slightest hope in any of the fighting factions. Concerning Solidarity there is no difference between them. They differ with respect to technique. During an interrogation one investigator screamed at me, shook his fist and threatened that I would end up rotting in jail if I didn't talk. Then another one came in and said, "But citizen major, why do you get so upset? Mr. Adam is a man of high culture and intelligence. He will say everything without your screaming." The second man thought like Jaruzelski, the first one like Olszowski. But both were officers of the security police and their goal was the same.

Even those in Solidarity and abroad who have been willing to grant the existence of complicated crosscurrents in the ruling circles within Poland tend to suspend such analysis at the Soviet border. They—we— speak of various sorts of Polish response to "Kremlin pressure," as if at least the Kremlin's pressure were some sort of invariable constant. Yet, as I review the record today, I see more clearly the vicissitudes and down-right contradictions in Soviet behavior over the past three years. It's not just that the Kremlin tried different tactical approaches at different times; rather, different circles within the Kremlin seemed to feel threatened by Solidarity in different ways and to differing degrees and hence reacted in very different fashions, *all at the same time.* Thus, to give but one recent example, the *New Times*'s attacks on Jaruzelski's close colleagues appeared in May 1983 and were followed throughout the Soviet press in the weeks leading up to the Pope's June visit by particularly shrill criticism of the Polish regime's excessive toleration of Catholicism. Yet, no sooner had the Pope left Krakow than Jaruzelski was being summoned to Moscow, not for the dressing-down everybody expected, but rather to be awarded the Order of Lenin, the highest honor conferred by the Soviet government on foreign dignitaries. Such sequences have occurred again and again, and they suggest that there is as much confusion, conflict, and jockeying for position within the Kremlin as among the Polish ruling circles.

Thus, when one "Western diplomat" quoted in a recent *New York Times* dispatch (July 1, 1983), commented that "There is only one real question—how big is the field of maneuver—and the field of maneuver is defined in Moscow," he was of course accurately describing the situation but at the same time begging the question. A future history of the Solidarity period will need to explore the constantly shifting power re-lations among the various contending factions in Moscow who were presumably defining the field of maneuver in Warsaw. One key element in such a history will be an evaluation of those relations during a period of precarious transition (Brezhnev's decline, debility, death, and replace-ment by an obviously ill Andropov). But here again, it may be some time, if ever, before anything like a full history can be put together.

At the very least, though, this precariousness aggravated the inherent edginess of Soviet response to what was happening in Poland. Soviet policymakers were concerned, for obvious reasons of self-interest as well as those of ideology, about having a communist party in power give way at all before the demands of a mass worker's movement; and they were concerned about the national security considerations involved in having a sudden romantic, nationalistic upsurge on their very border. (Nationalism itself is threatening to the Russian leaders of the USSR who must have continual nightmares about the possibilities for romantic revivals among any of the dozens of nationalities *within* their country's borders.) But I suspect at least some of them were particularly troubled by the implications of a Polish renewal for the world balance of power, and hence for world peace. The transition from the Brezhnev-Andropov era toward whatever will come next may well include a gradual loosening of the Soviet Union's hold over its Eastern European satellites. But such a loosening is still a fearsome prospect for the present leadership. Within their memory, political instability and nationalist excess in Central Europe have already occasioned two world wars, and although the Soviet domination of the region has entailed all the notorious ill effects with which we are so familiar, still it has at least frozen the volatility of the region for a period of over 40 years. One can imagine some younger Soviet technocrats who are only now approaching positions of leadership and who appreciate the historical inevitability of a loosening of Soviet control over Eastern Europe and yet who shudder at the prospect of just how such a loosening is to be accomplished without provoking a third world war.

That, at any rate, is a charitable view of the sort of considerations which may animate some of the Soviet leaders in their thinking about Poland. On the other hand, there is a more cynical and probably more justifiable interpretation of the prevalent Soviet attitudes. Ronald Steel captured it superbly in a recent article about an entirely different subject (Henry Kissinger's ascendancy to the chairmanship of the presidential commission on Central America; *Washington Post*, Outlook Section, July 24, 1983). "Nicaragua," Steel observed, "like El Salvador, is what Lyndon Johnson used to refer to as a 'piss-ant country.' Superpower managers don't like to admit that what makes them superpowers is controlling piss-ant countries. They need a more exalted name for it. They call it the global balance of power."

The trouble with piss-ant countries, like Nicaragua and El Salvador and Poland, of course, is that occasionally they refuse to behave like good little objects—simple pawns in the schemes of their superpower managers. Sometimes they take on a life of their own. . . .

Back on November 10th, General Jaruzelski chose to flaunt his victory over the Solidarity underground by touring local factories where their called-for eight-hour strike was most emphatically not taking place. The evening news showed him, behind the perennial dark glasses, touring the assembly line at the Rosa Luxemburg Electric Light Bulb Factory outside Warsaw. Few Poles missed the special significance of Jaruzelski's choice of backdrop: The Luxemburg Factory had been the one visited by Walesa over a year earlier on October 28, 1981, during the one-hour warning strike which had been aboveground Solidarity's last nationally coordinated action.[39]

"There is a law in psychology that an unfinished activity awaits its completion," noted a group of social psychologists commissioned by the martial-law regime last December to evaluate current approaches to propaganda. A pilfered copy of their report managed to find its way into the кos underground bulletin (and thence into the July 22, 1983 issue of the New York *Committee in Support of Solidarity Reports*). "Accordingly," the psychologists continued, "Solidarity and its activities remain—psychologically speaking—unfinished." These experts then gingerly went on to suggest to the regime that rather than attacking the memory of the union, "it is better to say that the people should continue some of the threads of Solidarity's activities and that we ourselves wish to do so . . . that those goals of Solidarity which were correct were also the goals of the party." Well, one can *say* whatever one wants, but the political fact remains that the goals of Solidarity which were correct were most emphatically not the goals of the party—were not and cannot ever be—and that the contradictions inherent both in such propaganda and in the policies which it disguises will become all the more evident with the passage of time. For, notwithstanding the currently low spirits evident throughout Polish society, it is also a *political* law—and no one knew this better than Karl Marx—that unfinished activity awaits its completion, and it is a political fact that Solidarity and its activities await theirs.

In the weeks just after the coup—this seems years ago, now—Adam Michnik wrote his fellow-prisoners a long letter urging them not to accept the regime's offer of release provided they agreed to emigrate:

I know you do not believe in a quick victory, in a rapid rebuilding of the pre-December Solidarity. You know that before you lies a road of drudgery marked by suffering defeats and by the bitter taste that remains after contact with human smallness. And it is not as if you idealized that pre-December Solidarity either. . . . You must have seen . . . the symptoms of a betrayed revolution and the beginnings of degeneration. But you also saw, during those months which you would not exchange for any others and which you were always ready to pay for with years in prison, you also saw people rising from their knees, people thirsting for true and free speech, people receiving free speech like communion, people with lit-up faces and eyes full of trust—all this you saw, and you know it cannot be trampled underfoot and destroyed by tanks. And you will not see such faces on the boulevards of Paris.

Or, he might have added, on the streets of New York, either.

During my visit to Warsaw last October, one of the most frequent bits of graffiti I saw was a simple logo:

In Polish, CDN stands for *Ciag Dalszy Nastapi* and means, "to be continued." These are the initials one finds, for example, at the ends of installments of serialized writing. The Western press has a tendency to focus on news stories during climactic developments and to fade out during the interim—the long, slow periods when revolutions gestate—so that we may expect Poland to be receding, further and further, into the back pages of our news journals during the months ahead. We should not, however, be misled. The saga of Poland is definitely CDN.

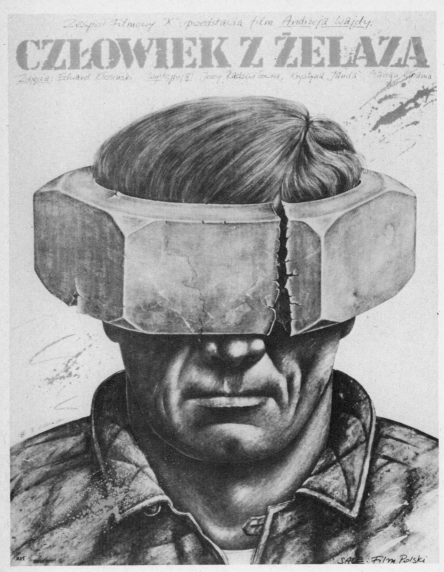

The poster for Andrzej Wajda's film *Man of Iron* (1981). The archetypical Stalinist worker hero is revealed to have been blinded by shackles he is only just now beginning to break. (*Artist: Rafal Olbinski*)

APPENDICES

———— + · + ————

The Twenty-One Demands

These are the Twenty-one Demands which the Interfactory Strike Committee (the MKS) presented to government representatives on August 23, 1980, in Gdansk, and which formed the basis for the negotiations that culminated in the agreements of August 31, 1980.

1. Acceptance of Free Trade Unions independent of both the Party and employers, in accordance with the International Labor Organization's Convention number 87 on the freedom to form unions, which was ratified by the Polish government.
2. A guarantee of the right to strike and guarantees of security for strikers and their supporters.
3. Compliance with the freedoms of press and publishing guaranteed in the Polish constitution. A halt to repression of independent publications and access to the mass media for representatives of all faiths.
4. (a) Reinstatement to their former positions for: people fired for defending workers' rights, in particular those participating in the strikes of 1970 and 1976; students dismissed from school for their convictions.

(b) The release of all political prisoners (including: Edmund Zadrozynski, Jan Kozlowski, and Marek Kozlowski).

(c) A halt to repression for one's convictions.

5. The broadcasting on the mass media of information about the establishment of the Interfactory Strike Committee (MKS) and publication of the list of demands.

6. The undertaking of real measures to get the country out of its present crisis by:

    (a) providing comprehensive, public information about the socio-economic situation;

    (b) making it possible for people from every social class and stratum of society to participate in open discussions concerning the reform program.

7. Compensation of all workers taking part in the strike for its duration with holiday pay from the Central Council of Trade Unions.

8. Raise the base pay of every worker 2,000 zlotys per month to compensate for price rises to date.

9. Guaranteed automatic pay raises indexed to price inflation and to decline in real income.

10. Meeting the requirements of the domestic market for food products: only surplus goods to be exported.

11. The rationing of meat and meat products through food coupons (until the market is stabilized).

12. Abolition of "commercial prices" and hard currency sales in so-called "internal export" shops.

13. A system of merit selection for management positions on the basis of qualifications rather than Party membership. Abolition of the privileged status of MO, SB [Internal Security Police], and the party apparatus through: equalizing all family subsidies; eliminating special stores, etc.

14. Reduction of retirement age for women to 50 and for men to 55. Anyone who has worked in the PRL for 30 years, for women, or 35 years for men, without regard to age, should be entitled to retirement benefits.

15. Bringing pensions and retirement benefits of the "old portfolio" to the level of those paid currently.

16. Improvement in the working conditions of the Health Service, which would assure full medical care to working people.

17. Provision for sufficient openings in daycare nurseries and preschools for the children of working people.

18. Establishment of three-year paid maternity leaves for the raising of children.

19. Reduce the waiting time for apartments.

20. Raise per diem [for work-related travel] from 40 zlotys to 100 zlotys and provide cost-of-living increases.

21. Saturdays to be days off from work. Those who work on round-the-clock jobs or three-shift systems should have the lack of free Saturdays compensated by increased holiday leaves or through other paid holidays off from work.

During 1981, thousands of Poles jammed a travelling exhibition of photodocumentation of the grim (and previously taboo) events of December 1970 (right), including amateur photographs of the Gdansk Communist Party headquarters on fire and a surging crowd carrying the corpse of a worker atop a torn-off door frame.

Chronology

I.   Before Solidarity (1939–79)

1939

  As the year opens, there are 32,347,000 Poles, of whom 3,351,000 are Jewish. Josef Stalin is 60 years old. Nikita Khrushchev is 47. Leonid Brezhnev is 33. Wladyslaw Gomulka is 34. Edward Gierek is 26 and is organizing mine workers in Belgium. Stefan Wyszynski, who will become Primate of Poland, is 37. Karol Wojtyla, who will become Pope, is 19. Andrzej Wajda is 13. Marshal Josef Pilsudski has been dead for four years. It will be four years yet before Lech Walesa is born.

Jan. 30   Hitler requests annexation of free city of Danzig (later, Gdansk).
Aug. 23   Nazi-Soviet Non-Aggression Pact signed (with secret provisions on partition of Poland).
Sept. 1   Nazis invade Poland, igniting the Second World War.
Sept. 27   Soviet armies invade from the east, capturing thousands of Polish officers, many of whom will later die at Katyn.
Sept. 30   German-Soviet treaty settles the partition of Poland.

1940

Polish government reconstitutes itself in exile, first in Paris, then in London, under General Wladyslaw Sikorski. Meanwhile, in Poland, the Home Army consolidates resistance.

Apr. 29 Himmler chooses a marshy site in southern Poland for a prison camp: Auschwitz. Meanwhile, Nazis herd Jews into ghettos, build wall around Warsaw ghetto.

1941

June 22 Nazis attack Soviet Union.

July 30 Stalin establishes diplomatic relations with Sikorski's London-based government-in-exile; releases some Polish soldiers, previously held prisoner, to form Polish Division under General Wladyslaw Anders, and sends them to Middle East.

1943

Polish Home Army continues to mount stiffest indigenous resistance in any Nazi-occupied country.

Feb. 2 A German army surrenders in Stalingrad.

Apr. 13 Nazis uncover mass graves at Katyn; this revelation leads to a rupture between Stalin and the London-based Polish government.

Apr. 19–May 8 Warsaw Ghetto Uprising ruthlessly suppressed. Most Polish Jewish ghettos ordered liquidated.

July 4 General Sikorski dies in mysterious plane crash off Gibralter. Replaced as head of London-based government by Stanislaw Mikolajczyk.

Sept. 29 Lech Walesa born near Lipno, between Warsaw and Danzig.

Nov. Wladyslaw Gomulka becomes first secretary of Polish Communist Party.

1944

March Polish Division plays particularly distinguished role in battle at Monte Cassino, Italy.

July 22 Lublin Committee formed (Stalin's alternative to the London-based government and the precursor of Communist rule in Poland).

July 23 Soviet Army forges across Curzon line into Poland.

Aug. 1 Home Army launches its own liberation of Warsaw; the approaching Soviet forces stop at the Vistula to allow Nazis time to liquidate the uprising.

Oct. 2 Warsaw Uprising collapses: 200,000 Warsavites have died. Hitler orders survivors deported and the city razed.

1945

Jan. 17 Soviet army liberates the ruins of Warsaw.

Feb. 4–11 Yalta Conference: London-based regime subsumed into a Government of National Unity, with the Communists in the lead.

March Soviet army has "liberated" most of Poland: 6 million Poles have died, 3 million Polish Jews; 38% of Poland's industrial capacity, 35% of its agricultural resources, and 60% of its schools have been destroyed.

May 7 V-E Day: Nazis sign unconditional surrender.

June 28 Polish Government of National Unity transferred from Moscow to Warsaw (with Mikolajczyk as vice premier). Fighting between Communists and Home Army continues through the summer.

Aug. 2   Potsdam Conference: Polish postwar boundaries redrawn (in effect, the entire country is moved about 125 miles westward, resulting in mass migrations). Danzig becomes Gdansk; Stettin becomes Szczecin; Bromberg becomes Bydgoszcz.

Nov. 11   Marshal Josip Tito takes power in Yugoslavia.

1946

May 12   Stefan Wyszynski named bishop of Lublin.

May 26   Communist Party wins parliamentary elections in Czechoslovakia.

July 4   Anti-Jewish pogrom in Kielce: Poles kill 42 unarmed Jews returning from concentration camps.

Nov. 1   Karol Wojtyla is ordained priest and sent to Rome for further studies.

1947

Oct. 12   Mikolajczyk, accused of being an "ally of foreign imperialists," flees to London. Poland now falls completely under the domination of its Communist Party.

1948

Feb.   Communists seize power in Czechoslovakia; later this year, in Hungary as well.

June 24   Soviet blockade of Allied sectors of Berlin circumvented by Berlin Airlift.

June 28   Yugoslavia expelled from Cominform for its hostility to USSR.

Sept. 3   Gomulka, accused of "nationalist deviations" for supporting Tito, is replaced as head of the Polish CP by Boleslaw Bierut, on Stalin's orders.

1949

Jan.   Wyszynski is named Archbishop of Warsaw and Primate of Poland (elevated to Cardinal, Nov. 1952).

Mar. 2   Purge of Czech CP.

June 16   Purge of Hungarian CP.

Sept.   First Smith Act trials in U.S. result in long prison terms for leaders of CP-USA.

Oct.   East German government consolidated under CP control.

Nov.   Soviet Marshal Rokossovsky changes name to Rokossowski and, on Stalin's orders, is installed as Polish defense minister.

1950

June   Korean War begins.

1951

July   Gomulka is arrested and imprisoned for his "rightist deviations." These are the dark days of Poland's Stalinist period, with hundreds of arrests and imprisonments.

1953

Mar. 5 Stalin dies of brain hemorrhage. Power struggle over his succession eventually yields Nikita Khrushchev as new Soviet leader.

June 17 Berlin Workers' Uprising is violently suppressed in East Germany.

June 19 In U.S., Ethel and Julius Rosenberg are executed for espionage.

July 23 Armistice at Panmunjom ends Korean War.

Sept. 28 Cardinal Wyszynski is placed under house arrest.

1954

Dec. Senator Joseph McCarthy is censured by the U.S. Senate.

Dec. Gomulka is released.

1955

May 14 Poland becomes a charter member of the Warsaw Pact.

1956

Feb. 14 At 20th Congress of the Soviet CP, the world Communist movement is stunned by Khrushchev's revelations of Stalinist horrors. Destalinization begins.

Mar 12 No one is more surprised than Boleslaw Bierut who dies of heart failure without ever leaving Moscow. Moderates in Warsaw move toward a rehabilitation of Gomulka.

June 28 In Poznan, workers go out on strike over wage, food, and working conditions, march on Stalin Square, and are met by government tanks. Over 70 die.

Oct. 19 Khrushchev pays a surprise visit to the Polish CP Central Committee meeting in Warsaw as they prepare to reinstate Gomulka. Soviet armored divisions converge on Warsaw. Thirty-six hours of tense negotiations. The Soviets relent.

Oct. 21 Gomulka elected first secretary of the Polish CP.

Oct. 24 Hungarian uprising put down, during the ensuing weeks, through a bloody Soviet invasion.

Oct. 28 Gomulka releases Cardinal Wyszynski.

Oct. 29 The Suez Crisis.

Autumn Gomulka launches a period of liberalization, the Polish "Spring in October." Rokossovsky is removed as defense minister; Andrzej Wajda directs *Kanal*; Jerzy Andrzejewski publishes his parable of the Spanish Inquisition, *Darkness Hides the Earth*; Leszek Kolakowski edits the dissident journal *Po Prostu* (*To Put It Plainly*); etc.

1957

Oct. Gomulka clamps down on excessive revisionism; *Po Prostu* is shut down.

1958

Wojtyla is made Auxiliary Bishop of Krakow.

Wajda's *Ashes and Diamonds* depicts the fighting between Communists and the Home Army.

1961

Jan. Deterioration in Church–state relations: religion can no longer be taught in school.

Aug. 13 The East Germans erect the Berlin Wall.

1964

Apr. Letter of 34 Polish Intellectuals calls for greater freedom of expression.

Sept. 29 Free Speech movement in Berkeley.

Nov. 24 Karol Modzelewski and Jacek Kuron expelled from Polish CP, respond by releasing an "Open Letter to the Communist Party," a seminal critique of bureaucratic centralism.

1965

July Modzelewski and Kuron sentenced to three-year prison terms.

1966

Oct. 21 On tenth anniversary of Gomulka's ascendancy (and the brief "Spring in October"), Adam Michnik and other students at the University of Warsaw demand release of Kuron and Modzelewski; professor Kolakowski addresses rally.

1967

Wojtyla elevated to cardinal.

June 5–11 The Six-Day War. Israel's defeat of the USSR's Arab allies leads to an unseemly outbreak of pro-Israeli sentiment in Warsaw.

1968

Jan. 5 In Prague, Alexander Dubcek becomes first secretary of the Czech CP; the party begins reforming itself, the start of the Prague Spring.

Jan. 30 Warsaw authorities close down a production of Adam Mickiewicz's 19th-century romantic-nationalist, anti-Russian play *Dziady*. Students demonstrate; Michnik arrested.

Mar. 8–11 Further student demonstrations (featuring such chants as "All Poland is Waiting for its Dubcek") presently broken up by a violent onslaught of "angry workers," brought in by Interior Minister Mieczyslaw Moczar.

Mid-March Moczar orchestrates a virulent anti-Semitic purge of the Communist Party. Of the 30,000 Jews still in Poland, 20,000 leave during the coming months.

Mar. 25 Kolakowski is dismissed from his chair at the University of Warsaw, along with five Jewish professors; he presently chooses exile.

Apr. 22 Polish authorities have subdued their student troubles.

April–May Dramatic student demonstrations at Berkeley and Columbia Universities in U.S.; student-worker uprising in France.

Aug. 20–21 Soviet Union and Warsaw Pact countries (including Poland) invade Czechoslovakia, oust Dubcek, and replace him with the grimly Stalinist Gustav Husak.

1969

Power struggle with Moczar preoccupies Gomulka; purge of the liberal elements in the intelligentsia continues, while the general economic situation worsens.

1970

Gomulka introduces new Five-Year Plan featuring an "incentive system" which in fact reduces most workers' wages.

Nov. 18 West German Chancellor Willy Brandt visits Warsaw as part of his policy of *Ostpolitik*, signs trade and nonaggression treaties.

Dec. 13 "A realignment of prices" twelve days before Christmas: Food prices increase dramatically, while prices for certain luxury goods go down.

Dec. 14 Furious workers at the Lenin shipyards in Gdansk launch protest strike; students at Gdansk Polytechnic decline to join in.

Dec. 15–17 Strikes spread along the Baltic coast to Gdynia and Szczecin and are violently suppressed in tank and helicopter assaults.

Dec. 20 Gomulka resigns as first party secretary and is replaced by Edward Gierek. The Battle of the Baltic ebbs. Official toll: 45 dead, 1,165 wounded. (Unofficial estimates are much, much higher.)

1971

Jan. 22 New strike in Szczecin. Gierek visits the docks for an extraordinary nine-hour session, insisting that "I, like you, am a worker." Strikers relent.

Jan. 25 Gierek meets with representatives of Gdansk shipyard, including a 27-year-old Lech Walesa.

Feb. 13 Women textile workers striking in Lodz achieve a rollback of December food price increases.

June 24 Gierek's revised Five-Year Plan emphasizes expansion of consumer sector based on massive foreign loans.

1972

May 31 President Nixon visits Poland, encourages increased trade as part of his policy of détente.

1973

Polish debt to West is still only $2.5 billion.

Sept. 11 The government of Salvador Allende in Chile, a democratic-socialist experiment in the American sphere of influence, is overturned in a violent, CIA-backed military coup.

Oct. 6–24 The Arab–Israeli "Yom Kippur" War. Arab oil embargo and subsequent price increases signal the beginning of a decade-long economic slide which will upend Gierek's plans for exporting manufactured goods to prosperous Western markets.

1975

Poland signs the 35-nation Helsinki Agreements, recognizing existing European national boundaries and guaranteeing "fundamental freedoms including freedom of thought, conscience, religion, and belief."

1976

Polish debt to the West is now $11 billion. Veteran Polish economist Edward Lipinski addresses an open letter to Gierek, warning of economic disaster.

June 24   Gierek attempts to raise food prices 60%. Sit-down strikes sweep the country, notably in Ursus and Radom. Defense Minister Wojciech Jaruzelski insists, "Polish soldiers will not fire on Polish workers." There are fewer casualties than in 1956 or 1970, and the Baltic coast remains calm.

June 25   Prices are rolled back and strikes sputter out. Below the surface, during the coming months, retaliatory persecution of strike leaders is heavy. Lech Walesa fired and subsequently blacklisted in Gdansk.

Sept. 23   Establishment of KOR, the Workers' Defense Committee, by a group of intellectuals (including Kuron, Lipinski, Jan Jozef Lipski and Jan Litynski) who will monitor hearings of persecuted workers; extend legal, medical and financial help to their families; and offer advice in their organizing.

1977

Jan. 6   240 Czech intellectuals issue a manifesto demanding greater human rights, form the Charter '77 organization, and are met with severe repression.

Feb.   Wajda's *Man of Marble* premieres in Warsaw (with its final scenes, concerning the Gdansk events of 1970, cut).

May   Several KOR affiliates found NOWA, an underground printing house, which will publish Milosz, Solzhnitseyn, Orwell, Grass, etc.

May 7   Stanislaw Pyjas, a Krakow student who is loosely affiliated with KOR, is murdered.

Autumn   First issue of *Robotnik,* KOR-affiliated workers' bulletin, edited by Litynski.

Dec. 29–31   President Carter visits Warsaw. (The Carter administration's emphasis on human rights and the Gierek regime's growing reliance on American good will contribute to a climate in which Polish activists can continue to organize relatively unimpeded through 1980.)

1978

March   Early version of Free Trade Union of Silesia formed in Silesia.

Apr. 29   Committee of Free Trade Unions for the Baltic Coast formed, under the leadership of Andrzej Gwiazda, including Anna Walentynowicz and Walesa.

Aug. 6   Pope Paul VI dies. Albino Luciani of Venice is elected his replacement, takes the name John Paul I, but he too dies on Sept. 28.

Oct. 5   Isaac Bashevis Singer wins the Nobel Prize for Literature.

Oct. 16   Karol Wojtyla of Krakow is elected Pope and takes the name John Paul II.

Dec. 16   Walesa and Gwiazda organize an impromptu memorial service for the 1970 martyrs at the plaza outside the Gdansk shipyards.

1979

June 2–10   Pope John Paul II makes a triumphant pilgrimage through Poland, addressing huge throngs in Warsaw, Czestechowa, Krakow (and saying a special mass at Auschwitz).

Sept. *Robotnik* publishes a Charter of Workers' Rights, the basis for the eventual 21 Points of August 1980.

Dec. 16 Gwiazda and Walesa organize another 1970 memorial service outside the Lenin shipyards. Many participants arrested. Walesa vows that if there is no official memorial erected at this site in time for services on this date next year, then 35 million Poles will bring one stone each and build their own. Officials, presumably, scoff at the threat.

Dec. 27 Soviet troops invade Afghanistan. (As events now begin to take shape in Poland, Kremlin leaders will find themselves already tied down, to some extent, on this other front.)

II.   Solidarity Time (1980–81)

1980

The Polish debt to the West now exceeds $20 billion.

July 1 It all starts up once again with a government decree that effectively raises some meat prices by almost 100%. Localized strikes break out all over the country, beginning with the Ursus plant outside Warsaw. Within hours, the strikers are granted pay increases of between 10 and 15%. No sooner do these strikers return to work, mollified, than strikes break out at neighboring plants, with similar demands. The pattern continues throughout the country, throughout the month.

July 2 KOR announces it will henceforth serve as a strike information clearing house.

July 11 Managers of important factories confer in Warsaw, are told to buy "social peace" as cheaply as possible, but at any price.

July 11 Strike spreads to Lublin. By July 16, most of the city is paralyzed, including, for four days, the vital rail link to the USSR. The 35 Points of the Lublin committee anticipate the 21 Demands of Gdansk. On July 18, in another anticipation, Deputy Prime Minister Mieczyslaw Jagielski is sent in to negotiate. On July 20, Lublin strikers accept a compromise—one that the Gdansk workers will not—and return to work.

July 19–Aug. 3 Moscow Summer Olympics, badly truncated by the West's Afghanistan boycott. Poles are convinced that their meat is being diverted to Moscow.

July 21 Workers in Radom are granted unsolicited, preemptive pay raises.

July 27 Gierek leaves for a three-week vacation by Brezhnev's side in the Crimea.

July 31 Lech Walesa placed under the last of a ten-year series of 48-hour arrests. While he's in prison, his wife Danuta gives birth to their sixth child.

Aug. 7 In a preemptive move, the managers of the Lenin shipyard in Gdansk fire popular activist Anna Walentynowicz.

Aug. 8 KOR expresses willingness to serve as contact center between strikers throughout the country, reveals that since July 1, over 150 factories have struck.

Aug. 10 A delegation of Gdansk activists drives down to Warsaw to consult with Kuron and other KOR leaders.

Aug. 12   In Warsaw, the Politburo spokesperson tells Western reporters that the labor unrest has passed its peak.

Aug. 14   In Gdansk, 16,000 workers in the Lenin shipyard launch an all-out strike with the first shift. Initial demands include a pay increase; the erection of a monument to the 1970 martyrs; reinstatement of fired coworkers, including Walentynowicz; and the right to form an independent trade union. Local party leader Tadeusz Fiszbach arrives. Negotiations are broadcast live over the PA system, as they will be throughout the next 17 days; Walentynowicz is brought to the yard and addresses the workers; Walesa scales the shipyard walls. The workers close off the plant and refuse to leave.

Aug. 15   Over 50,000 workers in Gdansk are now on strike. Government imposes communications blackout. Gierek returns from Crimea, a week early.

Aug. 16   False reports of strike resolution. Walesa himself wavers, initially accepting concessions on monument, reinstatement of fired workers, and a big pay increase. Within moments, realizing workers are willing to stay out for more, he changes his mind—the strike continues. Two weeks later, workers will settle for a smaller pay increase in exchange for more substantial concessions.

Aug. 19   Strike spreads along the Baltic coast, notably to Szczecin. Students at Gdansk Polytechnic contribute to strike fund. Walesa emerges as leader of the MKS, the Interfactory Strike Committee, which now consists of 500 delegates from 261 striking enterprises.

Aug. 21   In Warsaw, 24 KOR activists and associates have been arrested, including Kuron, Michnik, Litynski.

Aug. 22   First issue of the strike bulletin is printed on commandeered mimeograph equipment in the shipyard. Its title: *Solidarnosc.*

Aug. 23   Deputy Prime Minister Jagielski arrives in Gdansk to head government team, is presented with 21 Demands and told further talks will await the restoration of communications.

Aug. 25   Seven expert advisers arrive from Warsaw to assist MKS negotiators. Late this night, communications are restored.

Aug. 26   Second round of talks with Jagielski. MKS now numbers 1,000 delegates. Cardinal Wyszynski in a mass at Czestochowa, part of which is broadcast over TV, appears to urge workers to return to work, although the Church subsequently protests the selective TV editing.

Aug. 28   Strikes spread to Gierek's home district, the Silesian coal fields.

Aug. 30   Negotiations reach climax. Breakthrough at Szczecin, followed a few hours later in Gdansk. Jagielski returns to Warsaw for consultations. Wajda, visiting the shipyards, is told, "Now you must make our story, Man of Iron!" He will.

Aug. 31   Jagielski returns. Some last-minute confusion as to applicability of these accords to the rest of the country, and as to fate of arrested activists. Walesa vows workers will resume the strike if activists' release does not come quickly. Government and strikers sign final agreement in large hall at shipyard. Essential points include sanctioning of free, independent trade union with the right to strike; improved health and working conditions; Saturdays off; Sunday masses to be broadcast over the radio; loosened censorship and political repression.

Sept. 1   Warsaw activists released. Gdansk strikers return to work. Strikes continue elsewhere as workers attempt to determine national applicability of the accords. Walesa takes possession of new union office.

Sept. 3   Jastrzebie Agreement settles strike in Silesian coal fields.

Sept. 5   Parliament meets in very open and critical session; Gierek is absent (reportedly hospitalized due to heart trouble); at late-night Central Committee meeting, Gierek is ousted and replaced by Stanislaw Kania (previously in charge, variously, of the army, the secret police, and relations with the Church).

Sept. 7   Walesa attends private mass in Warsaw with Wyszynski.

Sept. 8–15   Seventh Annual Polish Film Festival in Gdansk includes special midnight screening of the early rushes of *Robotnicy '80*, a documentary of the strike.

Sept. 15   Authorities declare Gdansk accords applicable to the entire country.

Sept. 21   For the first time since the Second World War, Sunday mass is transmitted by radio throughout the country.

Sept. 22   For the first time since July 1, there are no strikes in Poland. Delegates of 36 regional independent unions, meeting in Gdansk, unite under the name "Solidarity." Karol Modzelewski emerges from academic seclusion to become the union's spokesperson.

Sept. 24   Solidarity attempts to register with Warsaw court, as required by law, but there are ominous delays.

Oct. 3   Solidarity stages a tremendously effective nationwide one-hour warning strike to protest government delays; the strike receives extensive coverage on the evening news.

Oct. 9   Czeslaw Milosz, Polish poet and essayist living in the United States, is awarded the Nobel Prize for Literature.

Oct. 24   Crisis escalates as Warsaw court makes registration of Solidarity contingent on inclusion of language recognizing "the leading role of the [Communist] party." Solidarity refuses and sets November 12 deadline for resolution of the problem—or the union will call a general strike.

Oct. 29   East Germany announces severe travel restrictions between the two countries, taking what will continue to be an even harder line than Moscow.

Oct. 30   Kania in Moscow, Wyszynski at the Vatican.

Nov. 10   Polish Supreme Court rules that Solidarity's charter can stand without reference to leading role of the party. Solidarity withdraws strike threat.

Nov. 20–24   The Narozniak affair: Kuron and Walesa rush to mediate crisis in Warsaw as a Solidarity printer is arrested and subsequently released. Walesa appeals for an end to wildcat strikes but hardline bureaucrats keep concocting new provocations leading to local flare-ups.

Nov. 29   Students at the University of Warsaw end sit-in after authorities agree to register independent student organization.

Dec. 1–13   Increasing tensions as Soviets undertake military maneuvers all around Poland and the West warns of impending invasion.

Dec. 12   The Church condemns the behavior of political "extremists" (implying KOR).

Dec. 13   Kania says Poland must be left alone to resolve its problems, and for no particular reason, tensions subside.

Dec. 14 One thousand farmers from throughout the country gather in Warsaw to demand registration of their own union, Rural Solidarity.

Dec. 16 In Gdansk, dedication of the 1970 martyrs' memorial attended by leading cultural, religious, government, and Solidarity figures.

Dec. 30 Kania visits the Gdansk memorial.

Dec. 31 By year's end, the debt to the West has reached $23 billion and the government is pointing to scarcities in food and other supplies in urging an end to labor unrest.

1981

January The major themes for confrontation as the year begins are Solidarity's demand for a five-day work week and Rural Solidarity's demand for registration.

Jan. 12 *Robotnicy '80* premieres in Warsaw, moving on to a tremendously successful semi-underground run throughout the country.

Jan. 14–20 Walesa leads a Solidarity delegation on pilgrimage to Vatican, meets with John Paul II.

Jan. 24 As part of its ongoing conflict over the five-day work week, Solidarity simply has its members take this Saturday off.

Jan. 27 Farmers occupy official agricultural offices in Rzeszow, demanding recognition of Rural Solidarity.

Jan. 30 Compromise agreement on five-day work week.

Feb. 3 Solidarity's threatened one-hour strike is called off when government finally agrees to negotiate with the farmers in Rzeszow.

Feb. 8 Government announces inquiry into KOR.

Feb. 9 Defense Minister Jaruzelski is named prime minister as well. He requests a 90-day truce and Solidarity agrees.

Mar. 4 Moscow hardens its line and demands the course of events be reversed.

Mar. 5 Kuron and Michnik arrested and briefly held.

Mar. 8 At the University of Warsaw, 3,000 students and faculty commemorate the anniversary of the 1968 demonstrations and protest anti-Semitism. Meanwhile, nearby, an association known as Grunwald stages a rally of 500 people, featuring anti-Semitic speeches, and is subsequently praised by Politburo hardliner Stefan Olszowski.

Mar. 9 In Poznan, Rural Solidarity, still officially unrecognized, holds its first congress.

Mar. 19 A meeting in Bydgoszcz is broken up in a violent display of police force; dozens are hurt and three hospitalized, including the charismatic leader Jan Rulewski.

Mar. 20–30 A period of ever-increasing tension. As the Warsaw Pact begins its Soyuz '81 military maneuvers all around Poland, Solidarity threatens a general strike for March 31 unless those responsible for the Bydgoszcz violence are disciplined. Walesa confers with Deputy Prime Minister Mieczyslaw Rakowski.

Mar. 27 Solidarity holds a four-hour warning strike and continues to mobilize. Period of greatest tension to date.

Mar. 30 At the last moment, Walesa reaches a fairly vacuous compromise with Rakowski and rams it through his national commission. Meanwhile, at a

221

stormy session of the CP's Central Committee, hardliners Olszowski and Tadeusz Grabski are on the verge of being voted off the Politburo when a letter from the Kremlin stays the purge.

Apr. 1   Furious outcry within Solidarity at the lack of democratic process during the climactic stages of the Bydgoszcz negotiations. Modzelewski resigns as press spokesperson. Meanwhile, national meat rationing begins.

Apr. 26   Western governments agree to reschedule debt. Total Western debt now exceeds $25 billion. Polish passport law liberalized.

Apr. 30   Central Committee in its seventh meeting since August calls for an extraordinary full party congress in July to be preceded by an open, secret-ballot delegate selection process.

May 1   Unusually low attendance at official May Day celebrations. Rationing, meanwhile, is extended to a wide variety of products besides meat.

May 3   Massive celebrations commemorate 190th anniversary of the 1791 constitution (May 3 had been the official national holiday after 1919, although its observance was suspended after 1947).

May 8   Crowd in Warsaw suburb of Otwock, furious over police mistreatment of two drunk youngsters, is on verge of lynching policemen when Adam Michnik and other Solidarity activists rush over to defuse the situation. Lech Walesa leaves for a week in Japan as a guest of Japanese labor confederation.

May 12   Warsaw court registers Rural Solidarity.

May 13   At Vatican, John Paul II is seriously wounded in attempted assassination. Stunned Poles watch extensive coverage on TV. Situation is particularly tense because of grave illness of Cardinal Wyszynski.

May 26   A group of party hardliners, billing themselves the Katowice Forum, issue a declaration and gain support of Kremlin.

May 27   Wajda's *Man of Iron* wins the Golden Palm at the Cannes Film Festival.

May 28   Cardinal Wyszynski is dead at age of 79. Vast crowds throng funeral service.

June 5   Walesa addresses the International Labor Organization in Geneva.

June 7   Czeslaw Milosz returns for a visit to Poland and is given a hero's welcome.

June 13   Walesa denounces the defacing of a Soviet war memorial in Lublin, one of the first overt anti-Soviet manifestations, and has Solidarity crew clean it up.

June 27   In Poznan, 150,000 attend memorial service on 25th anniversary of 1956 massacres; monument is dedicated.

July 7   The bedridden John Paul II names Bishop Jozef Glemp of Warmia to succeed Wyszynski as primate.

July 14–20   Extraordinary congress of Polish CP (with 80% of the delegates attending their first party congress) yields few extraordinary results, despite high hopes, and nothing much changes.

July 27   In Warsaw, *Man of Iron* opens, uncensored.

July 25–Aug. 10   With food lines lengthening and supplies dwindling precipitously, food protests erupt throughout Poland. The regime, meanwhile, launches a withering propaganda offensive against Solidarity.

Aug. 3   Twelve thousand air traffic controllers in the United States launch a strike. President Reagan, who has nothing but praise for unionizing in Poland, quickly fires the strikers and busts their union (PATCO).

Aug. 5 Leaders of the ultra-nationalist KPN arrested.

Aug. 12 Solidarity leadership asks population to refrain from further demonstrations.

Aug. 18–19 Print workers strike in protest against regime's propaganda campaign.

Aug. 31 Poles observe first anniversary of Gdansk accords. Solidarity now claims 10 million dues-paying members, all of whom have participated in the delegate-selection process leading up to the upcoming national congress.

Sept. 4 Soviet navy launches war games off Poland's Baltic coast.

Sept. 5–7 A prison break and takeover in Bydgoszcz defused by Solidarity.

Sept. 5–10 In Gdansk, 890 delegates from throughout Poland convene the first session of Solidarity's National Congress. Glemp opens congress with mass. Issues of internal democratic process dominate early proceedings. Congress denounces the "workers' self-management" bill currently before parliament as a charade, proposes its own version, and demands a national referendum to decide the issue. Finally, the delegates send a provocative message of support to independent workers' movements throughout the Soviet bloc, and then adjourn for two weeks.

Sept. 11 Moscow describes first session of Solidarity Congress as an "antisocialist and anti-Soviet orgy."

Sept. 12–22 Tensions escalate rapidly as Polish CP leaders receive, and leak, a very threatening letter from their Soviet counterparts. Fiercest propaganda attacks yet on Solidarity. Meanwhile, government and union officials negotiate the self-management issue.

Sept. 15 Vatican releases papal encyclical entitled *Laborem Exercens (On Human Work)* in which John Paul II echoes many Solidarity positions.

Sept. 22 Walesa rams a mild workers' self-management compromise through his presidium, and the government parliament quickly passes it.

Sept. 26–Oct. 7 Second session of Solidarity Congress opens with new anger over lapse in democratic process in recent negotiations. KOR dissolves itself. Walesa defeats more radical opponents (Gwiazda, Rulewski, and Marian Jurczyk of Szczecin) but garners only 55% of vote for union chairmanship. Solidarity offers its own two-year economic program, and leaders attack excessive military spending.

Oct. 4 Government announces steep price increases on food and tobacco, provoking Solidarity's anger and widespread wildcat strikes.

Oct. 15 Temporary rollback of price increases.

Oct. 18 Kania resigns as first secretary of CP, is replaced by Jaruzelski who is now prime minister, defense minister, and party secretary. Jaruzelski proposes a ban on strikes.

Oct. 19 Walesa finds himself opposing both a ban on strikes and the strikes the ban would ban.

Oct. 20 Police provocations in Katowice.

Oct. 23 Jaruzelski fans small army units out into the countryside, allegedly to help rural administrators in food procurement.

Oct. 28 Solidarity stages one-hour nationwide strike. Both Jaruzelski and Walesa hope it will be the last, but it isn't.

Early November Faced with the increasingly evident counterproductivity of traditional strikes, workers in the Sosnowiec mines in Lower Silesia contrive an intriguing innovation: "the active strike." They continue working but they manage the mine and supervise distribution themselves.

Nov. 1 Thousands in Warsaw commemorate the victims of Katyn.

Nov. 4 Unprecedented summit meeting brings together Glemp, Walesa, and Jaruzelski.

Nov. 7 Most extensive ongoing strike since August 1980 continues in Zielona Gora province: 160,000 out in protest over a fired activist.

Nov. 9 Government proposes a seven-member "Front of National Accord," with Solidarity to have only one seat.

Nov. 11 For the first time since 1939, Poles mark anniversary of country's rebirth at end of First World War in ceremonies which commemorate the memory of Marshal Jozef Pilsudski.

Nov. 12 Zielona Gora strike ends, but 250,000 other Poles are engaged in wildcat strikes.

Nov. 17 Solidarity and government launch first substantive talks in over three months, but they get nowhere and are completely stalemated by Nov. 26.

Nov. 19 Polish army announces a surprise withdrawal of the hundreds of small units surprisingly sent out into the country on Oct. 23.

Nov. 20 Consortium of West German gas companies concludes last in a series of West European-Soviet agreements, clearing the way for construction of the $15 billion Siberian gas pipeline.

Nov. 23 Fifteen Solidarity members, including Gwiazda, resign from their positions in protest over Walesa's "too conciliatory stand."

Nov. 24 Soviet Marshal Viktor Kulikow, commander of the Warsaw Pact forces, in Warsaw for consultations with Jaruzelski.

Nov. 29 Jaruzelski tells Central Committee that "a state of war" is imminent if there is not a quick end to strikes.

Dec. 2 Helicopter-borne Warsaw police forcibly break up a week-long sit-in by 300 cadets at the Firefighters' Academy.

Dec. 5 Strikes in support of students at the Radom Engineering School (who are protesting the appointment of their new rector) now idle 70 of Poland's 104 institutions of higher learning.

Dec. 6 Warsaw regional Solidarity sets Dec. 17 as a day of protest against Dec. 2 police action and urges the national union to go along; also calls on national leadership to establish a force of "permanent worker guards."

Dec. 7 Warsaw Radio broadcasts tape recordings of a recent closed Solidarity leadership meeting in which Walesa and other leaders predict imminent confrontation and seem to advocate overthrow of the government. Solidarity claims the passages have been taken out of context.

Dec. 10 Soviet leadership fires off yet another angry note to Polish Central Committee.

Dec. 11–12 Solidarity's national commission convenes a weekend meeting in Gdansk. Increasingly radical rhetoric; national endorsement of Warsaw Solidarity's December 17 protest, calls for free elections to parliament, and, as Walesa looks on in frustration, a call for a February referendum in which the entire country will be canvassed for its opinion of Poland's current rulers and alliances.

III. The State of War (1981–1984)

Dec. 13 The eleventh anniversary of the beginning of the bloody week of martyrs on the Baltic coast (1970). During the night between Saturday, Dec. 12, and Sunday, Dec. 13, Polish army troops seal off town after town throughout Poland. Phone and telex lines are cut. Thousands of activists are interned, including Walesa, virtually all of the members of Solidarity's national commission meeting in Gdansk, and most of the former members of KOR. (In an attempt to soften the blow, the regime also arrests former party secretary Gierek and several colleagues.) All Solidarity offices are seized, and the union suspended. At 6 A.M., General Jaruzelski, in a radio address which will be repeated hourly throughout the day, declares "a state of war" and places the country under a 21-man Army Council of National Salvation (WRON). Within hours, 20 separate martial law decrees suspend basic rights, ban all public gatherings, institute strict curfew, sanction censorship, suspend mail and telephone service, militarize key enterprises, ban all unauthorized printing, restrict TV and radio to one Warsaw channel, institute summary courts, etc. The 30,000-man crack ZOMO forces are deployed throughout the country in preparation for confrontations the next day, Monday.

Dec. 14 Workers occupy their factories all over the country: Gdansk, Szczecin, Nowa Huta, Ursus, Katowice. . . .

Dec. 15 One by one, the government crushes individual strikes: Regular army troops surround factories while ZOMOS go in to forcibly evict the striking workers. Tremendous quantities of food start appearing in stores as the regime tries to convince Poles things are getting better, and only succeeds in convincing them that it was hoarding supplies all along.

Dec. 16 Eleventh anniversary of the worst violence in Gdansk in 1970 sees a daylong battle throughout the city. Government announces seven deaths the previous day at the Wujek mine in Silesia. Warsaw radio's list of 57 interned dissidents includes several who have not even been in the country for some time.

Dec. 17 ZOMOS complete occupation of the Lenin shipyard; in Warsaw, a tear gas attack on demonstrators seeking sanctuary in the Church of the Holy Cross.

Dec. 18 Government reports most of the country has been "normalized," except for a steel mill and a few mines in Silesia.

Dec. 19 Jaruzelski cables Brezhnev birthday greetings (the Soviet leader is 75) and thanks him for his help and understanding.

Dec. 20 Polish ambassador to U.S. defects, seeks political asylum.

Dec. 21 Katowice steelworks subdued in tank assault. Several thousand miners are still holed up in two Silesian mines.

Dec. 23 President Reagan blames Soviets but directs sanctions at Poles.

Dec. 24 Regime briefly lifts curfew for Christmas Eve. Jaruzelski, in a Christmas address, assures Poles that martial law is preferable to the civil war which would have been the inevitable alternative. Polish ambassador to Japan defects, asking for U.S. asylum.

Dec. 28 The last Silesian mine occupation ends.

1982

Jan. 6 In an Epiphany sermon, Glemp denounces loyalty oaths as "unethical," but appeals for public restraint to avoid bloodshed.

Jan. 7 First issue of *Tygodnik Wojenny (War Weekly)*, underground journal.

Jan. 9 Glemp meets with Jaruzelski.

Jan. 10 Telephone communications within towns restored, subject to wiretap and interruption.

Jan. 16 Zbigniew Bujak, the Warsaw region leader who managed to elude arrest and is hiding underground, tells the *New York Times* that the first shock of martial law has passed and spontaneous opposition movement is growing. Actors' boycott already in full force.

Jan. 27 Steep price increases, effective February 1, are announced.

Feb. 10 Intercity telephone service restored, via operator, with the exception of Gdansk.

Feb. 28 Government claims total of 6,647 internments so far, with 2,552 already released. Other sources claim somewhat higher totals.

Mar. 3 Government announces that all those interned may apply for permission to leave Poland on a one-way visa.

Mar. 9 Military uniforms will no longer be worn by television announcers.

Mar. 19 Polish Journalists Association dissolved.

Mar. 21 Lech Walesa is refused permission to attend the baptism of his seventh child, a daughter born just weeks after the imposition of martial law and given the highly symbolic name of Maria Wiktoria.

Apr. 6 In Frankfurt, agreement to reschedule part of Poland's debt.

Apr. 12 Easter Monday: Official monopoly over broadcast media is broken as Radio Solidarity transmits an eight-minute message in Warsaw, asking people to flick their lights on and off to indicate reception.

Apr. 22 Representatives from underground Solidarity regional organizations in Gdansk (Bogdan Lis), Warsaw (Zbigniew Bujak), Krakow (Wladyslaw Hardek), and Wroclaw (Wladyslaw Frasyniuk) form Temporary Coordinating Commission (the TKK).

Apr. 25 Glemp and Jaruzelski meet for second time.

Apr. 30 Fifteen-minute strike in Gdansk shipyard demands release of Walesa and other internees.

May 1 In response to a TKK call for boycott of official May Day celebrations, a big counterdemonstration in Warsaw—the first mass demonstration since Dec. 13. Solidarity badges everywhere. Chants: "We want Lech, not Wojciech!"

May 2 Regime lifts curfew, announces automatic dialing nationwide to resume on May 10.

May 3 Rallies in Warsaw, Gdansk, and elsewhere celebrate the 1791 constitution. Violent ZOMO response in some places. Crowds chant, "Gestapo, Gestapo." According to the regime, 2,269 people are detained during these early May demonstrations.

May 4 Authorities impose temporary phone blackout on Warsaw and Gdansk.

May 13 Fifth-month anniversary of martial law observed with strikes and demonstrations at universities throughout the country; several deans and professors interned.

May 19 Underground printing flourishes. Warsaw region weekly publishes open letter from Jacek Kuron.

May 20 Jan Jozef Lipski released from internment, given permission to go to England for medical treatment.

June 8 Radio Solidarity makes first Gdansk broadcast.

July 5 Glemp to Vatican.

July 6 Radio Solidarity makes its first Krakow broadcast.

July 12 Glemp indicates Pope's 1982 pilgrimage to celebrate the 600th anniversary of the Jasna Gora monastery in Czestochowa may have to be delayed.

July 21 On eve of official national holiday, Jaruzelski announces release of many internees (including all women) and restoration of international telephone service, but says Pope will not come this year.

Aug. 1 Large gathering at Powazki Cemetery in Warsaw, commemorating Warsaw Uprising (1944), hears a recorded appeal by Bujak.

Aug. 10 In Szczecin, 1,000 people attend funeral of son and daughter-in-law of interned regional leader Marian Jurczyk. They are said to have fallen from a window, and he is allowed out briefly to attend ceremony.

Aug. 13 Polish press agency reports that many internees released last month are being reinterned because of resuming activities "incompatible with state security."

Aug. 16 Jaruzelski to Crimea for a short working visit with Brezhnev.

Aug. 26 In Czestechowa, Glemp appeals for release of Lech Walesa but nevertheless calls on Poles not to take their grievances into the streets.

Aug. 31 Second anniversary of the Gdansk accords sees the biggest mass demonstrations yet throughout the country. Police detain over 4,000; zomos use firearms. There are at least seven deaths, including three in Lubin. In Warsaw, police arrest Zbigniew Romaszewski, the chief coordinators of Radio Solidarity (his wife and co-worker, Zofia, was arrested a few weeks earlier). They will be sentenced to 4½ and 3 years respectively.

Sept. 1 Demonstrations continue in Wroclaw and Lubin. Wladyslaw Gomulka dies at 77.

Sept. 3 Formal charges of attempting to overthrow the state are filed against KOR leaders Jacek Kuron, Adam Michnik, Henryk Wujec, Jan Litynski, Jan Jozef Lipski, and Miroslaw Chojecki. Although the first four are in internment centers and the latter two out of the country, the regime still blames them for the Aug. 31 disturbances.

Sept. 5 Bishop Ignacy Tokarczuk offers a particularly tough sermon at Jasna Gora, especially when compared with Glemp's of the previous week.

Sept. 16 Although still seriously ill, Lipski returns from England to face arrest in a show of solidarity with the other KOR defendants. (While in England, he has completed a book on the history of KOR.)

Sept. 22 Kuron is allowed to attend his father's funeral for 15 minutes. (Exactly two months later, Kuron's wife Grazyna dies as well, a victim of TB she contracted while in internment camp.)

Oct. 5 Glemp cancels trip to U.S. as Polish parliament prepares to meet. Wladyslaw Frasyniuk, arrested in Wroclaw, is replaced on the TKK by his lieutenant Piotr Bednarz.

Oct. 8 Polish parliament delegalizes Solidarity.

Oct. 10 In response, TKK calls for a four-hour strike on Nov. 10, the second anniversary of the union's registration. Meanwhile, at the Vatican, John Paul II canonizes Maksymilian Kolbe, a Polish martyr of Auschwitz.

Oct. 11 Spontaneous strikes in Gdansk. Workers demand reconstitution of Solidarity and release of Walesa.

Oct. 12 Authorities militarize the Lenin shipyard: the strike crumbles.

Oct. 13 Support demonstrations for the (already collapsed) Lenin shipyard strike in Warsaw and Nowa Huta, where 10,000 march and one young man is killed.

Oct. 20 In Nowa Huta, thousands attend the funeral of the man killed Oct. 12. The TKK, meanwhile, ups the ante, calling for an eight-hour strike on Nov. 10, actions during December leading toward a general strike in the spring, and a complete boycott of the new party-sponsored unions.

Oct. 26 The Polish parliament passes a variety of restrictive bills, most notoriously its "social parasite" legislation (men who are not engaged in socially useful work, as defined by the regime, can now be sent to work camps).

Oct. 30 Glemp in Italy openly admits the Polish Church hierarchy strongly opposes the planned November protests.

Nov. 8 Glemp and Jaruzelski confer, emerge declaring "a common concern for maintaining and consolidating calm, social harmony, and work" (i.e., *Don't strike*). Pope's visit is announced for June 1983. Meanwhile, Lech Walesa sends Jaruzelski a letter proposing a meeting; and in Wroclaw, the new TKK member Piotr Bednarz and eleven of his regional associates are arrested, thereby gutting a once-strong underground organization.

Nov. 9 Roman Laba, American Fulbright scholar, is arrested, accused of too close ties with the underground, and expelled.

Nov. 10 The TKK's eight-hour strike fails to materialize.

Nov. 11 Kremlin announces death of Leonid Brezhnev the previous day. Warsaw regime announces release of Lech Walesa.

Nov. 14 Walesa returns to Gdansk.

Nov. 15 Frasyniuk goes on trial in Wroclaw, will receive a six-year sentence.

Nov. 20 Glemp meets with Walesa.

Nov. 27 TKK regroups, acknowledges new conditions, and cancels December actions.

Dec. 1 Actors' union abolished.

Dec. 12 On eve of its anniversary, Jaruzelski indicates martial law will be suspended by year's end.

Dec. 16 Walesa detained at his home to prevent his participation at 1970 commemoration ceremony.

Dec. 23 All remaining internees are released with the exception of seven Solidarity activists who now have their status shifted to arrest: Gwiazda, Jurczyk, Modzelewski, Rulewski, Jaworski, Palka, and Rozplochowski. Those imprisoned for martial-law violations (estimates range from 1,500 to 3,500) remain in jail.

Dec. 24 At the behest of Cardinal Glemp, actors end their boycott.

Dec. 31 Martial law, its main features now codified into the civil code, is suspended. Late this night, two loudspeakers broadcast words of encouragement to the KOR prisoners in Warsaw.

1983

Feb. 2 Dr. Marek Edelman, the only leader of the Ghetto Uprising (1943) still living in Poland, announces his refusal to participate in the government's international commemoration of the 40th anniversary of the Ghetto Uprising, set for April.

Feb. 10 Walesa interrogated in the case of the KOR leaders.

Mar. 9 Anna Walentynowicz goes on trial, will receive a fifteen-month suspended sentence.

Apr. 9–11 Walesa holds secret meetings with TKK, returns to tell about it. He, his wife, and his chauffeur face interrogation by embarrassed police.

Apr. 14 Edelman placed under "protective custody" in Lodz.

Apr. 17 Solidarity holds alternative commemoration ceremony at the Warsaw Ghetto Monument.

Apr. 18–21 Official government ceremonies commemorate the Ghetto Uprising. The PLO lays a wreath, and the World Jewish Congress's delegates leave in protest.

Apr. 20 Union of Polish Visual Artists suspended.

Apr. 22 Walesa given permission to return to his shipyard job.

May 1 Unofficial May Day celebrations in 20 cities draw an estimated 100,000. Another death in Nowa Huta.

May 3 Plainclothes police beat up volunteers at St. Martin's Church in Warsaw. Wajda is dismissed as head of Film Unit X.

May 6 Soviet journal *New Times* attacks the Polish weekly *Polityka*, bastion of Rakowski and other party "moderates."

May 12 Eighteen-year-old Grzegorz Przemyk, son of poet Barbara Sadowska (a volunteer at St. Martin's), is halted by police as he and friends celebrate the completion of school exams, is taken to the station and beaten so badly that two days later, he dies.

May 19 Over ten thousand attend the Warsaw funeral of Przemyk.

June 14 Litynski fails to return to prison after furlough to attend first communion of his daughter, goes underground.

June 16–23 Pope John Paul II arrives in Warsaw at the start of his second Polish pilgrimage. During the next eight days, he meets twice with Jaruzelski; holds huge masses in Warsaw, Czestochowa, Poznan, Wroclaw, and Krakow (before throngs numbering as high as 2 million who cheer every reference to "solidarity"); beatifies three new Polish Church figures; and finally, on the last day, holds a private meeting with Lech Walesa in the Tatra mountains.

June 25 The Vatican's *Osservatore Romano* publishes a commentary praising Poland's independent spirit but suggesting that the time has come for Walesa to step aside in the interests of social peace. Its author, Jesuit father Virgilio Levi, resigns a few hours later, but the Vatican never explicitly denies the purport of the article.

July 6 On his 60th birthday, General Jaruzelski is awarded the Order of Lenin, the USSR's highest honor for foreign dignitaries.

July 12 A parliamentary commission clears Gierek and his senior colleagues of responsibility for Poland's economic debacle.

July 20–21 Parliament passes new, still tougher legislation in anticipation of complete lifting of martial law.

July 22   Martial law is formally lifted. A partial amnesty is announced, some prisoners are released, but the trial of the KOR and Solidarity leaders is still pending.

Aug. 1   Lech Walesa returns to work, wearing a Solidarity T-shirt, after taking the July vacation he wanted instead of the August one the regime wanted him to take. Conducts several interviews but is not reprimanded.

Aug. 3   TKK dismisses lifting of martial law as propaganda gesture, calls for actions on Aug. 31, including a two-hour transportation boycott.

Aug. 14   Solidarity's underground branch in Gdansk threatens a one-week work slowdown if the regime doesn't start negotiations with Walesa by Aug. 23. Bujak subsequently endorses the idea, recommends nationwide compliance.

Aug. 16   East German party leader Erich Honecker in Warsaw on official visit, the first by a Warsaw Pact leader since Aug. 1980.

Aug. 19   Polish writers' union banned.

Aug. 23   TKK founding member and head of Krakow region, Wladyslaw Hardek, appears on TV, urging his colleagues to come out of hiding and give up the pointless struggle. Walesa and others are dubious as to the statement's voluntary nature.

Aug. 24   The work slowdown in Gdansk and elsewhere appears ineffectual.

Aug. 25   Deputy Prime Minister Rakowski meets with workers in Gdansk shipyard, clashes with Walesa. Rakowski is booed, Walesa cheered and carried out of the hall atop workers' shoulders. Still, portions of the meeting are subsequently televised.

Aug. 31   Demonstrations throughout the country mark the third anniversary of the Gdansk accords, and although they are not as large as the previous year's, the Jaruzelski regime has still clearly not gained the allegiance of its subjects.

Sept. 1   Korean Air Lines Flight 007 shot down over Soviet airspace (269 die); this incident, along with the coming deployment of U.S. cruise and Pershing missiles in Western Europe, signals a precipitous decline in U.S.-Soviet relations.

Sept. 18   TKK sends letter of support to Chilean workers and trade unionists as protests there swell on the occasion of General Pinochet's tenth anniversary in power.

Sept. 27   Polish TV broadcasts a virulent documentary entitled "Money," which purports to present "evidence" of Walesa's penchant for financial self-aggrandizement. As the show begins, the announcer cautions, "Because the heroes of this program use vulgar expressions, we ask children and young people not to watch. We also inform you that we have removed from the conversation of persons appearing in this program excerpts which are insulting to the Pope, the Church, and Polish Church personalities." Because of the poor quality of various wiretaps, the announcer often reads his own version of what is being said—a version which includes several blatant internal contradictions.

Sept. 28   In Gdansk, 40,000 fans at a football match, noticing Walesa in the crowd, break into chants of "Solidarity" and "Walesa." Polish TV has to cut away from its coverage of the game.

Oct. 5   Lech Walesa is awarded the 1983 Nobel Peace Prize. The Polish regime lodges a diplomatic protest with the Norwegian government.

Oct. 12 According to Radio Warsaw 3.5 million members have by now joined the 18,000 new officially sanctioned unions.

Oct. 14 Two-day plenary session of the Polish Communist Party opens, after several postponements, focussing on ideology for the first time in twenty years.

Oct. 25 Urban suggests that the eleven KOR and Solidarity prisoners awaiting trial could be released if they would agree to emigrate to the West, at least until "complete stability" is restored. They have long refused such an offer and instead insist on a trial. Meanwhile, the United States invades the Caribbean island of Grenada, somewhat undercutting its right to complain about how the Soviets behave in their own sphere of influence.

Nov. 1 Rationing of butter, suspended five months earlier, is resumed. The regime begins preparing the population for major food-price increases, slated for the new year (butter up 40%, chicken up 70%).

Nov. 2 President Reagan offers mild concessions on some of his sanctions.

Nov. 3 Walesa announces he will not go to Norway in person to collect his Nobel prize, that it would not be proper for him "to enjoy such a glittering occasion while political prisoners are still behind bars." (It is also unclear whether he'd be let back into Poland.) He will try to send his wife, Danuta, instead.

Nov. 19 The regime warns Glemp to silence 69 dissident priests.

Nov. 20 Emerging from a second weekend-long secret meeting with the TKK, Walesa calls for a struggle against the upcoming food-price increases.

Nov. 21 Jaruzelski relinquishes his post as defense minister, but only after Parliament votes the creation of a National Defense Committee (a sort of military-government-in-reserve empowered to reimpose martial law at a moment's notice), of which he is named chairman.

Nov. 30 Czech party leader Gustav Husak in Warsaw on official visit; he and Jaruzelski endorse Soviet placement of missiles in Czechoslovakia and East Germany in response to U.S. deployment of Pershing and Cruise missiles this fall in Western Europe.

Dec. 5 At a Gdansk press conference, Lech Walesa advocates an end to Western sanctions "because what Poland needs now is not losses of millions of dollars but aid in thousands of millions." President Reagan promises to give Walesa's plea serious consideration.

Dec. 10 In Oslo, Danuta Walesa accepts the Nobel Peace Prize in her husband's name. Included in the audience, at the personal invitation of Walesa, are representatives of the free trade unions of Chile.

Dec. 13 On the second anniversary of martial law, Walesa and his newly returned wife travel to Czestochowa where, before the Black Madonna, he dedicates his Nobel Prize to the nation. On their way back to Gdansk, the Walesas' car is stopped thirteen times by the police.

Dec. 16 In the face of a massive police presence, demonstrations on this anniversary are only thinly attended. Walesa, sick at home with a cold, fails to attend a ceremony at the Gdansk 1970 memorial.

1984

Jan. 12   After thirty-nine years of rule, including over two years of martial law, the Warsaw regime still lacks the authority to announce food-price increases and then make them stick. Facing overwhelming public opposition, the regime completely revises its recently announced price schedule, cancelling some increases, lowering others, while further increasing the prices of certain luxury goods. The regime credits the new officially sanctioned unions with crucial intercession on society's behalf, thereby at least salvaging some propaganda benefits from the episode.

Notes

1. As for the situation of Western banks vis-à-vis Poland, there's an old Eastern European Jewish story that applies. Schlomo can't sleep one night; he's tossing and turning and itching and squirming, and finally his wife says, "Schlomo, what's wrong? You're driving me crazy with all this tossing." And Schlomo says, "Tomorrow's Friday." "So? So tomorrow's Friday. So what?" asks his wife. "Well, I owe Moishe ten rubles on Friday, and I don't have the money." "Ah, Schlomo," sighs the wife, climbing out of bed and heading toward the window. "Here, I'll take care of that." She opens the window, leans out into the still night air, and yells, "Hey, Moishe!" Across the way, a few moments later, Moishe's window creaks open. "Yeah," the old man grumbles, "what do you want at this crazy hour?" "Moishe," says the woman, "tomorrow's Friday." "Yeah, I know. So what?" "Well, Schlomo owes you ten rubles tomorrow." "Yeah, I know, so what?" "Listen," says the woman. "He doesn't have the money. He's not going to pay you." Whereupon she closes the window and returns to bed. "There," she says to her husband. "Now, *you* sleep and let *him* stay up all night worrying."

Or as one economist explained the situation for me: "When you owe the bank one hundred dollars and you can't pay them back, you're in big trouble. When you owe them a hundred million dollars and you can't pay them back, *they're* in big trouble."

In this case, as we have seen, the money owed is over 25 billion dollars, and it's owed to a consortium of over one thousand Western banks (principally American and West German). As of May, though, these banks were not exactly suffering. Poland has been rescheduling its debt, but none of the debt has been cancelled, and rescheduling merely means that Poland pays money now for the privilege of being able to forestall its payments on the principal until later. In other words, Poland will end up paying the banks substantially more in total than it would have had it been able to meet the initial schedule. The banks will do fine, so long as Poland doesn't default completely.

Some people wonder why Poland doesn't just default and refuse to honor its debts. "I suppose they could do so," one Western economist told me, "but then the country would be reduced to the status of a leper, a pariah among nations. No one would ever extend Poland credit again—it would be virtually impossible for an industrialized nation to proceed in an environment of such isolation. No, for all their exposure, the banks have Poland nailed."

In fairness to the Polish authorities it should be noted that theirs is a relatively modest example of a widespread international phenomenon—the burgeoning during the 1970s of the developing world's debt. During the same period, their counterparts in Argentina compiled a debt of $43 billion, in Mexico $80 billion, and in Brazil $88 billion! Profiteering was rampant in each of these countries during their development binges, and now revolutionary pressures likewise haunt many of their austerity drives. The difference, though, is that Poland was supposed to be a worker's state.

2. When portions of these essays first appeared in November 1981 in *The New Yorker*, this section on Jewishness and anti-Semitism in contemporary Poland evoked the strongest response among the readership—at least as far as I can gauge from the ensuing correspondence.

One man from New Jersey wrote: "Worse than an anti-Semite is an anti-Semitism apologist. Only a Jew could find a historical rationale for his own persecution. To claim that anti-Semitism is not deeply rooted in the Poles since they recognized the lie in Russian propaganda about Solidarity being a Zionist plot insults Polish intelligence. Until the Poles admit their cruelty to others and accept differences within their nation, they will never treat each other fairly. The Germans have at least expressed regrets for their treatment of the Jews. As far as I have seen, there is nothing of the kind coming from the Poles."

A woman from San Francisco who has worked with Soviet Jews "felt a disturbing familiarity in the accounts which you recorded and the intricate apologetics I've heard from Soviet Jews about anti-Semitism. It was hard to know what to say to these people when I would hear the most blatantly anti-Semitic 'analyses' of history being solemnly explained to me. . . . While deploring it, Americans can at least understand the process of government-sanctioned anti-Semitism in Eastern Europe. But it is much more difficult to comprehend the degree to which these racist attitudes have become woven into the fabric of those societies." This reader questioned in particular "the (supposed) facts about the percentage of Jews in the Polish Communist party. I've found that those stories turn out to be the Eastern

European equivalent of the 'Jews control the U.S. media and all U.S. corporations' type of misinformation with which we've all become too familiar."

On the other hand, a Brooklyn Heights Jewish emigré from Poland wrote to disassociate himself from the comments of the Los Angeles emigré quoted in my article who felt that the calamities currently visiting Poland couldn't have happened to a more deserving people: "I find this statement reprehensible and difficult to understand and accept as I too experienced hunger in Poland during the war and I am far from indifferent but rather very compassionate and troubled by the knowledge that in the country, in the city, in the house where I and my forefathers lived, there are children who are hungry. . . . Some of my friends who have the same background and have had the same experience as Jews in Poland feel exactly as I do and do not feel the vindictiveness expressed by our counterpart in Los Angeles."

3. This brief, curious war between the Soviets and the Poles in 1920 commands an extraordinarily important place in the Polish imagination. The various campaigns and countercampaigns of 1920 took place against a double backdrop. To begin with, there was the almost simultaneous upsurge of Bolshevism in both Russia and Germany at the conclusion of the war. (By some accounts, the Soviet army was in part attempting to cross Poland in order to lend assistance to the besieged Communist communes in postwar Prussia and Bavaria.) Secondly, these battles took place during the period of the Versailles Conference, when the newly sovereign state of Poland was attempting to lay claim to the widest possible territory— specifically, to reestablish its borders as they existed before the first of the partitions that completely obliterated Poland in 1772. The August battle on the outskirts of Warsaw had actually been preceded, four months earlier, by a battle just outside Kiev, in the Ukraine. Indeed, it was only because the Polish army's Ukraine offensive had become so ridiculously overextended during the spring that the Soviet counter-offensive was in turn able to drive the Poles all the way back to Warsaw during the summer. In the Treaty of Riga (1921), Poland managed to secure most of its claims on Soviet territory—an outcome that the Kremlin would not forget and that would contribute to Soviet diplomacy twenty years later (the Nazi-Soviet Nonaggression Pact).

It turns out that the unknown soldier in the Tomb of the Unknown Soldier in Warsaw died not in one of the world wars, but rather in the Polish-Soviet War of 1920. The Poles have long relished the spectacle of Soviet and Polish Communist Party officials delivering their ritual wreaths to the monument at official functions several times each year.

4. Following *Proba Mikrofonu*, Lozinski went on to concoct a remarkable feature film—part documentary and part fiction—entitled *Jak Zyc (How to Live)*. Shot before August 1980, it, like the earlier film, was only released after that summer. The film's poster, suddenly visible all over Warsaw this spring, gives a clue as to why release was delayed. It shows a large stone bust with a cravat dangling from the neck and instead of a face, a simple word engraved into the stonebulb: "TAK" ("Yes").

Jak Zyc documents an astonishing few weeks at a summer camp for young Communist families. The camp—a reward for "good behavior"—was used until recently as an incentive to keep young Party bureaucrats in line, and invariably turned into a festival for sycophants. Although Lozinski inserts a few actors of his own into the camp, most of the action in the film (specifically the Orwellian competition to determine "the best young Communist family," in which everyone was graded daily on a variety of numerical indices, children encouraged to rat on parents, and families to undermine one another's orthodoxy) was actually happening at the camp anyway.

In a recent interview, Lozinski noted that repression during the Gierek era may have been just as virulent as before, although it wore a different face: "Certainly during the seventies there were no mass arrests or (after 1970) bloody solutions. But please note that the mechanism was different. The dominant system of 'social education' was a system of rewards and privileges instead of a system of punishment." Later on in the interview, when asked how the people at the camp reacted to the presence of his cameras, Lozinski replied, "They were convinced that, since we were from Warsaw, we were something like another TV crew. Indeed, the staff people at the camp (the ones who were scoring the competition) may have performed their functions even more assiduously than usual, perhaps expecting that, in line with the reward system, the film would presently be seen by their own superiors."

5. It is an occasion for sad reflection to gauge the very different qualities of this interpenetration of film and politics in Poland and the United States today. In Poland, cinema and politics reflect and confirm each other's vitality and significance; in America, our actor-president merely highlights the emptiness of our image-addled political process.

6. The anchor, a longtime token of Polish-Catholic nationalism, has had a rich history in Gdansk. After 1970, several of the graves in the Gdansk cemeteries, otherwise unmarked, consisted of simple white crosses bearing small crucified Christ figures from the feet of which (an inverse image) hung modest anchors. These marked the graves of the noncorpses from the December massacre: shipbuilders who had died Polish Catholic martyrs.

7. This distinction between "political" and "social" concerns predates the current Polish situation. Indeed, throughout much of the early parts of his classic chronicle of the 1917 Russian Revolution, *Ten Days That Shook the World*, John Reed goes to great lengths to portray the different conceptions of revolution championed by the Mensheviks, on the one hand, and the Bolsheviks, on the other. Whereas the Mensheviks, according to Reed, were satisfied to limit their revolution to the "political" sphere, the Bolsheviks insisted on carrying it into the "social" realm as well. "Having at one bound leaped from the Middle Ages into the twentieth century," Reed concludes, "Russia showed the startled world two systems of revolution—the political and the social—in mortal combat" (Penguin edition, 1977, p. 36). Of course, its Bolshevik lineage renders Solidarity's position all the more interesting.

8. Contemporary economic policy in the United States affords an interesting contrast to this Polish approach. Under Reagan's tax plan, the recent cuts have been made on a same-percentage-for-everyone basis, with the result that rich peo-

ple are getting breaks amounting to thousands of dollars each, while poor people get nothing at all. The contrast could hardly be more galling.

9. Daniel Singer's book includes an appendix in which he details the extraordinary evolution of the consciousness of the Polish working class during the summer of 1980 (*The Road to Gdansk*, Monthly Review Press, New York City, 1980). "Although I was one of the few Western writers to go quite as far out on a limb as I did," Singer told me during a conversation in his Paris home, "I must say I did not anticipate the movement's being as mature or as adult as it's been. Much of that maturation however, occurred during August itself and perhaps couldn't have been anticipated. This is something which Western theorists have tended to downplay: the extraordinary capacity for people's maturing under pressure. I have spoken with several of the Polish intellectual 'experts' who were called to Gdansk by the workers about a week after the strike began, and they all tell the same story. Here they were, fresh from Warsaw, and their first bit of expert insight was that there was no possibility of obtaining an independent free trade union, so that they were coming in with all sorts of compromise proposals. And instead they were immediately told by everybody, from the first worker they met up to the presidium of the strike committee, that on that issue there could be no budging. Anything else was negotiable, but not that. Now, the idea of an independent trade union was something that, ten days before, maybe twenty people throughout the labor force of the Gdansk region had even thought of. I mean, implicitly perhaps, many thousands favored the idea, but they didn't even know it. And in ten short days, this demand for free and independent trade unions was to become the central expression of the will of the whole of the working class of the maritime region, and within a few more days, of the entire country. It's quite amazing."

10. "The only democratic counterforce to vanguard (Leninist) politics or to corporate politics," Lawrence Goodwyn, the historian of American populism, wrote in a recent article in the new quarterly *Democracy* "is a politically democratic presence in society—that is, some kind of empowered and democratic polity. Such an organized democratic presence is quite literally the most fundamental threat conceivable to the continuing dominance of corporate and vanguard elites. The historical evidence is overwhelming that both will, when confronted with even the beginnings of an autonomous democratic presence, move promptly to destroy it, divert it, buy it, or try in any way to gain effective control over it." ("Organizing Democracy: The Limits of Theory and Practice" *Democracy*, January 1981, p. 47)

Goodwyn's formulation helps explain a certain wary reserve which was evident among many American corporatists and bankers as they observed the burgeoning of Solidarity. Secretary of State Alexander Haig and some of the other alarmists in the new Reagan administration had some more immediate tactical considerations in mind as well during those days when they seemed almost to be wishing for a Soviet invasion. For starters, the Soviet Union's ongoing restraint in the Polish situation during the spring and summer of 1981 was running absolutely counter to everything the hard-line anti-Soviet ideologues in the new Reagan State Department would have had Americans believe about Soviet intentions and capabilities. Far from appearing power glutted and ambition crazed, the Kremlin leadership was appearing either too weak or too circumspect to take decisive action in its own interests on its very borders. Indeed, the Soviet Union seemed, if anything, a "pitiful giant"—hardly, at any rate, the kind of fearsome opponent that might justify "massive defense spending increases" on the American side.

Were the Soviet Union to have invaded Poland, on the other hand, hard-liners in the Reagan administration could have anticipated two very handsome side-benefits. First of all, the Soviet Union's macrostrategic situation would in reality have been decisively weakened. Its armed forces would suddenly have found themselves bogged down on two fronts—both in Afghanistan and Poland—neither with any hope of short-term resolution. At the same time, the Soviet Union's diplomatic standing would have suffered an overwhelming firestorm, particularly in Western Europe, where the longing for détente had failed to subside nearly as quickly as it had in the United States. Thus, the Soviet Union after a Polish invasion would in reality have constituted a substantially weaker opponent and yet—and here was the second side-benefit—it would have appeared to be a stronger, more threatening one. Imagine the ease with which the American military lobby could have subdued the growing disarmament movement in Europe were the Soviet Union merely to have cooperated by launching a few hundred thousand troops across its western borders.

Some commentators have noted that the Haig State Department's fixation on this question of Soviet intervention inadvertently (or, insist some cynics, intentionally) gave Polish authorities the impression that Washington would not object to an exclusively Polish military solution to the deteriorating political situation.

11. For a more complete discussion of the role of posters and graphic imagery in the achievement of Solidarity, see my article "Solidarnosc," in the February 1982 issue of *Artforum*.

12. The actual figure posted at banks and hotels early in September is 34.22 zlotys to the dollar. Point twenty-two. Since this rate bears no relationship whatsoever to the actual value of the currency, and since American banks and institutions aren't accepting zlotys in payment for their dollar debts in any case, it remains one of the enduring mysteries of travel in Poland just how the authorities come up with their official rates. Why point twenty-two? Why not point twenty-seven or point sixty-one? Somebody no doubt gets paid good money (probably dollars) to think these figures up and then monkey with them from week to week.

13. One afternoon in Warsaw I was speaking with a woman graduate student at the University. I asked her what kinds of political concerns she'd had before 1980. "Mainly involving feminist issues," she replied. "But since last August, I think a lot of us have set some of those concerns aside for the time being. They're important, but at the moment there are some things that are more important—the salvaging of the entire nation, for example—and the solidarity of the movement is the most important of all."

14. There were even some people I talked with who, in the tradition of Polish Romantic messianism, believed that if the Russians invaded, the Poles would *win!* The scenario I was frequently offered conjured up a Russian army bogged down in Poland for months, maybe years, of bloody guerrilla fighting, while one

by one the other Warsaw Pact countries—whose armies, incidentally, would like-wise be detained on Polish soil—would become engulfed in working class re-bellions of their own, rebellions that would eventually spread into the Soviet Union itself, leading to the collapse of the Kremlin regime. Q.E.D.

15. During the final days of the congress, KOR itself disbanded, and its 40 activists simply became members of the union their courageous stand had origi-nally helped to found. Many observers interpreted the group's dissolution as an attempt to calm Soviet hysteria: if so, the attempt failed. KOR had for some time served as a lightning rod, protecting Solidarity itself, in some perverse way, from the full brunt of Soviet attacks; now the Soviet media charged that the union was being infiltrated by the most antisocialist elements in Polish society.

This last charge was answered quite eloquently by Edward Lipinski, the 93-year-old economist who has served as a spiritual father to the Polish dissident movement for some time (indeed, KOR was founded in 1976 in his apartment). Speaking from the podium of the congress, the frail man read the delegates KOR's "last will and testament" with a booming voice and then concluded, "I consider myself a socialist. I have been a socialist since 1906. Socialism was to be the solv-ing of the problems of the working class, the liberation of the working class, the creation of conditions in which every man could become fully developed. But the socialism that was created here was a socialism of mismanagement and inefficiency that brought about economic catastrophe unequalled in 200 years. It is a socialism of prisons, censorship, and police. This socialism has been destroying us for 35 years as it has been destroying others. It is this socialism that is antisocialist and antirevolutionary."

16. There has been much speculation about the timing of the coup. Although Jaruzelski and his colleagues claimed that they had to impose martial law when they did because of the radical and provocative behavior of the delegates gathered at Solidarity's National Commission meeting—that Solidarity had, in effect, finally gone too far—there is little doubt that the seizure of power had been in the plan-ning stages for months (the initial official list of interned Solidarity leaders in-cluded the names of people who hadn't been in the country since the spring), and that the final deployment of troops, materials, and lines of communication was already well under way before the weekend session ever started. So, if there was any relationship between the coup and the National Commission meeting, it was that the convening of the latter allowed a more efficient perpetration of the former: All of Solidarity's leaders were in one convenient location, just waiting, as it were, to be interned *en masse*. There is, however, a strange crimp in this easy analysis: the National Commission meeting was scheduled to have ended on *Saturday afternoon*. According to a friend I visited in Warsaw in October 1982, who'd been present at the National Commission meeting that weekend in Gdansk, had the commission adjourned as originally planned, most of the regional leaders would have already left Gdansk by that evening, and the mass round-up would have been considerably more cumbersome. This woman feels that there were provocateurs at the commission meeting who were intentionally delaying things, prolonging the session into a third, never-to-be-realized day. By early Saturday evening, she continues everyone figured the meeting would have to be extended to Sunday. But then, somehow, to everyone's surprise, the commission did manage

to complete its deliberations by late Saturday evening. And this, in turn, is why a few of the leaders—notably Bujak of Warsaw—were not in their hotel rooms when the police barged in early Sunday morning: they'd already checked out, and they therefore eluded arrest.

17. The 40,000-figure proved inordinately high; chances are the initial figure of internees was closer to 10–15,000. It now appears that the 40,000-figure had its origins deep in the Polish foreign ministry. (It was first quoted, apparently, by the French Foreign Minister following consultations with his Polish counterpart, and within days it was being repeated as unquestioned fact.) If so, this was part of a tremendously ingenious disinformation campaign. By seducing the Western press into bandying about this inflated figure, the Warsaw regime both tried to undercut the future credibility of the Western media on questions of Polish repression and arranged to have the actual figure of 10–15,000 seem modest, indeed moderate, by comparison.

18. Notwithstanding which, Warsavites often deployed the Chilean analogy when considering their own situation. Within weeks of the coup, for example, they were referring to Jaruzelski as Pinochelski. The regime was not amused. The Warsaw correspondent for one of Sweden's top newspapers got into trouble when he filed a story about a Chilean shipworker who'd been active in the early seventies in Allende's revolution but had had to flee his country in 1973 with Allende's ouster by General Pinochet; the man had eventually found refuge as a shipworker in Gdansk, becoming active in Solidarity, only to find himself expelled from Poland following Jaruzelski's coup in December. The Swedish correspondent's story had run in his Stockholm paper flanked by two photographs—one of Pinochet, the other of Jaruzelski—under the headline "THIS MAN SHOULD BEWARE OF DICTATORS IN DARK GLASSES." Thanks to this little whimsical indiscretion, the Swedish correspondent managed to shoot his accreditation all to hell.

19. Rastafari: from Ras Tafari, Prince Tafari, the original name of the man who became Haile Selassie, the Lion of Judah, Emperor of Ethiopia, and the subject of a Black Jamaican religious cult—Rastafarianism—whose members worship him, smoke copious amounts of marijuana, and celebrate their worldview through the highly distinctive type of music known as *reggae*. It's this last bead on the chain—the music, with its fetching combination of millenarian Christian intensity and revolutionary social aspirations—that accounts for the curious epiphany of this magic-mystic Caribbean motto on a grey-flank wall in an Eastern European capital under martial law.

However, the image of Haile Selassie has surfaced in other guises in the recent Polish imagination. In 1978, Polish foreign correspondent Ryszard Kapuscinski published an extraordinarily supple, gorgeously written report on the final years of Haile Selassie's extravagantly corrupt regime, as seen from the point of view of the courtiers who up until the revolution in 1974 had swarmed around the imperial throne but who were now in hiding, fearing for their lives. The account first appeared in installments in the aboveground journal *Kultura* and then in officially sanctioned book form as *The Emperor*. Everybody in Warsaw knew it was a thinly veiled allegory of the Gierek regime. Thus, for example, following the description of a bloodily suppressed revolt "in the North," this passage: "His

Majesty sensed the spirit of the times, and shortly after the bloody rebellion he ordered complete development. Having done so, he had no choice but to set out on an odyssey from capital to capital, seeking aid, credits, and investment: our Empire was barefoot, skinny, with all its ribs showing. His Majesty demonstrated his superiority over the students by showing them that one can develop without reforming. And how, I hear you asking, is that possible? Well it is: if you use foreign capital to build the factories, you don't need to reform" (p. 90). Of course, the problem was that very little of the money made it to the countryside: most got lost in the coffers of the intervening bureaucracy. The analogy could hardly be more baldly obvious. At one point, one of Kapuscinski's informants notes that in a country of 30 million subjects. Selassie only allowed 25,000 copies of the national newspaper to be distributed, since "even the most loyal press cannot be given in abundance, because that might create the habit of reading, and from there it is only a single step to the habit of thinking, and it is well known what inconveniences, vexations, troubles and worries thinking causes. *For even what is written loyally can be read disloyally*" (p. 110, italics mine). *The Emperor* was just asking for disloyal readers! Why, it might be asked, was publication sanctioned at all? Partly, no doubt, for reasons of ideology, (Selassie had after all been overthrown by a Marxist-inspired group of soldiers who came to count themselves as Soviet-bloc allies); but also because to ban the book would have been to admit to the similarity between the two regimes. During Solidarity's time, seven separate stage productions of seven separate adaptations of Kapuscinski's book were being performed throughout Poland, and at one point even Wajda was slated to film his own version of the richly allegorical life of Haile Selassie. (The above quotations are taken from the 1983 Harcourt Brace Jovanovich edition.)

20. Some of the best critiques of the Polish Communist Party's administration of the country's economy over the last 15 years can be found today in the above-ground, government-sanctioned Polish press. Polish economists have an advantage in that they can be bitingly critical merely by being descriptive, and in the case of a recent article by Andrzej Zawislak, in a June 1982 issue of *Przeglad Techniczny* ("Technical Review"), analysis occasionally ascends to exquisite sarcasm.

"Being ineffective as it is," Zawislak notes, recalling the years before 1970 in an abstract-theoretical present tense,

> the system must pay its members as little as possible. But when it is impossible to go down too far (that is, down to the level of the real efficiency of the system), the payments must be made in undervalued money, or in money which has no equivalent in goods. But this will finally lead to a negative reaction on the part of society. If this reaction cannot be contained with adequately harsh measures, then the system intent on retaining its identity [read, a Communist Party intent on staying in power] is left with only one strategy: foreign loans. They make it possible to alleviate the shortage of goods as well as enabling further investment expansion. No one will lose by this expansion, it is said at the time, and its future effects capture the imagination of society. Owing to the loans obtained in the time of the so-called success, however, the economically active population [read, the working class] was receiving in the final analysis more than would be justified by their increases in productivity. This would not have necessarily led to disaster if the investment decisions had been correct. Unfortunately . . . correct decisions were only made by chance.

A few paragraphs later, describing the situation in the late seventies, Zawislak writes:

> With the opening of Poland to the influences of genuine market economics, our system was able to find a new creditor. The first creditor, the economically active population, was an internal one: it could be manipulated to a great extent. The other one was not susceptible to such manipulation. He was a capitalist banker, who lent in order to earn. As such, he was impermeable to our social and ideological rationales. To make things worse, the system's internal creditor was no longer prepared to make concessions, either.

However, Solidarity is not exactly spared the ravages of Zawislak's celestial irony. A few paragraphs later, he notes that:

> All this was taking place amid a general cry for economic reform and the earliest possible resumption of rational economic activity. But no sooner had a political force [Solidarity] capable of containing the previous violators of economic rules emerged and become consolidated than it began to show an inclination to follow suit. As it turned out, the representatives of the *ancien régime* and the militants of the . . . unions were linked by a common passion —an aversion to thinking in terms of assets and liabilities.

21. The warping effects of the discrepancy between official and black-market rates were as surreal and troubling for me in October of this year as they had been in September and May of last year: back at the hotel, to eat a lavish feast for what to me came to about one dollar after having interviewed a man who could no longer afford to buy sausage, was to eat a hungry meal. And then one evening I was brought up short by a Polish friend whom I'd originally met a few months earlier in New York City but who had returned to his family in Warsaw. "You know," he said, "there's a flipside to your situation vis-à-vis our currency, which was mine vis-à-vis yours. Those mornings in New York I'd find myself furiously battling with my conscience as to whether I could afford to indulge myself with a cup of coffee. After all, the 25¢ would really make a difference if I could save it to bring back here for my daughter. This is a battle that every Polish tourist now fights when abroad."

22. The full article was published in translation in the Fall 1981 issue of *Cross Currents*, pp. 334–42.

23. Before the advent of Solidarity, people's spiritual crises had often been the obverse: objects, they'd frequently been confronted with a decision as to whether to sign petitions or letters of protest, and they'd had to agonize over whether to assert their subjectivity. But the agony in both cases was basically the same. The Polish writer Kazimierz Brandys has written of one such meeting that took place a few months before the rise of Solidarity, where people were being urged to sign a protest petition:

> I have learned not to hold people's fear in contempt but to view it as suffering that deserves respect. Heroes and cowards—I don't trust such distinctions. I also cannot abide the division of people into those who sign and those who do not. Two intellectuals, a scientist and a film director, were once asked to sign

a protest. One refused, "I can't, I have a son." The other one unscrewed the cap of his fountain pen, "I have to sign: I have a son." . . . In the end, everyone must decide for himself what he fears most: life or himself (the *New York Times Sunday Magazine*, Dec. 5, 1982, p. 128; excerpted from *A Warsaw Diary*, Random House, 1983).

24. "Voices, familiar from our history," noted one underground pamphlet, "are sounding again: 'To the British propaganda, I declare that our organs are neutralizing only those elements which desire to reap a bloody harvest with foreign money, against the interest of the nation, and in the very place where, at the present moment, the principle of common effort in the service of common interests should guide everyone.' This is not a quote from Jerzy Urban. It is from Hans Frank." (Frank was the Nazi governor of occupied Poland, 40 years ago.)

25. John Berger, "The Moment of Cubism," in *The Look of Things*, Viking, 1973, pp. 143–44.

26. The general devastation of the Polish film industry in 1982–83 presented a particularly sorry spectacle when compared with its extraordinary vitality during the period from, say, 1975 to 1981. Ironically, although the increasing openness of Polish films is widely regarded as having contributed to the onrush of Solidarity, and although the Polish film industry enjoyed unprecedented freedoms during the 16 months that followed, relatively few of the films actually written and produced during the Solidarity flowering made it to the screen before the sudden truncation of those freedoms on December 13th. Perhaps the most celebrated case proved to be that of Ryszard Bugajski's *The Interrogation* (discussed in Part I on p. 35). The screenplay's commemorative witness to the victims of Stalinist incarceration metamorphosed during the film's production into an uncanny premonition. Bugajski was able to complete shooting on the film, starring Krystyna Janda (the protagonist in *Man of Marble*), just before the imposition of martial law, and he contrived to finish its editing, somewhat in secret, during the first months of the state of war. (See my report in the July–August 1982 issue of *American Film*, pp. 8–9.) The Culture Ministry, however, furiously banned exhibition of the film following its one showing before an advisory committee. A remarkable transcript of that body's deliberations was smuggled out to the West and published in the October 1982 issue of *The New Criterion*: it makes for chilling reading. Bugajski, himself, meanwhile was banned from making further films: during the summer of 1983 he was directing a Warsaw stage production of Tennessee Williams's *Cat on a Hot Tin Roof*, starring Janda.

In all, there were at least nine major films completed during the Solidarity period, which my contacts in Warsaw in October 1982 described as the finest work to date by their respective directors, all of which for the time being anyway have been "shelved," unavailable for exhibition or export, with some of them existing in the highly precarious form of an exclusive master print in a Culture Ministry vault. (For more details, see my report in *Cinéaste*, vol. 13, no. 2, 1984.) Virtually none of the brilliant younger generation of Polish directors—Falk, Kieslowski, Kijowski, Lozinski, Holland, et al.—were making films in 1982–83, although, Poland being Poland, some of them were still managing to be paid for turning in screenplays the regime had absolutely no intention of ever allowing to be realized. Meanwhile, the structure of the eight independent film units, each headed by a world-class director, which for years had been shielding the young filmmakers, itself came under attack. In particular, Wajda's "X" and Zanussi's "Tor" units became the focus of a witchhunt aimed at eradicating, in the words of angry officials, their "opportunistic, demagogic, and existential" line. Although Wajda was permitted to continue making films, notably his French coproduction of a very peculiar, allegorical *Danton*, he was dismissed, along with two of his top aides, from the leadership at "X."

27. There's an uncanny congruence between this sort of comment by Poles and the similarly incoherent positions advanced by some American evangelists who likewise display both thinly veiled anti-Semitism at home and unmitigated pro-Israelism abroad.

28. Daniel Singer recently wrote an article in which he tried to address those Western critics who feel Solidarity did not go far enough:

> In practical terms the advocates of a bid for power should also say more concretely how and when during the brief 16 months of Solidarity it should have been attempted. Everybody knows the one obvious date: the end of March. . . . Yet even then, had the strike toppled the party rule, the broad assumption is that the Russians would have come to its rescue. . . . In terms of formal logic, the critics are consistent when they claim the Poles should have taken on a mighty enemy as, for example, the Vietnamese had done. The snag is that everything—the terrain, the circumstances, the geography, the possibility of getting arms, was different. The odds are that the Polish movement would have been crushed like the Paris Commune or the Hungarian insurrection and would have taken decades to recover, whereas now, though having suffered a temporary defeat, it is potentially intact ("Poland in Perspective," in *Socialist Perspectives*, ed. Julius and Phyllis Jacobson, Karz-Cohl, New York City, 1983).

29. See Jan Nowak's *Courier from Warsaw* (Wayne State University Press, 1982), pp. 68ff.

30. "I didn't know they took Daddy," recalls Marek, a ten-year-old, one of the children whose testimonies were gathered in that issue of *Wezwanie*.

> I was sleeping with my brother and I heard nothing. But my brother must have heard something because he cried and Mommy kept hushing him. He is little, he barely speaks. The next day our neighbor cried when she saw me; she said Daddy was imprisoned because of Solidarity. At first I was ashamed that Daddy was in prison because in our family nobody was ever in jail. I remember that when a father of one boy was locked up for stealing, other boys laughed at him and shouted, "Son of a thief." In school our teacher gave me money and sausage and said the money was for us and the sausage was for Daddy. And then I said that Father was not in prison but just traveling. And I started to cry. Then the teacher said not to be ashamed because it wasn't father's fault but those bastards who locked him up. My little brother went with Mommy to see my father, and later he called for him all the time. I am

sorry for Daddy. Sometimes I wish very much that he would take me bicycle-riding, but I don't cry, I don't cry at all. My father said, and Mommy says too, that now I am the oldest man in the house.

Janek, a five-year-old whose father was also arrested, simply comments:

I want Daddy to come back very much. And Mommy wants, and Grandma and Mrs. Alinka and everybody, but they are keeping him there. The bad ones. And they beat him there. Mommy says they do not beat, but I know that they do. When I grow up I will steal a gun and shoot the one who took Daddy away. Even if Daddy comes back, I will do it, because Mommy is crying.

Adam, a 14-year-old, described a brief political demonstration in his class at school:

. . . Then came May 13th [1982]. All of us were getting ready for it days before-hand. Our class decided to stand up for a minute at noon. The ring was supposed to be the signal for our class. We did not arrange anything with the other classes, but it turned out that several classes in the school stood up. The teachers were taken by surprise, but before they could do anything the minute had passed. Only one teacher of Phys. Ed. beat two boys with a stick. When the time comes, that teacher will be punished.

Pawel, five years old, tells of a game:

We have a camp game. We sit on a bench and Jurek walks around and watches us so that we don't run away. When he turns away we shout, "The Crow will Die," and he hits us. We don't hit him because he is a zomo and he can shoot us. Jurek doesn't want to be a zomo but we give him candy. He fits his role because he is fat. Mother says it's a stupid game and that somebody may hear us and call the real zomos. But although she says that, she herself turns the lights on and off on the war's birthday [as per the instructions of Radio Solidar-ity]. She doesn't tell Father because he is in the party. Yesterday we were play-ing at an uprising. The zomos were Germans and we killed them. But this time instead of the zomos there were only benches because Jurek did not want to be a zomo, even for candy, although two pieces were filled with chocolate.

Marta, 13, whose father is apparently active in the underground, contributed the following composition:

I don't know what my father is typing. They are papers or documents. He is hiding them away after that. And I even know where he keeps them. My par-ents get home later than me and I take them to my friend and we read them and copy them. . . . One day my father noticed that somebody touched his papers and shouted at me. And he hid them somewhere else. Now I've found that place. We do understand everything in these papers, and when we go to work, we will join Solidarity. Me, my friend and the whole class—except two girls, because their fathers are in the army.

The *Wezwanie* article even included a poem by a child whose father is de-scribed as being in the militia:

My father said: Shut your mouth and shhh
So I won't say anything even what I am eating
Because my father said everything is a secret
My father sleeps with his eyes open
I'm not kidding.

For more on children's reactions to the state of war, see Victoria Pope's article in the April 5, 1983 issue of the *Wall Street Journal.*

31. "You have the Golden Horn." This last comment, as every Pole would surely recognize, was an allusion to an incident in Polish folklore, immortalized in Stanislaw Wyspianski's turn-of-the-century symbolist play, *The Wedding*, in which a victorious uprising of the Poles is guaranteed to begin if one of the wedding guests will merely blow on the magic golden horn which has suddenly appeared on his lap—only, in his drunken stupor following the revelries, he fails to notice, and the moment is lost. Awakening, he is left with but a piece of rope, a symbol of the lost chance and continued slavery.

32. The strike in the shipyard did in fact crumble on October 12th, but the regime was extremely lucky. That afternoon the winner of the 1982 Nobel Peace Prize was announced. Everyone in Poland had been eagerly awaiting the announcement (it had been expected any day), because everyone in Poland just *knew* the prize would be given to Lech Walesa. It did not: the prize instead was awarded to veteran disarmament campaigners Alva Myrdal and Alfonso Garcia Robles. Without doubt, the announcement devastated morale in the shipyard. Similarly, without doubt, had the announcement gone the other way, morale would have been bolstered and the strike might well have spread.

Ironically, October *1983*, which is when the Nobel committee in fact did get around to awarding Walesa the Peace Prize, might in turn have been a better time for awarding the prize to Robles and Myrdal, what with the then rising crescendo of antinuclear protest in Western Europe. For further thought on this subject, see my article in *In These Times*, October 19–25, 1983.

33. As things developed, it turned out that Walentynowicz did in fact undergo six weeks of psychiatric testing at a prison hospital in Warsaw during fall 1982. Her prosecutors were apparently hoping she would be found mentally unfit, but the examing psychologists failed to oblige, pronouncing her lucid after extensive testing. She did eventually go to trial, in March 1983, on charges of having continued her union activities after the imposition of martial law (in particular, of having encouraged strikers at the Lenin shipyards on December 14 and 15, 1981). Following three weeks of deliberations, the court found her guilty but meted out a surprising 15-month *suspended* sentence, and she was released.

34. One Polish documentary, by the young filmmaker Krzysztof Lang, which for some reason *was* passed by the censors, concerned the start of a typical day for one Polish woman: She wakes up in her small apartment, dresses, wakes her family, gets them off, leaves the building, stands in line at a shop, then eventually arrives at her workplace where she enters a studio, crammed with recording devices, tape-machines, etc., sits down, places earphones over her head, leans forward

toward the microphone before her, and then enunciates, very distinctly, over and over again: *Rozmowa kontrolowana, rozmowa kontrolowana, rozmowa kontrolowana . . .*

35. "Even were a war in Europe somehow to be confined to non-nuclear weapons, Poland would still be in a lot of trouble. Indeed, conventional weaponry has become so advanced and so lethal that some military experts have taken to wondering if there would be that much difference between the two types of war. John Keegan detailed some of the most harrowing prospects in an article in the July 1983 issue of *Harper's* entitled "The Specter of Conventional War" (pp. 8–14). He points out that the immediate devastation would not be the only problem. One of the more notorious characteristics of cluster bombs, for example, is that "some bomblets fail to detonate, yet remain primed. The area where they lie therefore becomes extremely hazardous for humans to enter." Such remains of battle can at least be detected, however, which is more than can be said for some of the more recent mines: "Most modern mines are plastic and return no echo to the electronic devices used by mine-clearing teams. Lightness and cheapness mean that they can be manufactured in enormous quantities and dispensed mechanically in clouds. As a result, wide areas can be sterilized against military use— since it is now so easy to broadcast mines, this is probably what will happen, as indeed did happen in the Falklands campaign. Large areas of those islands are now closed to human use, it is believed permanently, and the presumption must be that a European war would leave the same aftermath." Keegan concludes: "Both the great wars of this century were almost unmitigated disasters for the peoples on whose territories they were fought. The ingenuity and productiveness of the industrial nations ensure that any conventional war into which they might stumble in the future, even if they were able to keep their fingers off the nuclear trigger, would be yet more unbearable." (See also Michael Klare, "The Conventional Weapons Fallacy," *The Nation*, May 25, 1983, pp. 438–444.)

36. This sort of comment—and indeed the general tenor of most popular rhetoric in Poland since the coup with its heightened cold-war fervor (the tendency, for example, to see the Soviet Union in exclusively Satanic terms) has caused many in the Western peace movements to shudder in frustration. Recently, a well-known British peace activist and historian commented that, in the long term, peace in Europe will require a dismantling of both bloc systems—NATO and the Warsaw Pact—and ideally, an eventual, complete demilitarization from Ireland to the Urals, but that this in turn will require particular maturity on the part of citizens in the Soviet Union's client states in Eastern Europe. They will need to understand that even without a Soviet military presence within their borders, and even following extensive loosening of their internal totalitarian political systems, their countries must still remain within the Soviet sphere of influence—somewhat like Finland. From his talks with independent peace activists in Hungary, East Germany, and Czechoslovakia, he was convinced that people there understood this basic reality. "Poland, however," he said, "is the fly in the ointment. This unbridled nationalism of the Poles could someday be the end of us all."

Perhaps. Most Poles at any rate do look upon the Western peace movements with condescension and suspicion (in part because of the outrageously one-sided accounts they get of those movements through their own regime's propaganda— accounts which only feature the posters and speakers attacking American and NATO nuclear policy and never show the balancing criticism of Soviet bloc policy —propaganda which in this one regard, for some reason, most Poles seem willing to take at face value). But there were in Poland throughout the Solidarity period and continuing through to the present, voices that recognized the interrelationship of their internal struggle and the wider European peace movement. Thus, for example, at the Solidarity congress in September 1981, Bogdan Lis called for a diminution in Polish military spending precisely because of the desperate needs in the civilian sector. In May 1982, the Solidarity underground committee in the Krakow region called for demonstrations in June to commemorate the sixth month of martial law, with a pamphlet headlined, "WE PROTEST THE STATE OF WAR; WE DO NOT WANT A CIVIL WAR; WE DO NOT WANT A WORLD WAR; WE DEMAND A REDUCTION OF ARMS IN EUROPE AND WORLDWIDE; WE DEMAND THE DESTRUCTION OF NUCLEAR ARSENALS; BEGIN US–USSR DISARMAMENT TALKS NOW! . . .SOLIDARITY AGAINST ALL WAR! SOLIDARITY WILL CONQUER HATRED!" (*Solidarity Information Bulletin*, No. 10, May 29, 1982).

Addressing the fears of the previously quoted English peace activist more directly perhaps, Adam Michnik in a recent prison letter suggested an alternative vision of Solidarity's eventual historic role:

There is in today's world a great need to seek ways to peace and mutual agreement. . . . It may well be that one of these ways leads through Poland. . . . But dialogue requires the existence of partners. Solidarity, pushed into the underground, calumnied and persecuted, pays a high price to keep the chance of dialogue alive. I wish the peace campaigners in the West took this dimension of Solidarity's actions into account, for it is certainly not unthinkable that a spectacular peaceful solution in Poland will become the starting point for the resolution of international tensions; that it will become a source of strength and hope for all who prefer negotiations, however difficult and protracted, to dialoguing by means of truncheons and tear gas, tanks and guns, and finally missiles of tactical, medium and strategic range (*Uncensored Poland News Bulletin*, July 29, 1983, p. 28).

One of the most consistently interesting underground journals in Poland today is KOS (the acronym for its parent committee, the Committee for Social Resistance, which incidentally, in Polish, means "blackbird," as opposed to the regime's "crow"). In an issue in the early summer of 1982, the pseudonymous Dawid Warszawski published a fascinating essay on the relationship between Solidarity and the Western Left. Among other things, Warszawski noted, "Only the Left can be our true ally, because it is only for the Left that Polish society and the Polish working class in particular exists as an autonomous subject. The Right's true interlocutor is Moscow, not Poland, and we are useful only as a means of making life difficult for the Soviets. As Yalta has shown, a Poland subjugated by Moscow is of little interest to the Right. Financial and industrial circles, the Right's social base, have already begun to support Jaruzelski on their own initiative, hoping that he will be able to squeeze 28 billion dollars out of us." (The entire essay, as translated by Andrzej Tymowski, was published in the November 3–9, 1982 issue of *In These Times*.)

On May 9, 1983, the anniversary of Victory-in-Europe Day, KOS issued another interesting document, a direct appeal to the peace and antinuclear movements in Western Europe. It stated:

World peace is threatened. The threat of nuclear annihilation hangs over all the inhabitants of this earth. An unbridled arms race is against the interest of all people, regardless of where they live. It threatens you, the inhabitants of Western Europe, just as it does us, the inhabitants of Eastern Europe. It is therefore with respect and understanding that we view your protests against the growing frenzy of the arms race and the build-up of the worldwide nuclear potential. We view your protest as a defense of the most basic human right—the right to live.

Like you, we are convinced that war can bring the world nothing but death and destruction. Like you we say No to the arms race. We are aware that the frontier which divides the two huge military blocs carries incalculable consequences for us all. We believe, however, that protest against the threat of war will be successful only when it is taken up by people living on both sides of the frontier dividing the two military blocs, in unison and on the basis of a joint program of demands. We believe that to demand an arms freeze by NATO countries, without simultaneously demanding a reduction of the military potential of the Warsaw Pact does not serve the cause of peace.

The KOS authors went on to warn the Western peace movements against letting themselves be manipulated by the "expansionist policy of the USSR, based on military blackmail and aggressive and mendacious propaganda." But, in the final analysis they concluded, "We want the same as you. We want to live in peace and security in conditions which guarantee us the basic human and civil rights. In order to make the world in which we live more human, we should unite our efforts. Let the international solidarity of people who live in peace be expressed in united action against all acts of violence, blackmail, and lawlessness throughout the world" (*Uncensored Poland News Bulletin*, London, June 17, 1983, pp. 32–34).

37. As of September 1983, the regime still seemed unsure about how to proceed with the show trials of the five imprisoned KOR activists—Jacek Kuron, Adam Michnik, Jan Litynski, Henryk Wujec, and Jan Josef Lipski—on charges of conspiracy to overthrow the state. A sixth KOR activist, the eminent physicist Zbigniew Romaszewski, who has already been tried and convicted of antistate activities (for his role in launching Radio Solidarnosc) and is serving a 4½-year sentence, has had his name attached to the list for the upcoming trial. Again and again the government's press spokesman Jerzy Urban has declared the trial to be imminent, and again and again nothing has happened. Meanwhile, the defendants remain under arrest, although Lipski has been allowed to return home due to his critical medical problems, and Litynski, one of the Jewish defendants, was permitted out on leave for one day to attend the communion(!) of his daughter and then somehow managed to disappear from sight.

Meanwhile, the KOR prosecution appears to have been hooped together with that of the seven Solidarity figures whose status was shifted from internment to arrest in late December, just before the suspension of martial law and the release of all the other unindicted internees. These seven include: Andrzej Gwiazda (the electrical engineer who was vice-chairman of the original strike committee at the Gdansk shipyards and who subsequently challenged Walesa for union leadership at the September 1981 Solidarity congress); Seweryn Jaworski (a foundry worker and leader of the union branch at the Huta Warszawa steelworks, as well as vice-chairman for the Warsaw region); Marian Jurczyk (leader of the Szczecin region and another challenger to Walesa at the September congress); Karol Modzelewski (the medieval historian from Wroclaw who coauthored, with Jacek Kuron, the famous 1964 Open Letter to the Party, spent years in prison during the sixties, and subsequently served as the union's first press spokesperson); Gregorz Palka (a leader from the Lodz region specializing in economic problems); Andrzej Rozplochowski (a steelworker activist from Katowice); and Jan Rulewski (the charismatic leader from Bydgoszcz whose beating during the notorious police violence there led to the March 1981 crisis and who subsequently also challenged Walesa for the union leadership in September 1981).

The appearance of Gwiazda's name on this list is especially ironic. One of the most compelling scenes in *Robotnicy '80*, the remarkable documentary of the August 1980 strike negotiations in Gdansk, occurred when Gwiazda faced the government representatives across the table and asked, "What guarantee do we have that these agreements won't someday be repudiated and we on this side of the table all treated as criminals?" Deputy Prime Minister Mieczyslaw Jagielski, in a moment every Pole remembers and many used to love to mimic, threw up his hands in feigned insult, puffed up his cheeks, and insisted that such an outcome could not possibly occur in People's Poland.

In addition to the fact of their continuing incarceration, these prisoners are having to cope with a variety of nasty stratagems contrived by their jailers with the intention of breaking their spirits. Thus, for example, the regime several times intimated to these gentlemen that they might get to take part in the July amnesty. When Jacek Kuron, for instance, requested a one-day leave in order to attend the wedding of his son earlier in the summer, he was told that his son should reschedule the wedding for after July 22nd; that way, Kuron was told, there wouldn't have to be any special arrangements since he'd be out anyway. After considerable trouble, the son did reschedule the wedding, but Kuron, of course, was not released. There are, furthermore, increasing reports of failing health among these prisoners. Gwiazda, for instance, is said to be suffering from both ulcers and gallstones, and has lost all his front teeth due to untreated paradentitis. All the prisoners complain of cold, cramped quarters and unsufficient exercise.

In an interview smuggled out of prison in early August 1983, Adam Michnik related how he'd been reviewing the dozens of volumes of alleged evidence compiled against the defendants. "We are eager for the trial to begin," he claimed. "The trial can't possibly disgrace us, but it may disgrace them. Our prosecution dossiers are a gold mine of information, not so much about KOR as about its present overseers. At the trial I will recount what I discovered in these files about 'the gloomy conductors of the prison trains,' as Milosz would describe them. Jaruzelski may trust the discipline of the judges who will be sentencing us, but he should not hope for such discipline from the accused."

"We are reliably informed," the UPNB reported November 4, 1983, "that legal circles in Warsaw [who have read the official papers in the case] are puzzled by the indictment. In the words of one eminent lawyer, it's unclear whether the intention is to send the men to prison—or to build a monument to them."

And the regime itself seemed to be having misgivings about the trial. Late in October 1983, Urban publicly offered the eleven defendants freedom if they would merely consent to exile. None, however, seemed interested in the offer. In December, Michnik, for his part, dashed off a defiant open letter to Interior Minister Kiszczak. "General," he wrote, "I well know why you need our departure from this country: So as to be able to defame us in your newspapers with redoubled ferocity as people who have finally shown their true colors, who previously were only fulfilling someone else's orders and have now, blatantly, let themselves be bought by Capitalist comforts. To show the world that you are generous liberals and we nonentities without character. To be able to tell the Poles, 'Look, even they gave up, even they lost their hope for a democratic and free Poland.' For all of these reasons, but most of all to improve your image *in your own eyes* so that you'll be able to breathe a sigh of relief: 'There, they weren't any better than us after all.' For the very existence of people who associate Poland not with a ministry portfolio but with a prison cell, people who prefer Christmas in an investigation prison to a vacation on the Cote d'Azur, makes your life a torment. . . . After all, none of you would hesitate if offered the choice. You are unable to think about us in a different way because, thinking differently, you would be forced to discover—if only for a moment—the truth about yourselves." Michnik continued, "I cannot know the future and do not know if I'll yet live to see the victory of the truth over the lie, and of Solidarity over this present anti-worker dictatorship. But the thing is, General, that for me the value of our struggle lies not in the possibility of winning but, rather, in the value of the cause on behalf of which we launched this struggle in the first place. . . . For me, General, prison is not such a painful punishment. That December night, it was not me who got proscribed. It was freedom. And today it is not me imprisoned, it's Poland. Punishment for me would be if, under your orders, I had to spy, to brandish the staff, to fire on workers, to interrogate prisoners and pronounce shameless conviction sentences. I'm lucky that I happen to be on the right side: among the victims, and not among the victimizers."

At the conclusion of his letter, Michnik alluded to the coming Christmas holiday: "I want you to think for a moment, while you sit at your Christmas Eve table, that some day you will be called to account for breaking the law. Those whom you harmed and humiliated will send you the bill. It will be a very dark moment. Well, Christmas Eve is a time for toasts and wishes. My wish for you is that you will be able to keep your personal dignity at that moment. And your courage. Whatever happens, please don't stammer, as your colleagues from former governments did, that you didn't know. Because such claims don't arouse mercy, but only contempt. . . . As for myself, I wish that, just as I managed to be on the scene that afternoon in Otwock (in May, 1981) when I helped save the lives of those men of yours who were surrounded by that angry crowd, so I will be able to be on the spot that next time, when you will be in danger, and that I'll be able to help you, too. You see: I hope that I will always be able to be on the side of the victims and not among the victimizers. Even if you were to throw me right back into prison immediately afterwards and still be amazed by my stupidity."

38. The full text of Baranczak's poems, as translated by Richard Lourie, will appear in the Winter 1984 issue of *Dissent*.

39. Rosa Luxemburg was a prominent Polish Socialist and revolutionary during the first quarter of this century. Daniel Singer has been quoting her a good deal lately. As an epigraph to one article, he used the mocking prophecy she hurled at the czarist forces following their suppression of a Polish rebellion in 1905:

> You claim to have achieved order in Warsaw.
> Fools, your order is built on sand!

More recently he's quoted her observation that, "The revolution is the only kind of 'war' in which final victory can only be prepared by a number of defeats."

Index

This is principally a name index, supplemented by listings for a few general themes (such as "Polish economy" and "Polish army"). References to the chronology are indicated by a *c*., those to the notes by an *n*., and those to the illustrations by *illus*. In addition, at the tail-end of the index, there are listings for the key years 1830, 1863, 1956, 1968, 1970, 1976, 1980, and 1981.